PSYCHOLOGY IN THE CLASSROOM

A MANUAL FOR TEACHERS

HARPER & ROW, PUBLISHERS

Psychology in the Classroom

RUDOLF DREIKURS, M.D.

Professor of Psychiatry, Chicago Medical School
Director, Alfred Adler Institute of Chicago

Second Edition

NEW YORK · EVANSTON · LONDON

Contents

Preface

MANY CHILDREN of all ages need help and guidance beyond what most teachers presently can provide. Counselors have been assigned to schools to work with children, teachers, and parents in overcoming the obstacles to social and academic progress. A new professional discipline has emerged: child psychiatry. It is based on an assumption we cannot share, that children who need help are "emotionally sick." Few of them are really sick; most are misguided. Who is best qualified to help them—the teacher, the parent, the counselor, the psychiatrist, the social worker, the minister, or any adult friend or relative? In our experience, any one of them can be effective in influencing the child and helping him to adjust. The disturbed child has wrong ideas about himself and life and uses socially unacceptable means to find his place. Anyone who can win his confidence, who understands him, who can show him alternatives can redirect the child.

The teacher has one advantage over all the others; she can work with the whole class and solicit the help of the group in the adjustment and improvement of each individual child. Not knowing what to do, our teachers feel increasingly unable to cope with difficult children. They are caught in a period of transition, shackled with the autocratic methods of the past and faced with conflicting ideas of the present. If they become familiar with psychological and group approaches, they can exert strong and effective influences on the child, for both the prevention and the correction of maladjustment. Using psychological methods to promote adjustments does not make the teacher a psychotherapist. Nor does using group dynamics and discussion methods to overcome the child's deficiencies make her a group therapist. Nevertheless, the dynamic process which can be instituted in the classroom may, in many cases, avoid referral for psychiatric treatment.

At present, training in psychological methods specifically applicable to the classroom is almost unavailable to teachers. For this reason, the classes conducted by the author primarily for teachers actively engaged in their profession have provided them with a unique experience. This book attempts to reproduce it.

Part I presents the theoretical premises for the application of the psychological approach in the classroom. A specific concept of man underlies any educational philosophy. Ours is based on the philosophy of democracy, with its implied principle of human equality, and on the socio-teleological approach of the psychology of Alfred Adler. In this frame of reference, man is recognized as a social being, his actions as purposive and directed toward a goal, his personality as a unique and indivisible entity. We are teleo-analytically oriented, concerned with the goals of the child's behavior and the means of changing goals when necessary.

Part II consists of a discussion of selected reports on actual classroom situations in which children with problems were involved. Most of the reports were provided by the teachers of the school system of Gary who attended my classes at the University of Indiana, Gary Extension. A few were from students of the School of Education, Northwestern University. Many of these reports reflect the shortcomings of initial efforts; they are included primarily for didactic purposes, to facilitate a clearer distinction between a correct and a futile approach.

The author gratefully acknowledges the cooperation of the following teachers who, knowing that reports written in a learning situation are often subject to criticism, were still willing to have them published so that others might benefit from their experience:

James E. Anderson, Doris Bell, Doris Boese, Althea Brach, Harriet Cohen, Bernice Collins, Mabel B. Cox, Iona Crisman, Carl L. Durkel, John Farley, Bernard Fax, Evelyn Ferguson, Inex Fox, Phyllis Franzman, Ruth Goshorn, Ann Gracin, Joseph Jaco, John

Jancose, Joan Janda, Arella Johnson, Mary Johnson, Evelyn Joseph, June Kinser, Sonia Leskow, Marion Levy, Vivien McCray, Ruth Martindale, Max A. Mason, Elinor Monnix, Doris Neuton, Mary F. Peckenpaugh, Ann Roland, Neal Roland, Helen Scott, Gladys Smith, Sophie Sollers, Anna May Thomas, Ruth Thompson, Doris S. Travis, Ruth VanLiew, Elsie Wendt, Dorothy Werblow, Howard Williams, George T. Wood.

The author wishes to express his special gratitude to Muriel and Frederick Reed for their untiring efforts in evaluating the material from the point of view of educators. Their most valuable contribution was their guidance in the selection and analysis of the examples and their presentation.

To my dear friends in Jamaica, B.W.I., Mr. and Mrs. Harold Wheeler of Hartmont and Mr. and Mrs. Richard Temple of Paradise, sincere thanks for having provided an inspirational setting for the compilation and integration of the material.

In addition, the contribution by Mrs. Bernice Grunwald to the revised edition is gratefully acknowledged.

RUDOLF DREIKURS

Introduction

IN OUR DAILY CONTACT with a child, in pleasant and unpleasant encounters, in satisfaction or struggle, we experience his personality through his overt behavior, through the character traits which he exhibits, through the abilities and deficiencies which we can see. But these impressions do not permit any direct conclusion concerning the psychological mechanisms which propel him, or the factors which have influenced the development of his personality in the past. On the contrary, our close personal contacts make it almost impossible to consider him in terms of underlying causes and motivations or of past developmental influences. Thinking of them while we are actually dealing with the child would inhibit and confuse us. When we enjoy the child or are annoyed with him we act impulsively, without too much thinking and analysis. The more involved we are personally, the less we are able and willing to think objectively. Many of our contacts with children consist of such immediate, impulsive, and emotional interpersonal reactions, of a meeting or clash of personalities, of actions without evaluations.

Such behavior on the part of parents and teachers is the daily routine. If we are satisfied with the child, if we enjoy him, if we get along with him, then there is no need for upsetting this natural and spontaneous relationship. However, when we encounter difficulties, when our relationship becomes unpleasant, when we are faced with deficiencies or faults that we would like to change, then it is not only futile but dangerous to follow our natural inclinations and impulses. By so doing we may fortify a child's mistaken attitudes and intentions, intensify past damaging influences, and perpetuate failures and deficiencies. This is because our immediate response often gratifies the child's conscious or unconscious intentions.

Furthermore, this inclination to react impulsively prevents any understanding of why the child behaves as he does. In a moment of anger we do not care to know. It requires a different frame of mind to be willing to make such an inquiry. Anger, annoyance, disgust, or similar feelings of antagonism must be eliminated first. Only then can we investigate and draw our conclusions about possible constructive steps. No effort toward correcting a child's behavior or personality can have much success unless it is based on an understanding of the child's personality and of the factors contributing to the disturbance. Such an understanding requires emotional preparation and a readiness to reason, plus sufficient knowledge. Only when we are thus prepared can we understand the child and our own role in the present difficulty.

The necessary psychological knowledge includes recognition of the basic needs of children, insight into the factors which influence their development, and an objective method for recognizing the child's present goals and motivations.

To perceive the basic needs of children, one must consider the child in all his aspects. He is first a physiological organism with biological mechanisms and requirements. Apart from this, he is a psychological entity following psychological dynamics. But more than anything, he is a social being who wants to belong and acts within the social atmosphere of group life. His basic needs are fulfilled at any age only if he has a chance to function adequately on all three of these levels.

Understanding a child's development presupposes knowledge not only of the stimulations and frustrations to which he has been exposed but—even more important—of his responses to these stimulations, be they biological, psychological, or social. His current condition is the logical consequence of his development up to now and constitutes the link between past and future; it is merely the present segment of a continuous development.

Nobody will take issue with such a formulation. However, in

establishing specific principles on which to base educational procedures we meet confusion and controversy, because scientific investigation of the factors in personality growth has not brought unequivocal results. We have failed so far to reach a generally accepted evaluation of the basic needs of children, of the factors which influence their development, and of the psychological dynamics at work. This unfortunate condition of contemporary knowledge has had a detrimental effect on the application and usefulness of psychological principles in the field of education. Some educators try to avoid theoretical confusion and conflicting technical recommendations by confining their attention to facts that cannot be disputed. This limits the extent and significance of their data. Others, instead of analyzing the various *factors* affecting the development of children, are satisfied with the description of developmental *phases* observed in the majority of children at a given age. Instead of looking for deeper dynamics in the child, they try to rely on inventory tests which compare the individual child with a "norm," based on an average of a great number of children.

Emphasis on certainty, acceptance restricted to what is proved and agreed upon by all, often prevents the understanding of important psychological dynamics. At the present stage of scientific progress a formulation of the deeper dynamics acceptable to every investigator is impossible, but the lack of generally acceptable formulations need not delay or paralyze progress. All we need is the courageous spirit of the pioneer. Certain observations, which have not been generally accepted or statistically proved, can be accepted as working hypotheses, and we can examine their validity through our own experience. Every educator becomes thereby an experimenter.

We are witnessing a revolution in the field of education. Rapid changes in concepts and methods are occurring with varying speed and extent throughout the school systems of our country. They reflect a democratic evolution with its far-reaching changes in interpersonal relationships and social settings. The traditional superiority of adults over children is fast disappearing, in line with the disintegration of masculine superiority, the supremacy of the white race, and the power of capital over labor. Democratization implies a process of equalization. Consequently, in our growing democratic atmosphere it is impossible to treat children as inferiors. Neither parents nor teachers can any longer "make" a child behave or conform; pressure from the outside has lost its effectiveness and must be replaced with stimulation from within.

Since traditional methods have lost their efficacy, new methods have to be found which can bring results in a democratic setting. Teachers are aware of this requirement, but unfortunately in their groping for democratic approaches they often become confused. Many suffer from the illusion that to be democratic requires nothing more than to stop being autocratic. They do not realize that avoiding autocratic approaches does not make a teacher democratic, but may merely create anarchy. A democratic atmosphere combines freedom with order, and is thus distinguished from autocracy's order without freedom and from anarchy's freedom without order.

This state of transition leads inevitably to confusion concerning educational policies. On one hand, the teacher is confronted with the increasing independence and rebellion of a new generation at war with adult society. And on the other, the teacher is subject to the criticism of all those forces within the community that try to stifle democratic progress because they see in it dangers to the status quo. Caught between the opposition of the children, the pressure of school authorities, and the demands of perturbed parents, and exposed to public scrutiny of a not always benevolent nature, the teacher is in a precarious position. Every effort must be made to alleviate this hardship.

This book presents such an effort by offering teachers information which they may utilize to increase their effectiveness. It reflects psychiatric observations and practical experiences in dealing with the problems of children who need help. A better understanding of the dynamics involved and the methods available in dealing with them may be of help for a profession which carries the burden of a whole generation and is preparing the way for the future of mankind.

Part I

BASIC PRINCIPLES

CHAPTER 1

The Teacher's Role

IN THE PAST the role of the teacher was to "teach," to impart knowledge, which the child was supposed to absorb. If the child failed to absorb such knowledge, the process of learning stopped. However, outside pressure could induce the child to apply himself. In an autocratic society such methods brought good results, so that most children exposed to a school situation showed progress and acquired some knowledge.

Today these methods of teaching no longer bring about the desired results. Our schools produce an increasing number of illiterates and many of our pupils simply refuse to study. In order to be effective, the teacher has to know more than the subject matter. In the past it made little difference how material was presented; children were forced to learn it. Now, however, children decide whether or not they will study. Efforts to force them to study usually fail, increasing antagonism to learning.

This situation is now widely recognized and efforts are under way to remedy it. Some progress in improving teaching methods has been achieved, but far too little to meet the needs. The pleasurable sensation that a student experiences when he suddenly comprehends something is far too rare in our classrooms. We are confronted with insufficient knowledge about the process of learning, but indications are that a major breakthrough in learning theories is imminent. Such a breakthrough probably will be greatly stimulated by the realization of the ease with which children can learn before they enter school, in contrast to the slow progress they make thereafter. We are wasting the tremendous learning potential of young children. Revolutionary changes in methods of teaching are needed and probably will be developed in the near future.[1]

There can be no doubt that good teaching methods will enhance the teacher's ability to impart knowledge. But no technical procedure will help her to overcome a child's resistance to learning, unless she understands the child's motivation and knows how to improve it, if necessary. Any teacher can acquire this knowledge by studying psychodynamics and group dynamics, but some do not have to be taught. They are the so-called naturals. Through their intuition and empathy they know what the child needs and wants. However, we cannot rely on natural teachers alone, for there are far too few of them. All teachers should acquire this essential knowledge, and this means that a change is required in the training of teachers, both on the undergraduate and postgraduate level.

One hears a frequent objection to this suggestion. Teachers are already overburdened with work. How can we now demand additional responsibility from them? After all, it is the duty of the family to raise children who will have proper motivation to study, apply themselves, and behave well. The teacher is confronted with behavior patterns, assets, and deficiencies developed during the child's early formative years in his family. Can she offset the detrimental influences to which the child has been and still is exposed in his family and community? According to our experience, she can.

The teacher who cannot take time to understand the child and change his faulty goals will spend much more time with the disturbing child whom she cannot reach or influence. And if she has acquired the skill to overcome the child's opposition, she is actually in a position to counteract detrimental influences outside of school.

We cannot blame teachers for their failure to teach successfully, for they have not been provided with the tools needed in their job.

---

[1] Our present forms of curricula will probably also have to be revised. Carlton Washburn, *A Living Philosophy of Education*, New York, John Day, 1949, suggests that one of the best ways to eliminate the deadwood of the curriculum is to subject all curriculum material to the acid test of whether the children can be led to see its value, to feel a need for learning it, to pursue its attainment with zest.

They are excellent teachers as long as the children study and behave themselves, but few know what to do if the children do not cooperate. The teacher is also exposed to many other pressures, tensions, and demands for which she has not been prepared. We shall examine the five primary arenas of conflict—with children, with parents, with the principal, with the community, and with herself.

THE SKIRMISH WITH CHILDREN

Most teachers are interested in teaching and in stimulating the child to learn. When they take on the teaching assignment, they have a clear goal. In the past, children went to school understanding that they had to learn. Is this still true today? One can safely say it is not. The development from submissiveness to authorities to increasing defiance and self-determination was probably gradual and related to the democratic evolution.

Why do our children go to school? The vast majority go because they are obliged by law. Others, because their friends are there. An increasing number of children seem to have only one purpose in going to school: to make the life of the teacher as miserable as possible. For them it is a game to defy her power. Some children go to learn, but for the wrong purpose. They study because they want to be better than others, to look down on those who are not equally successful; or they study in order to get good grades for college entrance so that they can earn more money. There are children who really like to learn, for learning's sake, more frequently in the lower grades. But around the fifth grade, the first peak of resistant learners is reached in the underachievers. The children are no longer interested in learning and study only enough to get by. Later the antagonism to learning increases and culminates in the final dropouts. They have by now learned the skill of how not to learn.

Whether the teacher wants it or not, whether she is aware of it or not, she is usually drawn into a power contest from which she cannot extricate herself. There is a war on in our schools.

The war between the generations is as old as our civilization. But the smoldering rebellion against the domination of the young by the old has not been able to break into the open because society has upheld the power of adults. This power has diminished with the democratic evolution and its concomitant sense of equality for all, expressed by each person's self-determination, which frees him from the submission to autocratic demands. After World War II, all previously subjugated groups began to claim their right to equal treatment—women, members of colored races, laborers—and children. Now the conflicts come into the open and will increase in violence until we find the means by which we can learn to live with each other as equals. Only a few educators have so far recognized the reason for our predicament in dealing with children.

The German educator Wyneken, the founder of the Free School Community in Wickersdorf, pointed out in 1910[2] that life in our schools suffers frequently from the division of two armed camps of teachers and of students, who oppose each other with varying degrees of hostility. This is as true in the United States as in Germany. Maria Montessori[3] in 1950, shortly before her death, made a touching plea for a truce between children and adults. She saw a state of warfare in education, a war between the grown-up, who is strong, and the child, who is weak. The teacher is often the persecutor of the child, although an unconscious persecutor. Nor is this conflict confined to the school; it is everywhere, even in the home. Kvaraceous[4] speaks of the "continuum of norm-violating behavior" of our children. On one end of the continuum is the child you cannot get up in the morning or put to bed in the evening, who does not take care of his belongings, fights with his brothers and sisters, eats either too much or too little, does not take a bath, refuses to do his homework, and so on—in other words, the "normal" American child. And on the other end is the juvenile delinquent, who is openly at war with society. There is only a quantitative difference between them; one fights more violently.

The opposition the teacher finds in her classroom obstructs her

[2] Gustav Wyneken, *Schule und Jugenkultur*, Jena, Diederich, 1920.

[3] Maria Montessori, "Disarmament in Education," *Montessori Magazine*, Vol. IV, 1950, pp. 9–12.

[4] W. C. Kvaraceous, *Delinquent Behavior*, Washington, D.C., National Education Association, 1959.

best intentions and undermines the idealism with which she may have entered her profession; she feels thwarted in her best efforts. The conflict with the children may start in the first grade, or even in kindergarten, when the teacher encounters children who cannot sit quietly or cannot concentrate on anything. (One should never say that a child "cannot" sit quietly; all the teacher knows is that he *does not* sit quietly or concentrate.) Since few educators have any training in understanding the motivation of children who are deficient, and since it is human to desire an "understanding," it has become general practice to use labels which seem to explain the child's behavior. Consequently, we call him immature, lazy, passive-aggressive, prone to daydream, endowed with a short interest span, and so on. This does not "explain" the child's behavior, but merely describes it.

Research has recently added a series of "explanations" for the teacher's difficulty with some children. There was first the concern with the low I.Q. The intelligence test is still most frequently used to evaluate the child. The routine use of testing gives some semblance of important information, but actually is harmful. If the child's score is low, one cannot expect much from him, and consequently the teacher reinforces the child's discouragement. And when the child's score is high, the teacher becomes discouraged if he does not perform according to his potential. Actually, the child's real abilities, his creativity, and spontaneity are hardly measured by our present testing methods, which do not even provide a valid evaluation of the child's intellectual capacity. Tests are helpful if they are used judiciously, with knowledge of their limitations.

There are many other research results which provide the teacher with some consolation for her inability to teach certain children successfully. One discovered that boys, because of their slower development, do not show reading readiness at the age of six. Therefore, we considered postponing reading instruction of boys until the age of eight, notwithstanding the fact that in other cultures all boys read at the age of four. But there they do not know yet about the slow development of boys! And now we are discovering that the proper age at which children can learn to read and write may be two and a half or three.

While some teachers succeed in teaching all their first-grade students to read, others find solace in the discovery of "dislexia," particularly the effects of sidedness. If the child is hyperactive and uncontrollable, then he may suffer from minimal brain damage, about which the teacher naturally cannot do anything. More recently we have discovered the tremendous learning handicap of "culturally deprived" children. It is more than questionable that any one of these attempts to diagnose the child's learning deficiency will continue once teachers learn to understand the motivation of the child, his "private logic," his goals, and how to change them. Then the teacher will no longer be frustrated by the child's sabotage of her efforts, but may in turn discover how she can influence him despite any handicap he may have.

This brings us to a frequent dilemma of teachers in dealing with their pupils. How strict should they be, how permissive? There is a tendency to vacillate and to assume that there should be a happy medium. This, however, is not a solution. A democratic classroom, based on mutual respect, has no provisions for either vacillation or the happy medium. What is important is that the teacher learn to become a match for the child. Then she will no longer be outwitted by those children who combat her.

At the present time teachers are inclined to manipulate the students according to the old autocratic principle of divide and conquer. They side with the conformists against the rebels, with the good against the bad student, thereby extending the warfare. Their fight with some elements in their class leads to animosity and hostility among the students.

Many teachers are afraid that anarchy will erupt if they do not "enforce" compliance. But countless difficulties result from such ill-advised efforts to press children into submission. Children become only more defiant, for their cooperation cannot be gained through humiliation and suppression. Without realizing it the teacher then becomes more interested in her own power and authority than in the welfare of the students. As soon as she becomes resentful, frustrated, annoyed, she stops being a leader and an educator and becomes just a fighting human being, fighting for her right, her position, her prestige and superiority. No understanding of the situation and of herself is then possible; the teacher is in no condition to recognize those of her actions that may be responsible for the child's behavior.

THE ENCOUNTER WITH PARENTS

Every teacher tries to meet the parents of all her children, especially in the lower grades. If the child functions well, these encounters are pleasant. But if the child is not doing well, a tug of war may ensue. The teacher may blame the parents for the difficulty she has with her students. She often demands that they exert their influence to improve the child's academic progress or deportment. Usually she gives them the responsibility to help the child with his studies, particularly with his homework. In doing so she contributes greatly to the unhappiness of the family and to the child's increased antagonism to learning. If the parents had known how to exert a beneficial influence on their children, the present difficulties would not have arisen. They are the last ones to be charged with the responsibility to improve deficiencies; usually they only aggravate the situation further.

The parents, on the other hand, feel that the teacher is failing in her assignment. They expect the teacher to know how to teach, and most important, they expect the teacher to use her influence so that the child gets good grades. They also expect her to know what to do when the child misbehaves.

We witness here the old game of passing the buck. There is a general rule about the parents: the less mother knows what to do with the child, the better she knows what the father should do. This applies equally for the relationship between teacher and parents. If the teacher were able to deal effectively with her pupils she would not need to complain about the lack of cooperation on the part of the parents. However, what kind of cooperation can she really expect? Unfortunately teachers can make demands on parents, but they cannot tell them how to meet these demands successfully. Unless the teachers are exposed to and trained in parent education procedures, they cannot make feasible suggestions. Once instructed in the methods which parents can use to influence their children, the teachers are in the most promising position to provide parent education. Because of the cultural changes which make traditional methods of raising children obsolete, parents must get acquainted with training methods which are effective in a democratic setting. No one is in a better position to assist the parents in their difficult task than teachers who are familiar with effective methods of influencing children.[5]

The lack of cooperation from parents about which teachers so often complain can be well understood. Those parents whom the teacher tries to influence, understandably enough, do not enjoy their contact with her. One sure method to drive the parents into opposition are the notes the teacher sends home, what we call the "love letters." "Johnny does not bring his homework, Johnny cannot sit quietly, Johnny is a daydreamer, Johnny fights with the other children." It is a generally accepted practice to send such notes to the parents. Why? If you ask the teachers they will tell you that the parents *want* to get this information. But do the teachers always do what the parents want? Of course not. They will say that the parents ought to know. Why? Does the teacher really expect the parents to improve the situation? If the teacher is honest with herself she will know that nothing will change. After all, she probably has sent similar notes to the same parents many times before. Then why does she send them? In our discussions with teachers it became quite clear. The teacher feels so defeated by the child in her class that she wants to cause a little trouble for him at home. And in this she succeeds. But it does not improve her relationship with the parents, although they feel compelled to carry on her battle with the child.

RELATIONSHIP TO PRINCIPAL

Besides his administrative obligation the principal has to supervise the curriculum and the process of instruction. More important for the teacher is the help he can give her with difficult and disturbing students. When she feels unable to cope with one, she sends him to the principal. But what can he do?

At present most principals are in a precarious position. Not trained

[5] See R. Dreikurs and V. Soltz, *Children, The Challenge*, New York, Duell, Sloan & Pearce, 1965.

in the psychology of children, not acquainted with effective means of exerting corrective influences, he tries to maintain discipline in the traditional way of scolding, preaching, threatening—and punishing. It seems that the principal is the last remnant of an autocratic figure who has the right and the obligation to lay down the law, to enforce rules. The extent to which this autocratic role is accepted by many principals is evidenced in their conviction that the child needs the paddle.

There can be no doubt that such drastic methods sometimes have a beneficial effect, at least superficially. The child improves, for a while. The detriments of such a procedure are usually overlooked. It is obvious that the apparent good results are fallacious; otherwise no repeat performance would be necessary. What is worse, such display of power only reinforces the child's conviction that power is all that counts in life. And after the display of force, the child uses his own power very effectively against his teacher, until she, in despair, sends the child again to the principal.

It has become apparent that the principal needs almost the same training as the counselor in understanding and correcting a child's behavior. In the past, one considered such a function as the domain of the school psychologist and counselor. They were called upon to help individual children and to advise teachers about the needs of the child. It seems that more important than counselors are principals and supervisors. If they are sufficiently familiar with the effective means of influencing children, they are in the best position to help teachers in applying these methods. Then the teacher will be justified in expecting helpful suggestions, instead of being afraid of the evaluation by her supervisors if she is unable to control the child.

Whether the principal is aware of it or not, he cannot escape being in the middle between teacher and child. He follows the pattern of a distressed mother who is informed by the teacher about the misdeeds of her child. She either sides with the child against the teacher or with the teacher against the child. In either case her influence will only aggravate the situation. The principal will also be inclined to side with one or the other, although usually not openly. He may also try what parents do when their children quarrel—to find out who is right and wrong, as if that would do any good. In any warfare one or the other combatant is often right and often wrong. Exploring who is right and wrong in a given situation does not diminish the warfare.

This brings us to the crucial function of the principal. He establishes the atmosphere of his school; he can bring peace or friction. The ability to integrate all for the common purpose is as important for the principal as for the teacher in her class. Many of the group techniques which the teacher needs to know are equally vital for the principal. Without regular discussion with his staff he will find it difficult to exert his influence on his faculty. Instead of blaming and censoring, the teachers need understanding and support in their difficult assignment to teach reluctant learners and antagonistic rebels.

Being left alone with her difficulties in teaching, maintaining discipline, and covering her assignments, she is inclined to be afraid of the criticism by principal and supervisors. In turn, she may expect the impossible from the principal; she may be disappointed and critical if he does not resolve the conflicts with the child and his parents. The principal becomes the butt of antagonisms between teacher and child, and between teacher and parent. Trying his best to resolve the conflict, his lack of training often merely brings temporary relief. Usually the fighting lines become deeper and the mutual antagonism and distrust increases. He cannot help but become resentful of the teacher and the parent who caused his predicament. And he, in turn, usually gets little encouragement from any one.

THE TEACHER AND THE COMMUNITY

In most cases the expectations of the community are not in conflict with the educational goals of the teachers. However, in many communities, especially those with considerable racial or economic differences, the teacher is not considered a friend, but a critical and imposing authority. We find the same principle here as in the classroom. The teachers are excellent if they do not meet opposition and often helpless or even provocative if they encounter it. The community may have an exaggerated expectation of what the schools can achieve or may oppose the schools if they wish to incorporate new ideas and procedures.

There is a peculiar imbalance between the rights and duties of the school and those of the community. The parents are obliged by law to send their children to school. But the school takes it upon itself to expel a student if the teacher is unable to cope with him. Do the parents have the right to expect the school to provide their children with the necessary education? At the present time, even though they may have the right to expect this of the schools, the schools are likely to fail them, simply because educators share the parents' lack of training in dealing effectively with disturbed and difficult children. We find also that pointing out what each opposing group is doing right or wrong is of no value. Means have to be found to reconcile differences of opinion and interests on the basis of mutual respect. And the technique for doing so is not known; we have not learned how to resolve conflicts by agreement instead of fighting.

The teacher experiences the pressure of the community in the reactions of the parents of her students. She has a difficult decision to make, when to give in to the demands and when to resist them. And most important, how one can stand up without provoking and antagonizing. This depends again on the teacher's attitude, whether she resents the pressure or understands it, whether she feels superior and contemptuous or is willing to assume leadership. The crucial factor in determining her performance is her attitude toward herself.

THE TEACHER'S STRUGGLE WITH HERSELF

The teacher is faced with a professional handicap. She is often threatened by her students in her authority. Then she feels obliged to assert her authority, not realizing that in our time authorities are no longer recognized, but fought. She feels personally responsible for each child's failure or uncontrollable behavior, when she no longer has any means to "make" a child study or behave himself. She can acquire methods to stimulate children to do so, but most of the effective means are not known to teachers. Moreover, what actually is merely lack of information is often construed by her as lack of her own ability, as a sign of personal failure.

This fear of being a failure is another professional handicap. It is characteristic for our neurotic society that nobody can be sure of being good enough, each one trying to be superior and afraid of being inferior. This whole yardstick of success and failure, superiority or inferiority is even more ingrained in our contemporary educational system. The teacher is almost obliged to impose it on her students. How could she extricate herself from it? Yet such an extrication is essential if she is to function as a free agent. The desire to be perfect makes spontaneity and creativity almost impossible, because they imply the danger of making a mistake. How can the teacher acquire the necessary courage to be imperfect if she, in her daily routine, constantly has to watch for every infraction of perfection?

Unless the teacher can tolerate making mistakes, she cannot be spontaneous, and spontaneity is one quality most needed in dealing with children, who are naturally spontaneous and creative, although they frequently use their creativity to fight the teacher. The teacher, moreover, often offers herself as a willing target, because the child has it within his power to deal her a devastating sense of failure.

As long as the teacher is concerned with how good she is as a teacher, she remains highly vulnerable. She may actually succeed in being a good teacher and influencing her students to cooperate, to learn, and to conform. However, if she is frustrated in her attempts and finds she cannot be a good teacher, she may then become the worst kind, fighting with and abusing the child. The only solution then is to expel the child or transfer him to another class. Such incongruities in one teacher have often been observed. They are the result of a teacher's excessive ambition. And most teachers are overly ambitious. They cannot tolerate a gifted child who does not work up to his capacity, as if anyone does.

For this reason it may be difficult for a teacher to maintain an unbiased attitude toward each child. Yet a certain detachment is necessary for correct analysis and interpretation. The educator who becomes involved emotionally through anger, annoyance, or sense of failure acts impulsively and defensively, becomes self-centered rather than child-centered.

These conflicts and tensions can also be found in the teacher's dealing with other teachers, with the principal, with parents, and with the community. Supposed to be an authority, to be listened to, she may construe every criticism as intolerable, as personal insult. Conflicts are inevitable, but they remain utterly unsolvable if the question of personal value, prestige, and status becomes involved. Freedom from such fears is possible if one stops being concerned with oneself and considers instead the needs of the situation. When one can let the chips fall where they may, then one can forget oneself and instead concentrate on the task at hand. This is indeed a difficult assignment for the teacher. But if she can bring herself to this inner freedom, she can then impart it to her students and provide them with a healthy philosophy of life.

CHAPTER 2

Understanding the Child

TO UNDERSTAND CHILDREN, to influence them, and to correct their deficiencies requires knowledge about the development of personality. Our approach to children will vary, depending on our concept of human nature, and especially on our views about how they grow and become what they are.

The desire to be a part of the group is basic to all human beings. Man is a social being and can fully function only within a group. As long as he feels that he belongs, he can devote his energies to meeting the needs of the situation. The degree and the extent of belonging depend on the development of his "social interest," as Adler called it. He is born with the innate potential to function as a social being, to develop sufficient social feeling. Fully developed, it implies not only the awareness of having a place, but also the ability to play a constructive part in life. It is the basis for what can be called "normalcy," the basis for cooperation and fulfillment. Deficiency in its development restricts social function.

HEREDITY, ENVIRONMENT, AND CREATIVE POWER

The child experiences two sets of stimulations. One originates in his own body through his physiological functions and his hereditary physical endowment; the other comes from his environment and the people around him, first of all his mother.

16

Discussions of heredity and environment often raise the question of which one is more important in molding the individual. Such discussions miss the essential point: the individual is not simply a reactive organism, but an active participant in the solution of conflicts around and within himself. His behavior and development are not directly affected by either his inner or outer environment, but only by his perception and evaluation of them. Long before he can think consciously, or on the verbal level, the child has the ability to take attitudes toward what he experiences, to interpret—in a vague way, perhaps—what he encounters, and to draw conclusions which are the basis for his actions. The child not only reacts; he also acts. What he is born with is less important than what he later does with it.

His perceptions are always tinged with value—desirability, requirements, appraisal of his position in relation to other people. A crippled child, for example, does not perceive himself merely as having a defect, though this is all that the physical stimulus would tell him. Nor does his defect "cause" his subsequent development in a mechanistic way. He may perceive his handicap as an inferiority, a hindrance to full group acceptance and participation, or as an asset, entitling him to special privileges. Experiencing a sensation of inferiority, he can take various attitudes toward it. These attitudes, not the original deficiency, determine the resulting condition. Depending on his evaluation of himself in relation to the situation, and depending on the extent of his courage, he will compensate, overcompensate, or give up in despair and sustain a permanent deficiency.[1]

The same three types of responses are possible in regard to any difficulty a child encounters. Discouragement, resentment, and feelings of frustration do not result from external conditions, but from an individual's appraisal of his own ability to meet them. His appraisal of his ability is subjective and may be fallacious. Thus the past experiences of the child cannot be regarded as determining factors; they are only challenges.

[1] See the author's paper, "The Socio-psychological Dynamics of Physical Disability," *Journal of Social Issues,* Vol. IV, no. 4, 1948, pp. 39–54.

THE FORMATION OF THE LIFE STYLE

As the child interprets his experiences with the inner and outer environment, he draws conclusions about effective approaches toward social living. His attitude toward life in general constitutes his life style or life pattern; it is the key to the personality of each individual. It encompasses the unity of his personality; all acts and attitudes are only facets of this general life style, based on his central evaluation of himself and his abilities. Generally, dangers and disappointments play an important part in the formation of the life style, which includes a scheme of action by which the child hopes to avoid future humiliations, setting up a fictitious goal of assumed security. For example, a child who feels endangered in his position within the family by the arrival of a younger sibling may consider his position to be the prime objective of his life. Only when he is first in whatever he may do can he feel secure. On the other hand, a child who has been the youngest and who has succeeded in compensating for his position of weakness and smallness by putting the older and stronger members of the family into his service may consider it important for the rest of his life to secure the support, assistance, and protection of others. A child who has felt neglected and pushed aside may have reached the conclusion that he can be a part of the group only if he makes people feel sorry for him. His "martyr complex" becomes his basic guiding principle, giving him moral superiority over the physically and socially stronger. One child, on the strength of his earlier childhood impressions, may consider pleasing others his only way to acceptance, whereas another may rely on fighting as the only means of securing a place for himself.

In his efforts to play a part in group life (within his first group, his family), the child is guided by the example of, and his experiences with, other members of the family. Again, the influence is dynamic and not mechanistic. Human relations are based on mutual interactions which, for the most part, take place without awareness. The resultant relationship between any two people is actively established by both parties simultaneously. In his interactions with others, the child selects his individual approaches long before conscious thought develops.

Consciousness is correlated with verbalization and is often over-rated in its significance in human motivation. In the past, most educational approaches were on the moral, verbal, and logical level, directed toward developing the child's conscience. Yet while it is essential that the child accept social conventions and recognize right and wrong, this is not enough. Behavior springs not merely from rational thought, but even more from basic, only partially conscious, attitudes toward life. The child's concept of himself may prevent him from conforming to social demands. He may have wrong impressions about his position in the group and his chances of obtaining a place by antisocial methods. Such misconceptions about social living result in faulty approaches.

In his first experiments with others, the child operates by trial and error. Whatever is found to be effective is continued. In the beginning the child tackles each problem as it arises. Consequently, he may behave differently in dealing with father, mother, a favorite aunt, an older or younger sibling. As he grows older and perceives the group as a whole, he begins to look for guiding principles which permit a general line of action. Usually by the age of four or five, the child has integrated his subjective impression of group living into a total picture of life. His style of life is established. He no longer gropes on the basis of trial and error, but acts on the premise already established; henceforth he integrates every new experience into his stabilized concept. He has developed a basic personal bias and regards any new situation with his biased apperception. For this reason a change of the child's personality is more difficult after this period and becomes increasingly so as the child's intellectual development permits him to maintain his basic assumptions despite obvious evidence of his misjudgment. He has learned to rationalize, i.e., to be logically correct in his misinterpretations.

Such basic assumptions can be recognized easily in children, because in contrast to adults they exhibit their attitudes openly. It requires deeper psychological analysis to discover the basic life style in adults, who have learned how to hide it. In either case, the individual is unaware of his own basic convictions. He cannot see his own misinterpretations, because if he recognized his errors he could not maintain them, and their maintenance has become necessary to his security.

THE DYNAMICS OF INFERIORITY FEELINGS

Because of the primacy of the desire to be an accepted, participating member of the group, the most painful experience for any child—as for any adult—is the feeling that he is inferior to others. Any hardship, tragedy, pain, and inconvenience is relatively tolerable as long as it does not imply a lowering of social status. Only then is the feeling of belonging to the group impaired. And not to belong is the greatest hardship for any human being. Inferiority feelings inhibit or restrict the development of the necessary social interest.

Unfortunately, we do not provide our children with the sense that they are good enough as they are. We are afraid that doing so would stop them from developing and improving. There are two ways to stimulate growth. One is on the vertical plane, striving for self-elevation; the other is on the horizontal plane, through the desire to contribute, to expand, to discover—moving toward, not ahead of, others.[2] Progress can be achieved in either way: However, the price of success on the vertical plane is too high. There can be no security, not through achievement, power, love, or anything else provided by the outside world. Whatever one may have obtained, it may not be sufficient or one may lose it. Our present methods of raising children present them with a sequence of discouraging experiences. It deprives each of the experience of his own strength, which alone can provide a sense of security, the confidence in one's own ability to face whatever may come.

The study of the effects of inferiority feelings is hampered by semantic difficulties with the term "inferiority." Inferiority *feelings* should not be confused with actual *inferiorities*. People who are in

[2] Lydia Sicher, "Education for Freedom," *American Journal of Individual Psychology,* Vol. 11, 1955, pp. 97–103.

reality inferior in certain regards may not recognize their deficiency and consequently may develop no inferiority feelings. Conversely, many people with inferiority feelings have no objective justification for their assumption that they are inadequate: they may be persons with high status and accomplishments. Besides actual inferiority and inferiority feelings, we must also recognize the *display* of inferiorities that is called an "inferiority complex." This term refers to the use of a real or assumed inferiority as an excuse, as a demand for special service or consideration; it is a frequent neurotic escape mechanism.

The distinction between inferiority feelings and an inferiority complex has practical significance, since the psychological effects of each are distinct. The sense of inadequacy or inferiority, regardless of how conscious or unconscious it may be, permits compensatory endeavors and thereby may lead to the development of positive qualities and accomplishments. This is not the case with the inferiority complex; it inhibits progress. It is a final conclusion of hopelessness, whether it is limited to a certain area of activity or encompasses the total social scene. While inferiority feelings are generally perceived in a vague way, the inferiority complex is not only fully felt but openly exhibited; the individual "knows" that he is no good or cannot do something, even though objective evidence might not support this assumption. Maladjustment, dysfunction, or misbehavior may only occasionally represent an inferiority complex, but they can always be traced to a sense of inferiority of which the individual is often unaware.

A feeling of social inferiority is experienced by every child as he grows up in a world of giants and realizes painfully his weakness and smallness. Our present methods of education, far from alleviating the sense of inferiority in children, actually accentuate and intensify it. The child becomes unsure of his social position not only in relation to the adults around him but even more by comparisons (made by himself and others) with older and younger siblings or other children and their accomplishments and abilities.

This social inferiority affects a child's relationships and leads him to seek individual compensations. His basic urge to participate is sidetracked by a desire for self-elevation. To be sure, self-elevation is also part of the desire to belong. But the ability to win acceptance from the group seems first to require a compensation for the feeling of inferiority. If this is not possible, then nothing remains but to withdraw from participation altogether.

Thus we see the possibility of two responses to any experience of inferiority feelings. The child either tries to compensate or withdraws. This compensation can be direct or devious: it can be by useful means or through methods which Adler called "on the useless side of life." There is no single rule as to which direction a child will take.

Inferiority feelings are an important dynamic factor in the development of abilities and character traits. To understand the reasons for the choice of a given life style requires knowledge of the opportunities and difficulties which the child encountered in his inner environment—in his physical constitution and in possible organic deficiencies—and particularly in his outer environment, with its obstacles and advantages.

THE FAMILY ATMOSPHERE

Father and mother provide the atmosphere in which the child first experiences and recognizes the values and conventions of social living. His orientation toward social living derives from the attitudes which he develops toward the social conditions characteristic in his family. The economic, racial, national, religious, and social influences of the community reach him through his parents, who express all these influences in their behavior toward each other and toward their children. They not only impress the child with the standards characteristic of the various social levels but also set the example for human relationships.

The relationship between father and mother establishes the pattern for all interpersonal relationships within the family. If they are competitive with each other, the spirit of competition will characterize all the family relationships. For instance, it has been observed that competitiveness between father and mother, with its constant mutual challenge for superiority, can offset the natural tendencies of identical twins to develop similar personalities. On the other hand, if the parents are cooperative and friendly, their children will have a better chance to develop these trends in their dealings with each other and later on with persons outside the family. Whether the parents are orderly or disorganized, cooperative or antagonistic, the family atmosphere will present its characteristic pattern to the children as a standard of life.

The family pattern, however, by no means *determines* the child's behavior. It may induce quite opposite behavior patterns. Nevertheless, children of the same family do by and large show an inclination to similar behavior, developing characteristic values and moral concepts, especially when these are clearly defined and accepted by both parents. We can therefore say that the similarity of character traits in brothers and sisters is an expression of the family atmosphere, while differences in the personalities of siblings reflect the particular role of each child in the so-called family constellation.

THE FAMILY CONSTELLATION

The child's development depends to a large degree on his function within the family. In his early relationship to other members of the family, each child establishes his own approaches to others in an effort to gain a place in the group. The sequence of birth provides each child with a different point of view within the family set-up. His position as the only, the oldest, the youngest, or the middle child, as the case may be, gives him different opportunities for exerting his influence and presents him with particular challenges. A child's place within the family group may also be affected by being an only boy among girls, an only girl among boys, a sickly child, or a child born after the death of a predecessor. Physical characteristics either shared with an outstanding member of the family or considered of highly important positive or negative value may influence a child. So may the favoritism of the parents, their special concern with one or the other child.

In our competitive society the desire of each child to find his place within the group meets at once with sharp challenge from his siblings. This occurs almost regularly between the first and the second child. The first one feels dethroned and must give up part of his mother's time and affection to the newcomer. He tries to maintain his superiority over the intruder, who in turn constantly challenges the position of the older sibling and his advantage of age. This competition must be distinguished from sibling rivalry, although the two often coincide. Rivalry means open contest and fights for immediate gratification; competition is possible without such open resentment, envy, and antagonism. Competition has a much deeper impact on each child, leading to the development of opposite character traits, abilities, interests, and temperaments, as each child seeks success where the other one fails. This explains why in most families the first and second child are so different.

Such competition is not limited to the first two children. The position of the middle child is particularly precarious; having neither the rights of the older nor the privileges of the younger, he often feels unfairly treated. In the resulting competitive struggle he may be pushed down by the two others or he may succeed in pushing them down into failure.

The youngest child—similar in some ways to an only child—can find a variety of methods to compensate for a position that often evokes inferiority feelings. He may solicit the service of others by being helpless and weak; he may gain special attention through his charm; or he may shine with brilliance and accomplishments. Whatever he chooses for his compensation, it will reflect his dependence on others for value, status, and significance. Similarly, any child who has received special treatment and privileges is under the pressure of competitive strife from his siblings and develops his own personality in interaction with those who try to challenge him.

Whereas children reach an agreement as to which method each one will employ to find his place, parents, unaware of their choices, reinforce each child's plans. They make the good better and the bad worse. The first child may be spoiled by his parents, becoming the favorite, which leaves the second to navigate for himself. The direction in which the first will move will depend less on what his parents do than on how the younger sibling will proceed. If he, all by himself, develops strength and independence and manages to succeed in life, then all the love and favoritism of his parents will not prevent the older from becoming deficient. Or, vice versa, the first one may emerge as the better, with the help of his parents, which may prompt the other one to fail. It is the children who reach their decision in their interplay with each other. The parents could exert constructive influences, but then they would have to extricate themselves from the unconscious decision of the children and not thereby reinforce it.

Personality traits of children are thus movements indicating their responses to the power politics within the family group. The relationship between each of the members of the family can be described almost diagrammatically by the existing similarities and differences of personality; they indicate alliance and competition. The children who are most different in character, interests, and achievement are the competitors, and those who are alike are the allies. The strongest influence on the development of each child is exerted by his main competitor, the one who is most different from him.

The problems of each child therefore become an integral part of the family relationships and cannot be understood—or solved— as isolated problems. When the problem child improves, his competitor, the good one, always becomes worse. Their behavior is coordinated. The parents are not the cause of maladjustment; they merely make it possible and reinforce faulty goals.

THE METHODS OF TRAINING

The family atmosphere generally provides some constancy in the child's experiences and, therefore, leads to the development of his individual life style. Although the methods of training used in a specific family are part of the general atmosphere of the family, and of religious, national, racial, or cultural standards, they vary with each child, and frequently even with each new situation. In consequence, a child's attitudes and goals also vary. His behavior, good or bad, is only a logical outcome of the response he gets from his parents, which in turn is evoked by his actions. Parents, often not recognizing the child's intentions, unwittingly fall victim to his provocations.

Rearing children has been made difficult by changes in the social structure of contemporary society. The development of democracy requires new methods in the solution of conflicts. Past social patterns were based on the relationship of dominant-submissive; the dominant maintained his control through bribe and threat, reward and punishment. These methods are inefficient in training a child in a democratic setting in which a state of equality is achieved by everyone, based on his freedom to decide for himself. Equality has become a reality; the difficulty lies in the fact that we do not know how to live with each other as equals, because we have no tradition to guide us.[3]

A relationship between equals requires respect for others and for oneself. Most of the mistakes made in the rearing of children today are a violation of either the adult's self-respect or respect for the children. The parents who let the child "express himself" without restraint, damage their own self-respect and "spoil" the child. In their misconception of the idea of democracy and freedom, they let the child disrupt family order and impose his will upon them. Spoiling is the most frequent mistake of our time. It includes a variety of ill-advised procedures, such as overprotection, indulgence, oversolicitude, worship, and the like. When such methods fail to stimulate a child to proper behavior, adults are apt to revert to the old

[3] The term *equality* is widely used but little understood. In which way can people be equal, since they are so different in personality, ability, physical attributes, etc.? Equality can pertain to equal rights and equality of value. (In other languages, this difference is expressed in special terms, like the German *Gleichwertigkeit* and *Gleichberechtigung*.) Democracy implies both kinds of equality—but not equality of opportunity which never existed and cannot exist; it is a subterfuge of pseudo-democratic tendencies which refuse to recognize the fundamental rights of each human being.

Regardless of individual differences in race, sex, money, age, education or any other individual trait or quality, each individual has to be recognized in his equal rights, expressed in his right of self-determination, and in his equal value, commanding respect for what he is. Equality is not an ideal or a hope for the future; it exists. The sense of equality motivates all groups of heretofore dominated people, like women, colored races, children, and the poor, to demand to be treated as equals. Disregard for this demand creates the present upheaval in our society.

principles of humiliation and punishment, which disregard the dignity of the child. This approach includes all forms of overmanagement, scolding, nagging, and moral and physical punishment.

It is evident that these methods do not induce a child to respect order. Generally less recognized is the similarity of their psychological effects. Spoiling and suppression equally give rise to discouragement. It is obvious that a child who is humiliated is impaired in his development of self-confidence. But it is not always realized that the same effect is achieved through spoiling. The spoiled child is deprived of the necessary opportunity to experience his own strength and ability. Furthermore, as a corollary to overprotection and indulgence, parents and teachers often reveal a lack of confidence in the child's ability, intelligence, and sense of responsibility. Many adults do not recognize the child's capacity to take care of himself in difficult situations. By their lack of faith in him, they increase his doubt in himself.

THE FOUR GOALS OF THE CHILD'S DISTURBING BEHAVIOR

Every action of a child has a purpose. His basic aim is to have his place in the group. A well-behaved and well-adjusted child has found his way toward social acceptance by conforming to the requirements of the group and by making useful contributions. But even the child who misbehaves and defies the needs of the situation still believes that his actions will give him social status. He may try to get attention or attempt to prove his power, or he may seek revenge or display his deficiency in order to get special service or exemption. Whichever of these four goals he adopts, his behavior is based on his conviction that only in this way can he function within the group. His goal may occasionally vary with circumstances: he may act to attract attention at one moment, and assert his power or seek revenge at another. He may also obtain his goal by different techniques; and conversely, the same behavior pattern may be used for different purposes. Its dynamics can be generally recognized by the *effect* it has on others, and by their reactions.

These four goals of disturbing behavior can be observed in all young children up to the age of ten. We are often accused of arbitrarily and haphazardly putting every disturbing behavior of a child in one of these four categories. We did not invent them; we merely observed them. If someone could show another goal of a misbehaving young child, we would be glad to incorporate it. It is difficult for many parents and teachers to believe that the disturbing behavior is directed against them. It is a means by which the child tries to find status, and at this age his status depends on the reaction he can get from adults. These four goals can be also observed in teenagers and even in adults; but there they are not all-inclusive. There are many other ways in which adolescents can find their place in a destructive way, through smoking, sex, heroism, and excitement. The sad fact is that the increase in status and personal value which we consider essential for everyone, is more easily obtained through useless and destructive means than through accomplishments.

1. The *attention-getting mechanism* (AGM) is operative in most young children. Its predominance is the result of the method by which children are brought up in our culture. When young, they have few opportunities to establish their social position through useful contribution. Whatever has to be done for the welfare of the family is done by older siblings or adults. This leaves only one way for a young child to feel a part of his family group. Prevented from gaining status through his own constructive contributions, he seeks proof of his acceptance through gifts, demonstrations of affection, or at least through attention. As none of these increases his self-reliance and self-confidence, the child requires constant new proof that he is not lost and rejected. He may try first to get results through socially acceptable and pleasant means. When, however, these methods are no longer effective—when a younger sibling steals the show, or when the adults expect the child to give up his "childish" behavior as he grows up—he will try any other conceivable method to put others into his service or to get attention. Unpleasant by-products like humiliation, punishment, or even physical pain do not matter as long as his main purpose is achieved. Children prefer being scolded, punished, and even beaten to being ignored.

2. Efforts to "control" the child lead to a deadlock in a struggle for *power and superiority* between child and adults. The child tries

to prove that he can do what he wants and refuses to do what he ought to. No final "victory" of parents or teachers is possible. In most instances the child will "win out," if only because he is not restricted in his fighting methods by any sense of responsibility or moral obligation. The few times that parents are able to score a "victory" and overpower the child make him only the more convinced of the value of power and the more determined to strike back, the next time with stronger methods.

3. This battle between parents and children for power and domination may reach a point where the parents try every conceivable means to subjugate the culprit. The mutual antagonism may become so strong that each party has only one desire: retaliation, to *revenge* his own feeling of being hurt. The child no longer hopes merely for attention or even power; feeling ostracized and disliked, he can see his place in the group only by his success in making himself hated. Children of this type know where they can hurt the most and take advantage of the vulnerability of their opponents. They regard it as a triumph when they are considered vicious; since that is the only triumph they can obtain, it is the only one they seek.

4. A child who is passive, or whose antagonism is successfully beaten down, may be discouraged to such an extent that he cannot hope for any significance whatsoever. He expects only defeat and failure and stops trying. He hides himself behind a *display of real or imagined inferiority*. He uses his inability as a protection so that nothing will be required or expected of him. By avoiding participation or contribution, he tries to preclude more humiliating and embarrassing experiences.

In pursuing one or more of these goals, disturbing children may be either *active* or *passive* and may—as in the case of attention getting—use *constructive* or *destructive* methods. Only if the child feels accepted will he use constructive methods; antagonism is always expressed in destructive acts. On the other hand, whether the child responds actively or passively depends on his self-confidence and courage. This basic pattern of activity or passivity is one of the first established in early infancy and is difficult to change. It reflects the infant's evaluation of himself, perhaps based on prenatal experiences and early training, perhaps on innate predispositions.

Later discouragement may move the child down the ladder of antagonism and rebellion; but the degree of activity often remains unchanged.

The two pairs of factors lead to four types of behavior pattern:
1. Active-constructive
2. Active-destructive
3. Passive-constructive
4. Passive-destructive

A few characteristic behavior patterns so often found in school children may serve as examples of these four basic patterns. *Active-constructive* behavior is the extreme ambition to be the first in the class, the helpfulness exhibited by the "teacher's pet." *Active-destructive* is the clown, the bully, the impertinent and defiant rebel. *Passive-constructive* is the children who with their charm and adoration manage to receive special attention and favor, without doing anything themselves. *Passive-destructive* is laziness and stubbornness.

As seen in the chart, attention getting (goal 1) is the only goal which is achieved by all four behavior patterns. Power (goal 2)

Diminished Social Interest →

Useful		Useless		
act. constr.	pass. constr.	act. destr.	pass. destr.	
"success"	a — "charm"	"nuisance" b	"laziness"	AGM
	c	a "rebel"	"stubborn" b	Power
		"vicious"	"violent passivity" b	Revenge
		c	"hopeless"	Assumed Disability

Social Discouragement ↓

or revenge (goal 3) are obtained mainly through active- and passive-destructive methods. (Power and revenge through "good deeds" is possible, but rare in children.) The display of inadequacy (goal 4) can naturally only use passive-destructive methods.

The most frequent deteriorating sequence is from active-*constructive* AGM to active-*destructive* AGM to active-destructive *power* to active-destructive *revenge* (line a). Another frequent line goes from passive-*constructive* AGM to passive-*destructive* AGM to display of *inability* (line b). In most cases this development goes through a passive demonstration of *power*, but not so frequently through passive *revenge* which we call "violent passivity." Sometimes passive-constructive behavior can turn directly to the open display of inability (goal 4) (line c). Improvement does not follow the same lines. Even a revengeful child, who generally presents the most disturbed behavior patterns, can become adequately adjusted if he can be convinced that he is liked and can be useful.

The relationship between the life style and the prevalent goals can be described through the example of two of the most frequently found personality patterns. A child who thinks he must be first to have any place in the group, because he was dethroned by a sibling and had to fight to maintain his superiority in the family, can try to establish his superiority first through an active-constructive AGM. If this avenue is blocked, he may try to steal attention by being tough, or silly, by clowning, and so forth. These are active-destructive methods of getting attention. He may then turn to a display of destructive power: he can still be first in being bad. And if he turns to revenge, he may try to be the first in viciousness, and he may succeed.

On the other hand, a child may consider his only chance to find his place in the group through being served by others, because he was an only, a youngest, or a sickly child. He may first succeed through a passive-constructive AGM, being cute and a clinging vine. If these methods fail, he may become destructive to gain attention and service. Passive-destructive behavior may help him also to prove his power by forcing others to be occupied with him, to coax him. Revengeful violent passivity or a display of utter inadequacy and feebleness may equally move others into action for him. The same life style can be at the root of any one of the four goals.

THE THREE PHASES OF CHILDHOOD

On his way to adulthood each child passes through various stages. Developmental psychology describes a variety of them. Here we touch on only three main divisions which imply a fundamental distinction of function: the preschool child, the child in school, and the adolescent.

The preschool child functions mainly within his immediate family group, including close relatives and neighbors. During this time he tries to find his place as an individual within this group. He learns to function biologically and socially and to integrate his physiological, mental, and psychological capacities into his individual pattern of social functioning, his life style.

When the child enters school, he becomes a part of the community and tries to find his place among individuals of different economic, cultural, social, racial, and religious backgrounds. At this time work, duty, and responsibility become important aspects of his life.[4] His personal pattern of functioning, of interpersonal relationships, becomes settled. The teacher and a group of peers take an important part in stimulating his individual responses to social living. Today there is a tendency to lower the age of school attendance so that the characteristic dynamics of the school period take effect when the child is only three or even younger and enters nursery school. This is a necessary compensation for the increasing difficulty

---

[4] In the past an important distinction was made between play and duty. First the child learned through play. When he reached school age, he had to learn to "work," to accept "duties." One did not make learning easy for him, because then he never would learn to "work." Duty had to be a more or less unpleasant task to be fulfilled. We still find remnants of this philosophy in our schools. The less the child likes studying, the more unpleasant we make it for him. Experiences with teaching very young children to read and write indicate that early learning takes place with ease as part of a natural development like learning to talk and to walk. Today when the child does not want to learn, we have no means to force him to do so, as we had in the past.

of the family to provide sufficient stimulation for emotional and social adjustment.

The rebellion of youth which begins in early childhood, when the parents are defied in their authority, culminates during adolescence. During this period the child tries to find his place in society at large, which leads him into inevitable conflict with his parents and teachers. He questions what is handed down to him, particularly the values established by the preceding generation.

The conflict between the generations has become greatly accentuated and intensified in our era. The increase in juvenile delinquency is only a symptom of the generalized warfare that exists today between adults and children.

Parents have difficulty in changing their once established relationship with their youngster when he reaches adolescence; for them he is still "only a child," whereas his development in size and ability induces strangers to treat him as an adult. The confusion about his social position is intensified by his confusion about sex. New sensations are experienced, new desires, new impressions about the opposite sex. Parents are not accepted as guides, because their values and moral concepts often seem antiquated in the rapid evolution of social patterns.

Sexual patterns in our time are changing, in accordance with the new social status of women. Not only the inevitable uncertainty about sexual behavior but the thin line between freedom and license baffles each adolescent. There is no longer any rule that he can discover in regard to the particular social function allotted to each sex. In our present state of anarchy, in which each man and each woman has to establish his own equilibrium with the opposite sex, it requires great courage, common sense, and social responsibility to find an adequate equation. But our generation of children is further handicapped by a general lack of these very qualities. To the extent that they are spoiled and overprotected, they have learned more to demand than to contribute and are, therefore, more inclined to seek the easy gratifications which sex offers. Status and excitement are becoming the most highly esteemed values amongst our teenagers. Boredom justifies lack of participation; for the sake of excitement, almost every deed is permissible.

Another educational and cultural pattern burdens our generation of adolescents. They have been trained by adults to compete, and made to feel inferior if they do not excel. Their ambition, which their parents and teachers have tried to stimulate, now becomes the greatest obstacle to their adjustment. They all want to feel important, to be something special. Yet in our present culture the community offers little that gives them a feeling of significance. Some few are fortunate in finding eminence in school, academically, athletically, or socially. The great majority rarely find avenues for experiencing importance in a useful way. Only in their defiance of order and discipline can they feel some semblance of power and superiority. Driving a car, easy money, gambling, drinking, and sex are the easiest ways for them to achieve a sensation of significance. Perverted overambition is often at the core of juvenile delinquency. But instead of help and proper guidance, those youngsters who run afoul of the law encounter more humiliation, which in turn pushes them further in the wrong direction. Recreational facilities to give them wholesome fun and to keep them off the streets are not adequate resources to meet their problem. Unless society finds avenues in which the adolescent generations can take on responsibilities as equal partners in school and in the community, the ambitions instilled in these youngsters will tend to express themselves, logically and naturally, in useless or undesirable ways. And it is much easier to get status through useless means and misbehavior than through accomplishment.

It is significant to watch how the child responds in the various phases to psychological disclosure of his goals. At no time is he aware of the purpose of his misbehavior, any more than he is aware of his life style and his goals. If the child under ten is approached in the proper fashion and informed about his goals, he will show the characteristic "recognition reflex," which indicates that he recognizes the correctness of the interpretation.[5] But more than this: a child up to this age is able to give up a particular behavior as soon as he recognizes its purpose. (This refers only to distinct and special actions, not to his general life pattern.) In other words,

[5] The recognition reflex is more fully described in Chapter 3.

the young child can easily recognize his goals and change them. An adolescent has no great difficulty in recognizing his goals when they are explained to him; but it takes time and retraining to alter them. Adults find it difficult both to recognize their goals and to change them. This is the result of the process of "maturation," which permits an increasing power to rationalize and put up a front.

CHAPTER 3

Specific Methods of Correction

IS IT POSSIBLE to get along with children and to guide them without insight into their psychological dynamics, their motivation? The answer to this question is *Yes*, because there are specific and non-specific methods of correction. The specific approaches are geared to the needs of any particular child, whereas the nonspecific methods are applicable to all children. These are the establishment of a good personal relationship, encouragement, use of the group, integration of the class, and, most important, group discussions.

Any teacher can acquire the knowledge and sensitivity to understand the behavior of children. Some have a natural ability to sense psychological processes and to respond almost immediately to any situation; others need training. Even those who at first seem incapable of grasping what is going on in a child can develop the necessary skills if they wish to acquire them.

OBSERVING THE CHILD

Observation of a child can provide valuable information if the teacher knows what to look for and how to interpret what she sees. The behavior and the actions of the child provide opportunities for insight into his motivations. To understand a child properly, one must realize that his every act is purposive, and expresses his attitudes, his goals, and his expectations. The classroom is a natural setting for revealing them, through the child's interactions with other children, his deportment, his cooperation or lack of it, his academic work. The teacher who can find the common denominator for a child's actions can recognize his life style, the unity of his personality, the basic concepts upon which he operates.

Systematic observation may reveal that a particular child can participate only if he is on top. In subjects where he excels he does a fine job; but as soon as he lags behind, he gives up trying altogether. He may even become obstreperous when he sees an opportunity to take leadership among children who are defiant or who in other ways try to gain eminence in the class through disturbance The outsider and lone wolf becomes equally understandable to a teacher who can observe. As he does not believe that he can be liked and accepted by others, he may do well academically but be disturbing through his uncooperative relationships with others. Effective observation misses no detail of the interaction between all children. Many teachers, concerned with their own duties and dealing with each child separately, pay too little attention to the interplay of the whole group. It requires training to extend the field of vision so that the teacher can encompass the whole class at all times. If she can do so, she can spot a center of disturbance at the onset before it becomes a problem and can respond effectively to any child's bid for attention or power.

The child's attitudes are obvious even if he apparently does nothing. The way he sits, the expression on his face show his attitude and deserve notice. In a training class for teachers an experiment was conducted in which several children were called, one at a time, into the room for a few minutes. The teachers were advised to remain silent and passive, while watching closely in order to interpret what they saw. It was an artificial and—one must admit—embarrassing situation for the child. Most teachers, confronted with this situation for the first time, found it difficult to make any interpretation after the child left the room. The trained observer, however, was able to recognize one child as trying hard to get attention and help, a second as defiant. Another, the observer noticed, just sat helpless, and still another reconciled himself in a short time to the situation and amused himself. If such a situation of inactivity can reveal such basic attitudes in a child, how much more material is offered by the constant give-and-take of a classroom!

PSYCHOLOGICAL INVESTIGATION

Although the teacher's time for exhaustive studies of each child in her class is limited, she has many avenues of insight into their backgrounds. Sometimes short talks between classes can provide sufficient information to explain a child's attitude. The teacher can, and should, find out about the child's family constellation, the sequence of brothers and sisters and their personalities. In this way she can see the interrelationships within the family, the sources of discouragement, the handicaps which the child has encountered. An occasional contact with the mother can provide some impressions. As the mother is the most important person in a child's life and helps to set, by her own relationship with the child, the pattern for his future relationships to other people, so the behavior of the mother may offer an important clue to the child's attitudes. Often the child imitates his mother. His rigidity, bossiness, self-pity and righteousness, perfectionism, or disorderliness may be a mere continuation of maternal attitudes. Or the child may be the opposite of his mother. An overefficient mother can contribute greatly to the helplessness and inefficiency of her child. Mothers are often puzzled as to how their child can be so slow when they are so quick. The teacher may understand and perhaps explain.

The teacher must be warned against using the family influence on the child's difficulties for justifying her pessimism. Information about the family situation can be constructive only when it is used to understand the present attitude of the child. Then the past is no longer an obstacle; information about past detrimental influences can guide toward better present approaches. A clear picture of the child's life style, of his attitudes, and the goals that he developed in his family situation enables the teacher to offer new stimulations and experiences so that the child may reconsider his concepts and gain a more appropriate evaluation of himself and of his efforts to find his place in the group.

The curriculum can be used effectively to obtain pertinent psychological material. Themes can be devoted to information about earliest recollections,[1] or about brothers and sisters, unveiling the child's stimulations and frustrations. Dreams, plans for the future, happy or unhappy episodes in the child's life may be gleaned through class assignments. A teacher who wants to discover what is going on in the minds of her students can find many ways to look behind the overt behavior she faces in the classroom.

Of vital importance is information about the child's present attitudes toward school, work, his classmates, and—most of all—his teacher. Such information may be obtained through short personal talks and through written assignments. Class discussions are revealing. Sociometric approaches, discussed later, offer new avenues with great potentialities. A teacher who is trained in using all these various techniques will no longer use the term "problem" as an admission that she is at her wit's end, but rather as an indication that a child poses an interesting challenge.

Such a dynamic approach to children's problems is no longer concerned with qualities and faults, abilities and deficiencies, but with the child's movement, his attitudes, and his specific goals. The qualities, abilities, and performances are merely expressions of deeper dynamics which must be recognized and influenced before behavior can be changed.

A misbehaving or deficient child is mainly a discouraged child. His disturbance may show up in his scholastic deficiencies, in his deportment, or in his social relationships with his classmates. In either case, he behaves according to his convictions and concepts. It is they, not his endowment or his past, which determine his scheme of action. In a mechanistic and superficial approach, endowment and family conditions are overrated. Even the degree of intelligence, the I.Q., has less significance than the way in which a

[1] Their correct interpretation requires some training. They are of great psychological significance since we remember from the thousands of early experiences only those which support our general—and present—concept of life.

child uses his intelligence. A well-adjusted child is one who has found the way to make the best use of what he has, for the benefit of the whole.

RECOGNIZING THE CHILD'S GOALS

1. Through the Meaning of Behavior

The four goals of misbehavior described in Chapter 2 will be discussed here as the teacher experiences them in dealing with individual children. Correct evaluation of each goal requires careful observation and experimentation. It is advisable to consider in each case the possible goal and see how far the various acts and the conduct of the child fit into its pattern.

ATTENTION GETTING. The attention-getting mechanism (AGM) characterizes the behavior of many young children. The teacher is inclined to recognize the AGM only if it employs destructive means. Constructive methods of getting attention are often not recognized for what they are, and are actually fostered and commended. Especially the active-constructive AGM's are mistakenly valued as the answer to a teacher's prayer. A child who tries to excel and to gain his status through approval, admiration, and praise seems to be the ideal student. However, his goal is unmistakably self-elevation, not cooperation. Such children often fail miserably in life when they do not receive praise and recognition, because actually they are self-centered and work only for their own glory. They cannot cooperate if they do not shine. Most teachers succumb to their tricks and thereby prepare difficulties for the next teacher, who may not respond so favorably. Grading pupils may intensify— or even inaugurate—such mistaken concepts of participation.

The overambition instilled in children easily becomes a handicap when the child meets a situation where he must take his part without any chance to excel. He then either loses interest and withdraws from participation or becomes tense, anxious, and ineffectual. If he has no opportunity to excel anywhere, then he may turn to destructive means of getting attention, especially during his first years of school. A competitive spirit in school fosters the idea that one studies mainly to be ahead of others. A competitive society reveres those who succeed in their self-elevation, and fills its mental hospitals and jails with those who gave up. The teacher is in a position to stimulate or to discourage in children such mistaken concepts of the meaning of social living.

The passive-constructive AGM is even more detrimental in the development of personality and is usually overlooked entirely. Such children may well serve as teacher's pets. Their charm and dependence flatter the teacher's ego. They do exactly as they are told, pleasantly tempting the teacher to give them special attention and help. They adore and worship—but have little initiative of their own. Because they are so pleasant, nobody bothers to redirect them. Their discouragement, which is the basis for their passivity, does not become apparent, at least as long as they can gain attention without irritating through their passivity. They are much more discouraged than children who use active-destructive methods to gain attention. The latter can be induced to use constructive methods, if such channels are opened to them; but it is difficult to change a passive child into an active one.

The destructive AGM's are easily recognized, but teachers nevertheless succumb to them. The most frequent methods used by active children are noisiness, restlessness, chattering, talking out of turn, wild tales, standing up, throwing things, and various other forms of minor mischief. (Major mischief is not for the purpose of attracting attention.) Although these children are less discouraged and maladjusted than both passive-constructive and passive-destructive ones, they cause more trouble to the rest of the group and are, therefore, often regarded as worse problems. Actually, a teacher who recognizes the desire of these children for special attention can easily provide them with chances to receive it in a positive way. But a teacher who is annoyed by them, who feels her authority threatened, who is frustrated in her desire to restore or maintain order and conformity may easily push them into a contest for power. Because this switch from one goal to the other may occur so easily, teachers often fail to distinguish between an active-destructive AGM and a more antisocial intention, such as the seeking of power or revenge.

The passive-destructive AGM must be distinguished from the goal of displaying deficiencies as an alibi. In the stage of seeking attention, the child is slow or helpless only for the purpose of getting attention and service. Some reading problems are based on the child's desire to have others read to him. Slowness is an effective means of keeping others busy. So are untidiness, clumsiness, and helplessness. Laziness generally has its origin in a passive-destructive AGM. The teacher must be careful in dealing with those children lest she discourage them with her criticism in such a way that the child actually loses confidence in his own ability; he then may progress to using his firm belief in his inability as an alibi (goal 4), as an escape from any performance where his deficiency may become obvious.

THE CONTEST FOR POWER. Children who are exposed to criticism and pressure soon learn to fight effectively against these forms of oppression. One way takes the form of fighting power with power. They expect and therefore provoke pressure, and respond violently to the slightest pressure put on them. Scholastically they may refuse to do any work and disregard order and discipline in their working habits as well as in their behavior. Spelling difficulties are often based on this disregard of order. The child rebels against any pressure, even against the conventions of spelling. He writes as he pleases, and therefore spells a word as the spirit moves him. When such children meet with constant criticism they may eventually get so discouraged that they no longer even try to spell correctly.

The outstanding sign of the drive for power is the aggressiveness of such children. They do not respect order and discipline, they defy authority, and may become truant. They either press their demands forcefully or stubbornly refuse to do what is expected of them. They are often insolent. Socially they may be bullies, gang leaders, or lone wolves. They are generally vain and can be swayed by an appeal to their power and superiority. They are usually overambitious, with a distorted tendency toward the useless side of life.

Under the present conditions of education, it is no wonder that this contest for power is most frequently found during puberty. By this time the pressure of parents and teachers has reached the stage where the contest for power becomes almost inevitable. It finds its climax during these years when the young person seeks his place in society and finds all the avenues of social significance closed to him. His natural inclination to question all values handed down to him and to scrutinize standards and prescriptions makes him a distressing challenge to any educator who wants to show his moral or intellectual superiority. The fight becomes acute when the youngsters seek socially condemned methods to gain significance. Both sides become cruel to each other, and the children are easily pushed into relinquishing completely the values and standards of adult society.

Until recently the most frequent goal of disturbing behavior in children up to the age of seven or eight was the demand for special attention. This has changed, however, during the last ten years. The fight between adults and children has taken on more violent form, and the greater vehemence of the struggle reveals itself much earlier. The contest for power, which previously characterized the relationship between adolescents and adults, now can be seen in children at an early age.

SEEKING REVENGE. The most disturbing children are those who have given up any hope of being acceptable and accepted by adults. They feel—and most frequently are—disliked, abused, and hurt. They do not realize that they themselves provoke such treatment by anticipating it. They pose the greatest problem, both scholastically and behaviorally. They are violent and brutal, or sullen and defiant. Although the only way of helping them is to convince them that they are liked, they make such attempts difficult and often impossible. They are too hurt to believe that anyone can really appreciate them. The only group to which they may feel they belong is their own gang. They are ostracized by the "good" children and can find their status in society only by hurting others. They are the group from which juvenile delinquents often recruit their leaders.

Juvenile delinquency per se is not, however, limited to this type of children. The overambition of discouraged youngsters, their desire for easy significance, may also move them to illegal and disorderly acts. Some infringements of law and decency occur in almost any child's life. But under the influence of devout enemies of society or when caught by legal authorities and classified as delinquents, children may grow to believe that they no longer have any place among decent people. As long as criminal acts are regarded as expressions of depravity and not seen as resulting from suffering and discouragement, parents, educators, and authorities will incline to push children with whom they feel unable to deal effectively into this category.

DISPLAYING INADEQUACY. These children are discouraged to such a degree that they see no hope for success. Therefore, they no longer make any effort. Their discouragement may be total so that they actually become failures. Or they may be only partially discouraged and their deficiency consequently limited to a few activities. Most failures in scholastic progress belong in this category. Often the discouragement begins with the first formal instruction. First-grade teachers have a tremendous responsibility. Certain children, who have had no training in doing things for themselves, are unable to believe in their own ability to accomplish anything. Whenever they encounter any difficulty, they are inclined to give up altogether. Others may have been predisposed to such a defeatist attitude by the accomplishments of a competing brother and sister. We often find a pseudo-feeblemindedness when the next older or younger sibling is particularly brilliant and successful. The fallacy of the child's own evaluation is seldom recognized even in a mental test because he may perform as if he were really retarded.

Difficulties in reading or in spelling, which may originate as an AGM or a power contest, often lead to complete discouragement. It is misleading to seek the cause in a physical condition. Difficulties in mathematics are most often found in children who doubt their problem-solving ability. Inability to draw or lack of musical talent is also based on discouragement, contrary to prevalent opinions. If a child has never learned to sing and then enters a group of children who can sing, he is likely to draw the conclusion that he is different and less able than the others. On this basis, he and the others become convinced of his lack of ability. Or he may have formed such an opinion of himself in his comparison with a gifted sibling. One can safely say that the degree of efficiency does not indicate the potential of a child.

2. Through the Spontaneous Reaction of the Teacher

The meaning of a child's behavior can be understood, as we have seen, through the movement which it implies, a movement which is always directed toward a goal. This phenomenological approach of observing from the outside can be supplemented by introspective exploration. The teacher can verify her impression of the child's goals by watching her own immediate reaction to the child's behavior or transgression. What she feels inclined to do, almost with impulsive coercion, provides an indication of the child's intentions. Her automatic reaction is generally in line with what the child wants her to do. If she feels annoyed and expresses her annoyance by scolding, admonishing, coaxing, and the like, the chances are that the child is misbehaving, actively or passively, just to get her attention, to keep her busy with him. But if she feels personally challenged and threatened and if her inclination is to show the child that he cannot do that to her, then the teacher is, with all probability, succumbing to a power contest. If she feels deeply hurt and outraged, wondering "how anyone can be so mean," then the child has achieved his probable desire for revenge. If the teacher feels like throwing up her hands and saying, "I don't know what to do with you," it is probable that the child wanted to impress her with his inability so that she will leave him alone.

It is of great importance that the teacher learn to observe her own emotional response to the child's disturbing behavior. Not only does such observation provide her with a training in understanding the child's goal, but it is an indispensable prerequisite for a more adequate approach to the child. For as long as the teacher gives in to her impulsive reaction, unaware of its meaning, she will fortify the child's mistaken goal instead of correcting it.

3. Through the Child's Responses to Correction

Another set of observations permits the teacher to verify her impression about the child's intentions. The purpose of his behavior will decide his reaction to the teacher's corrective efforts. In other words, the child's behavior is a movement toward a definite, although unconscious, goal; the teacher can recognize the goal by looking at the direction of the child's movement. Then the teacher can, introspectively, recognize her own inclination to respond. Finally, in the ensuing interaction between the child and teacher, the child's original goal becomes affirmed and even more clearly pronounced. This is a so-called corrective feedback.

To take a simple example: Johnny disturbs the class, either by talking out of turn, chatting with a neighbor, or getting out of his seat. As we have seen, the same overt behavior may serve quite different goals: by and large, it is the degree of hostility, determination, and provocation which distinguishes revenge from power or a mere play for attention. Consequently, the teacher's distress is usually commensurate with the child's intention. Johnny's response to the teacher's effort to curb him will also reveal his goal. If he merely wants attention, he will stop his disturbance—although not for long. Shortly he will attempt something else to keep the teacher busy with him. If he wants to challenge the teacher's power and authority, then her effort to curb him will have the opposite effect. All she has to do is to tell him to stop—and he will get worse. The teacher's comment is his cue to defeat her. For this reason any attempt to stop a child forcefully if he is in a power contest merely makes the situation worse. If a child is bent on revenge, his reaction to a teacher's effort to stop his transgressions will not merely be a continuation of what he is doing but probably a switch to a more violent attack.

Another example of behavior could serve any one of the four goals. The children are supposed to put on their wraps after school. Little Mary is slow and hardly moves. What happens now when the teacher reminds Mary or even tries to help her into her coat? If Mary wants attention and service, she will happily respond to the teacher's assistance. If, on the other hand, Mary wants to exhibit her power, she may turn to some other activity which prevents her from getting dressed, or she may pull away when the teacher tries to help her. If Mary is bent on revenge she will kick, scratch, or bite, trying to harm the helpful teacher. And if she is trying to display her utter inability, she will endure passively whatever the teacher may do, without any cooperation on her part.

For this reason it is advisable that the teacher always keep a close watch on the child's reactions to her own corrective attempts, as she should also watch her impulsive reaction to the child's disturbing behavior. Doing so, the teacher not only will become aware of the kind of interaction that takes place between her and the child (which includes her own role in provoking the child's misbehavior); she will also become sensitive to the differences between each child's possible goals.

Any correction of a child's behavior or academic performance presupposes a change in his attitudes and beliefs. They are the basis of overt behavior or action. Everybody acts in accordance with his convictions, although he may not be aware of his inner logic. Common sense, the knowledge of good and bad, conscience and consciousness, may prescribe *one* pattern of action; but the child often does not act in accordance with his own "better knowledge." He cannot "control" himself because he does not know his own "private logic." The trained teacher can recognize faulty attitudes and deal with them.

It requires alertness not to succumb to the child's goals when he expresses them through disturbing or inadequate behavior. Yet if the teacher falls for the child's provocation, she plays into his hands and fortifies his belief that his methods are effective. When in doubt about a child's goal the teacher can find a helpful guide in watching her own reaction to his behavior. It is good policy not to do what the child expects; this means not to follow one's first impulse, but to do the opposite. Such a procedure is particularly helpful if a teacher does not know what to do. Then she can simply watch herself and see what she would first be inclined to do—and do something else.

For example, the wisest response to the frequent classroom disturbance caused by children who seek undue attention is to give attention, but in a way which baffles the child and does not yield him the desired satisfaction. Here each teacher must experiment and, relying on her own resourcefulness and temperament, establish her own technique. Often it suffices to call a child by name, but without any correction or instruction, just waiting inactively until he responds. Humor helps. If a child whispers something to his neighbor in a disturbing way, it is permissible to express curiosity, though not anger or annoyance, which is what the child expects. If a child is inattentive, one may ask his opinion about the last remark of the teacher or of another child, as the case may be. In such a way the teacher draws the child's attention to the class procedure without talking about his inattentiveness. If a child clowns, one can stop and invite the class to watch him perform. Far from encouraging the clowning, such action inhibits it, especially when an element of the contest for power is involved and the child expects to be stopped.

Such actions can be combined with some psychological and direct interpretation. A child who demands constant attention may be approached between periods, in the manner suggested earlier in this chapter. After asking him whether he would like to know why he behaves as he does, the teacher may say, "Could it be that you want me to keep busy with you so that you won't be overlooked?" If the recognition reflex indicates that she was right, she may then suggest an agreement with the child as to how often during an hour he wants such special attention. "Are ten times enough?" The child will hardly give a negative answer, or may even think that this is too often. Then the teacher may suggest, "Maybe we will try ten [or five] times." The number depends on the intensity of the child's quest. After this agreement has been reached, the teacher can respond to each disturbance by merely counting, "Johnny, one." Such a procedure has been found effective, although no method works every time and no child responds equally well to the same approach. The resourceful teacher will find many different means of devising situations by which the child can automatically realize the futility of his efforts, and therefore change his goal.

As a general principle, in the case of an AGM, a destructive method should first be turned into a constructive one, a passive into an active one, until finally the need for special attention may disappear. In practice this means that a child who has tried to attract attention by destructive methods should be given opportunities to get special praise and recognition for useful efforts and accomplishment. This emphasis on his ability to find his place through constructive means will be effective only if he is deprived at the same time of any gratification which he might get through disturbing behavior. Unfortunately, most educators who try to correct the child are not aware that they are actually satisfying his desire by making so much fuss over his disturbance. One must be careful not to fall into this trap, and limit giving attention to the few occasions where the child may get it on account of some accomplishment, slight as it may be. It is not the praise which is effective, but the attention.

The passive child can be stimulated to more active behavior by a similar procedure. Neglect of his bid for special consideration through his passivity, regardless of how charming or provocative it may be, and deliberate encouragement and comment on any active effort may induce him to change his approaches. The last step is to bring out the child's best efforts without any need for attention, praise, or recognition. Good marks, gold stars, and so forth, are based on the opposite principle.

As the child overcomes his feeling of inadequacy and gains courage and self-confidence about his place in the group, he can enjoy participating and functioning without concern for prestige and status. Functioning for the enjoyment of usefulness is the goal of the educator who is trying to remove emotional blocks and assist the child in his social adjustment and academic progress.

The teacher should not be discouraged when her experiments with new approaches do not bring immediate results; she should remember that her reorientation is a learning process just like reading and writing, and requires time. Moreover, it takes at least as much time to change a child's attitude as it takes to teach him the fundamentals of the three R's. Impatience is detrimental in both endeavors.

Difficult as it is to resist the child's provocation when he seeks attention, it is even more difficult to restrain oneself when he strives for power; this challenges the teacher's authority, her prestige. Nothing is more pathetic than a teacher who attempts to impress a child with her power, then is defeated, and does not want to admit it. However, once the teacher succeeds in developing an understanding attitude, free of inferiority feelings and concern with her own prestige, she will find it amazingly easy first to resist and then to influence a child who seeks power. Obviously certain personality types have greater difficulties with such children than others. One teacher accepts the challenge, fights back, and is again and again defeated; another remains calm and composed and wins the child to cooperation.

A child driven by the desire for power is always ambitious. But his ambition is directed exclusively at the defeat of the power of those who try to suppress him. An understanding teacher can redirect this ambition to more useful achievements. The relatively easy triumphs over authority can be replaced by the pride of accomplishment. For example, the child can be encouraged to help other children, either in the form of physical protection of weaker ones, or of academic help to another child who knows less in a certain subject. Children who are concerned with their power grasp at any such opportunity. However, the teacher needs to watch for two pitfalls. First, such a child is inclined to abuse any power assigned to him. While it is a grave mistake to react to such abuses by taking the assignment away from him, thus abandoning the constructive path on which teacher and child have embarked, the child needs supervision and direction to fulfill his assignment adequately. This difficulty is linked with a second factor which requires special consideration. Although a child desiring power may outwardly display high spirits, inflated self-esteem, and even a sense of superiority, he is actually deeply discouraged. His manifest behavior is a front to save his pride; he is whistling in the dark. It would be fatal to accept his overt behavior at its face value and to ignore the frightened child behind all the manifestations of assumed grandeur. Trying to pull him down from his high horse only increases his underlying sense of inferiority and futility. But a direct approach toward the soft kernel, through sympathy and understanding of his troubles, opens the way to a good human relationship. This principle is particularly important in dealing with adolescents who are inclined to act big in order to conceal how small they feel.

A child who feels compelled to show his power and superiority to save his pride is more willing to realize his mistaken aim if the teacher openly admits that she has no power over him. This can be done without any loss of prestige on her part. In a short private conversation she can explain to the child that she does not intend to fight with him and to show him *her* power as she knows that he is in a position to defeat her. This often disarms the child. Unless children have already been overabused, they are as sensible and responsible as we let them be. An appeal to their intelligence, sympathy, and assistance is usually more effective than any threat or display of authority, particularly if they learn to trust the teacher's desire to help them. The child would like to get out of his predicament if he only knew how. The teacher must constantly remind herself that a disturbing child is an unhappy one who needs encouragement, not humiliation. In the proper emotional climate, he and his teacher may reach some agreement as to how they can help each other in their difficult task.

Children rarely realize the predicament in which the teacher finds herself as a result of her exposure to so many pressures. Making the child feel that he has it in his power to *help* her in her difficult task, and in her responsibility to the class and to the school authorities, may also give him a sense of significance, but a constructive one. If then he displays his defiance openly in class, the teacher, who has already put her cards on the table, can respond by referring before the class to Johnny's attempt to show his power, explaining in a matter-of-fact way that they all must acknowledge his superiority. There is no fun in showing power if nobody challenges it. Power is important only when it is contested, otherwise it becomes futile. And this demonstration of Johnny's useless power may stimulate him to reconsider his position. Such personal withdrawal from power contests does not preclude the use of logical consequences to curb a child's excessive demands.

The desire to demonstrate power may reach the point where the child aims at revenge and retaliation. Desire for power and for revenge can easily overlap. Dealing with a child bent on revenge constitutes one of the most serious problems for a teacher, since these children are almost unsusceptible to reason. Convinced that they are hopelessly disliked and have no place or chance within the social group, they respond with deep distrust to any efforts to convince them otherwise. It takes a great deal of stamina to con · vince the revengeful child through continuous efforts that he can be, and is, liked. Here the group can be of extraordinary help, but it can also be a dangerous accomplice. Only too eagerly will "good" pupils identify themselves with the teacher in a consolidated front against the troublemaker. And too often the teacher accepts this alliance readily because of her own insecurity in dealing with such provocation. Thus intensifying the rift between the "good" pupils and the "bad" ones aggravates the problem instead of solving it. Group discussions can, on the other hand, help to promote mutual understanding and assistance. In private conversations the teacher may solicit the help of some pupil by asking him to take special interest in the outcast, drawing him into the group, demonstrating appreciation and affection. In this way it is often possible slowly to build a bridge across the hateful and, most of all, fearful barrier which such a child has put up between himself and society. Teacher and children need to give each other moral support in this endeavor lest they become discouraged. The antagonism which a revengeful child shows in the face of friendliness and kindness is understandable, but it is difficult to withstand.

The most frequent task for teachers is to overcome a child's discouragement in academic activities. It may require some fundamental changes in our educational system and in the philosophy of teaching before the failing student can be understood and helped. Mere logical and moral condemnations or indulgence must be replaced by understanding. Instead of being concerned only with the quality of the child's performance, the teacher must consider relationships, attitudes, and goals. When it is less important to her how a pupil acts than for what purpose, then even an excellent performance may be analyzed to see if its structure is sound. If it is unsound, steps are needed to correct it before overambition or a drive for attention pave the way to eventual failure and conflict. But more important, any deficiency must be met with methods which will not perpetuate or increase it. To avoid this the teacher must be aware of her own contribution to the deterioration of the child's ability.

A failing child's already firmly established defeatism is only increased by poor marks, by having him rewrite a faulty paper, or by subjecting him to other humiliations. As it is, most children have no difficulty in convincing the teacher that their own disbelief in themselves is correct. The destructive powers of the child are only too rarely matched by the constructive powers of the teacher. Instead of the teacher influencing the child, the child takes the lead in convincing the teacher of his inability. While he evokes attention, friendly or unfriendly, he is pushed into deeper despair.

The most important objective for the teacher is to learn how to avoid and to overcome such inferiority feelings, discouragement, and compensatory desire for prestige and authority, in herself as well as in her pupils. Only then is the way open to friendship and a sense of human fellowship with her pupils. A teacher who is not the children's friend cannot be a good teacher. But friendly feelings are not enough; the teacher must have the technique to translate her friendly attitude into constructive actions, to guide the child in the difficult process of growing up.

PSYCHOLOGICAL DISCLOSURE

The teacher is not merely an instructor in various subjects but an educator in the broader sense. As such she has to provide guidance and leadership. Even if she tries merely to teach the three R's, she cannot do that effectively without taking into account the whole child with his problems. It is a mistake to assume that the learning process takes place only on the intellectual level. The intellectual function is influenced by personal traits and emotional responses. Without taking them into consideration one wages a futile battle with all the obstacles which child and teacher encounter in their common task. The neglect of psychological dynamics in the learning process is often responsible for conflict and for the failure of both child and teacher.

The search for new educational principles has reached a crucial stage where changes in our knowledge and concepts are paralleling changes in our human relationships. In the relationship of superior-inferior characteristic of the past, little attention was paid to how the child *felt;* his wishes, likes, or intentions did not matter. He had to submit. His submission was the goal of social relationships as well as of educational procedures. Cooperation meant doing what he was told to do. Today, it requires mutual agreement. In our democratic atmosphere we need new means of gaining and evoking willingness. It is no longer sufficient to lay down the law; the teacher cannot gain compliance just because she is right. Psychological factors affecting the relationships between two people become more decisive than is righteousness. The teacher may be *logically* correct and still be psychologically mistaken.

The teacher wants the pupils to learn and to behave properly. But it is not enough for her to impress the children verbally with the necessity of doing so. Every child will resist occasionally for reasons of which he himself is not aware. Repeating what he ought to do does not improve the situation; on the contrary, it creates conflict in the child and intensifies his overt clash with the teacher. But one who can determine the psychological mechanisms that block a child's proper function can help him to comply and to progress.

The class situation does not preclude direct attempts to influence the psychological attitudes of each child. On the contrary, it provides new and even more effective methods. The class approach can teach more than the subject matter; the child can learn to understand himself. He can be made aware of his own motivations, particularly those which interfere with adequate functioning. Such instruction has a dual purpose: it can remove the obstacles in the path of academic progress, and it may influence the child's whole life and stimulate his social adjustment, now and for the future. We must keep in mind that a child who disturbs and does not work or behave well does not know the reasons for his inadequate behavior. It would be a mistake to assume that he does not want to do better; he cannot help himself, as he is not aware of the purposes he is pursuing. This is why telling the child to behave better is futile—he already knows that he should. But telling him the purpose behind his behavior can be extremely helpful to him.

Such discussions do not require much time. They can be arranged in short private conversations as well as in class discussions. First consideration should be given to their timing. They should never take place immediately after some misbehavior; at such time both child and teacher are excited, and any discussion implies reprimand, defense, friction. Furthermore, these talks should always be un-emotional and factual. If they imply criticism and reproach, they provoke only opposition and find deaf ears. Psychology can be a tool of greatest assistance, but also a weapon of tremendously destructive power. Psychology applied in a humiliating way can damage more than any physical abuse. In order to offer psychological interpreta-tions the educator must be calm and friendly. No matter how correct an interpretation may be, its effects are futile and disturbing if it is given belligerently or at the wrong time.

An effective discussion with the child should not be concerned with *why* the child misbehaves or fails, why he acts as he does; it should lead to an explanation of the purpose for which he does it. This distinction between "why" and "for what purpose" may seem insignificant. However, it implies the difference between emphasis on the past and on present goals. There may be a thousand reasons for the present attitude of the child. The untrained person, the edu-cator who cannot possibly know all the past influences in a child's life, can hardly make an accurate evaluation of these factors. Fur-thermore, any reference to the past is pointless to the child; there is nothing that he or anyone else can do about it. It is quite different with the evaluation of his present intentions. There is only one purpose in his present behavior, and intentions can be changed.

The child, moreover, responds differently to an explanation of causes than to an explanation of the goals of his actions. References to jealousy, insecurity, lack of self-confidence, feeling of being neglected, dominated, or rejected, feeling of guilt or of self-pity, regardless of how accurate they may be in explaining behavior, are accepted by the child at best with friendly indifference. They tell a child only what he is, and may discourage him further. His reaction is quite different when he is made aware of what he wants: to get attention, to show his superiority, to be the boss, to demonstrate his power, to get special service or consideration, to get even, or to punish others. Such interpretations of his true intentions evoke, if correct, an immediate and characteristic reaction. This automatic reaction consists of a roguish smile and a peculiar twinkle of the eyes, a so-called recognition reflex.[2] The child need not say one word, or he may even say "no," but his facial expression gives him away. The recognition reflex is a safeguard against a wrong interpretation of the child's intentions; therefore, psychological discussions carried on in this fashion have little danger of misinterpretations.

The recognition reflex can be observed in almost all children if a correct disclosure is given in the appropriate fashion and at the proper time. There are only two types of children where it cannot be obtained. One is the child with a poker face, who distrusts every one and is unwilling to show what is going on in him. It is difficult to break through his façade. The other type is the child who responds with a silly and embarrassed smile to whatever you tell him. This is another form of covering up. A sincere and earnest relationship is required before the child will respond to disclosure with a recognition reflex.

Proper disclosures must avoid flat statements. Bluntly telling the child what his goals are is a mistake; even if the teacher is correct in her assumption, it is not conducive to acceptance by the child. The child feels "caught"; he may resent such information which sounds almost like an accusation, even if the teacher maintains a friendly tone. An interpretation should always be preceded by asking the child whether he would like to know why he is doing or not doing certain things. (In speaking with a child, the terms "why" and "what for" can be used interchangeably so long as the teacher is aware that she is discussing only purposes.) After the child agrees to such a discussion, the teacher may offer her interpretation in a rather vague and indefinite way. "I wonder whether you don't want to. . . ?" "Could it be that. . . ?" "I have the impression that you want to. . . ." Such suggestions can never do any harm. If the teacher is on the wrong track, she merely gets no reaction. Then she can make another conjecture, and the child's reaction will indicate if it is correct.

[2] This recognition reflex and its significance is described in detail in the author's *The Challenge of Parenthood*, New York, Duell, Sloan & Pearce, 1948.

After the goal is established, future discussions may be devoted to other possibilities for obtaining a place in the group. The teacher may talk with the child about the factors which may have influenced him in forming his intentions and attitudes. This is the place where the teacher may have to do more listening than talking in order to see and understand the child's side of the story. There is always a good reason why he interprets a situation in a particular way, even though his interpretation may be based on a faulty evaluation of facts. The child may feel disliked when actually he is not disliked at all; he may feel stupid, inadequate, endangered, without having any justification in fact. It is not important for his actions whether his interpretation is correct or not; but what he thinks about the situation is important. Before she can successfully correct his misinterpretation, the teacher must first show her understanding and sympathy for the child's feelings and attitudes. A few minutes of talk with the child before, between, or after school periods may permit her to establish personal contact, gain insight into the child's problems, and help him toward solutions.

The qualification of teachers to become involved in psychological discussions and interpretations is often questioned. It is assumed that this function should be limited to school psychologists or psychiatrists; a teacher, endeavoring to use psychology on the verbal and interpretive level, is considered to transgress her function. Yet it is our experience that a teacher needs to understand the psychodynamics of a child and talk with him about his mistaken concepts and attitudes in order to help him to overcome his deficiencies. Getting psychological information and conveying to the child the insight that the teacher was able to gain is an essential part of her function. In this way the meaningless talk which goes on between educator and child, consisting of "explaining" what the child already knows, and coaxing and nagging, can be replaced with meaningful talk of underlying attitudes and convictions of which the child is not aware.

Psychological interpretation should not, however, be confused with attempts to "analyze," to pry into the unconscious, to dig into deep sources of emotions. It is not the same as deep psychotherapy, as used by psychiatrists and trained psychotherapists. Psychotherapy deals with past development, the formation of deepseated concepts, the life style of the child; interpretation, on the other hand, is concerned solely with present attitudes and immediate purposes. The art of interpretation should be known to anyone who works professionally with children.

CHAPTER 4

Nonspecific Methods of Correction

IT MAKES LITTLE DIFFERENCE whether a teacher is dealing with a so-called emotionally disturbed child or with the manifold problems of a normal child. The methods that can bring improvement are similar. Under existing cultural conditions almost all children need help at times. Besides the psychological approaches which take into consideration the motivation of each particular child are a variety of means by which the teacher can stimulate learning, participation, growth, and cooperation.

WINNING THE CHILD

One cannot influence anybody unless one has first established a friendly relationship. This fundamental premise is often neglected. Most difficulties with children are the logical outgrowth of disturbed relationships between child and adult. The same child who seems unmanageable to one teacher may be, and often is, cooperative with another. If a good relationship exists, serious disturbances of cooperation hardly ever arise. Often, however, a teacher tries to influence a child and to correct his behavior or deficiency without paying attention to the kind of relationship she has developed. Then, in her effort to remedy a misbehavior or fault, she upsets the already deteriorated relationship even more. If we compare the teacher with a sales person, we can recognize the unfair privilege that she enjoys. If a salesman does not use proper psychology to overcome his customers' resistance, he is fired. If a teacher fails to use adequate approaches to overcome the resistance of the child, the child is failed.

Techniques of winning a child's cooperation require constant consideration. There are no shortcuts; there are no pat prescriptions. Much depends on the individual personality of each teacher, on intangibles, on subtle expressions of attitudes, of emotional dynamics and almost spiritual values. Each has to find his own way. One teacher may succeed with genuine sweetness, while another who tries hard to be sweet becomes ridiculous and obnoxious to the children. There is only one element which all effective methods share: *sincerity*. It alone can win children. They have learned to observe keenly in their formative years. They are able to size up any adult within a few seconds. If he tries to put on a front, the child immediately senses his pretense. Children respond to anyone who has the courage to be as he is with all the faults and shortcomings that human beings possess. Admitting one's own faults or mistakes is still the best way of winning a child's confidence. And trying to be superior, to know more and better, and to *be* better, is the worst offense against a proper relationship with children. They are eager and willing to accept the adult's superior experience and skill, which are unquestionable anyhow, if the adult is humble enough not to flaunt them.

An outgoing personality and warmth may facilitate the establishment of a good relationship; however, these qualities cannot be learned, nor are they indispensable prerequisites. Even a cold and rugged personality is acceptable to children if the fundamental requirements for good relationships are recognized and met.

A proper relationship between teacher and pupil is related to the basic rules of cooperation and embedded in a clear concept of order. This fact is often overlooked; consequently, we encounter opposite and often confusing ideas about the fundamental principles of a good relationship. If it depended on the satisfaction of emotional needs and personal gratification of each child, then the contemporary emphasis on warmth and permissiveness would be justified. Unfortunately this premise is fallacious, and the consequences are often disastrous.

A proper relationship in a democratic atmosphere requires mutual respect and trust, and a sense of equality which is independent of individual differences of knowledge, information, abilities, and position. A teacher with proper respect for each child, who treats him with dignity and friendliness, may induce him to accept the order and regulations necessary for any social function. On the other hand, the educator must also have respect for himself and not yield where firmness is needed. Many kind teachers are not firm, and many who are firm are not kind, and many are kind and firm but not at the same time. Kindness combined with firmness is the only basis for a good and stable relationship. Children want to respect their teacher and want to be respected too. Treatment as equals and a chance to participate actively in the responsibility for the common task of learning elicit their best efforts. A teacher can act in such a way as to be regarded by her pupils as a friend and at the same time exert an accepted leadership.

Establishing the right personal relationship requires the teacher's full attention when she first meets a new class, just as the children use the first moment of contact to establish their own attitudes. They evaluate the teacher immediately and know what to expect from her. They guess fairly accurately how much fun and how much trouble they will have, how far they will be able to get by, or whether they will have to behave. Devoting the first hour to desk work is a mistake. It is better for the teacher to get acquainted with the children and to establish herself as a friend and leader. Some teachers, even after months, do not know the names of their pupils. Such negligence implies lack of interest in the individual child and creates distance. Interest in the child cannot be expressed in words alone; it has to be demonstrated. It is not convincing for any child to be told that all punishment, criticism, corrections, and low grades are only for his benefit. Real interest is shown through a few personal remarks expressing concern and familiarity with the child's activities, interests, and troubles. Sympathy for each child in his many tribulations can be expressed as an act of human fellowship without permitting the child to make undue demands for leniency and indulgence.

Humor is an effective tool for taking the sting out of any unpleasant or tense situation. Often a mistaken sense of respectability or an overconcern with one's prestige and dignity prevents the overt manifestation of good humor. But care is needed, for humor can serve only too easily to humiliate. Good-natured laughter can be easily provoked in children, sometimes merely by an inflection of the voice. The teacher can even learn how to laugh from children if she makes it a point always to laugh with them. It is not advisable to stifle laughter in the class.

To be an effective teacher, however, requires more than good personal relationships with the individual pupils. Moreover, knowledge of the subject matter is not sufficient. More important is the teacher's ability to make her subject interesting. The process of learning depends greatly on a desire to learn. One can force a child to study, but such an approach does not guarantee success. On the contrary, it may prevent it. Full cooperation in any performance can be obtained only through proper stimulation of interest. If a subject becomes distasteful, the compliant child may continue his effort to learn, but his inner resistance will prevent the full benefits of learning. More often the child will give up, at least temporarily. The teacher must have the skill to overcome such emotional blocks. There are inevitably moments of dullness, of distressing obstacles, of distractions to be overcome. The resilience to meet such contingencies depends on the child's desire to improve and to progress. This desire may be squelched if the child is given only hard, disagreeable, or uninteresting tasks. Many teachers limit their efforts to stimulate children to a promise of personal elevation. They hold before the child the possibility of a high mark, of surpassing others. Such inducement may be effective with a few children, but hardly with the whole class. The price of such artificial stimulation of ambition is too high. For each child who responds and succeeds, there are many more who fail.

A teacher must stimulate a genuine interest in all the children if she wishes them to grow. The process of learning should become an enjoyable experience for all. This presupposes that the teacher is enthusiastic about her own function. Many teachers realize this and start with some degree of enthusiasm. But when they become discouraged by their inability to stimulate progress in their pupils commensurate with their own standards, or those of their superiors or the parents, they may then resort to pressure.

It takes considerable effort to convince parents and teachers alike that pressure hampers the child's progress and desire to learn. At present such reorientation is especially difficult, because some apparent success can be obtained by pressure methods. The child may not do any work without it, whereas some progress is achieved through coaxing, forcing, threatening, and close supervision. This implies, however, a waste of energy and torture for both educator and child; such methods bring little gain at a high cost. Much more can be accomplished by a stimulation of the child's interest, and with less effort for all concerned. One can force anybody at the point of a gun, but as soon as the threat is removed, cooperation stops.

The prevalent methods of pressure are responsible for many bad working habits. They are maintained only because effective methods of stimulation are too little known. A teacher who wishes to exert a favorable influence on the development of a child, both personally and academically, will gain her objective best by avoiding any pressure, and seeking and experimenting instead with methods of winning the child and stimulating his cooperation and growth.

ENCOURAGEMENT

Every misbehaving or deficient child is discouraged. As long as he has confidence in his ability, he will use constructive means to find a place in the group. Discouragement is at the root of mistaken approaches. Every child would like to be good and is "bad" only if he sees no chance to succeed. Children are going to be deficient as long as our methods of training constitute a sequence of discouraging experiences. Overprotection and indulgence have the same discouraging effect as severity, humiliation, and punishment, for they deprive the child of the necessary experience of his own strength, of his ability to overcome difficulties and take care of himself. He learns to depend on others and not on himself. Criticism and humiliation do not add to a child's self-confidence and courage; yet these two qualities are the basis for social adjustment and academic progress. They alone provide a sense of security.

The modern teacher is confronted with children who are too often already handicapped by their home training. While she should be trying to counteract their discouragement she finds herself only too easily provoked into perpetuating the discouraging methods used by their parents. The child expects the same treatment from his teacher and induces her to fit into his scheme. It requires a great deal of understanding, strength, and patience to resist such anticipations.

The teacher occupies a crucial position in the child's life. She is the first person besides his parents to exert deliberate educational influences. And she is often the first to emphasize work and responsibility. If her influence is discouraging, she may permanently block a child's function in one or another field of endeavor. Many adults suffer from unnecessary deficiencies as a result of their initial experiences in school, because their teacher convinced them unwittingly of their total or partial inability. Some intelligent persons, well read and well informed, cannot spell correctly because their teacher failed to convince them that they could. Some learn to hate books, which become a symbol of their "inability." Mathematical problems may remain a torture. A lasting and strong distaste for any formal knowledge may result from the discouraging experiences of school years. Teachers with the best intentions of developing knowledge and intellectual capacities in children often operate on false premises and do not realize how much harm they can do.

Deliberate use of encouragement, and the knowledge and skill to use it effectively, are prerequisites to any constructive and corrective influence. They are mandatory for any teacher, not only to avoid doing harm but also to offset any previous unfavorable experiences to which the pupil has been exposed. We all know how to discourage; we find it easy to criticize and look down on others. But when faced with the need to encourage, we are clumsy and often do the opposite. We do not know where to start. Consequently, if we want to help somebody we resort to correction, pointing out his mistakes. We rationalize that we are doing it for his benefit, unaware that far less benefit accrues to him than to our own ego. The child seldom changes behavior patterns which have been the object of criticism. Yet the same ineffectual procedures continue, partly because many do not know what else to do. Whenever we feel frustrated in our efforts, we are inclined to look for a scapegoat. And any teacher who does not know how to influence the child is inclined to blame *him* for her own ineffectiveness. Even if she tries to assume an encouraging attitude, she may do it in a discouraging way. Telling a child that he could do so much better, he could be such a nice child, "if only . . . ," means clearly that he is not nice, that it is his fault if he does not do better. This is not encouragement, and it seldom helps.

It is difficult to define the method of encouragement, as all depends on the child's reactions. The same words spoken to two different children may encourage one and dishearten the other. For instance, telling the child how well he has done may lead one to increased self-confidence and stimulate further effort, while another may think this was just an accident and never in the future will he be able to do as well again. Therefore, encouragement requires constant observation of the effect. How to encourage cannot be learned in a mechanical way. It is more than a single action; it expresses the whole interrelationship between two persons. The difference between encouragement and discouragement is subtle. We may discourage a child by expecting nothing of him or by expecting too much. And again, the decision of "too little" or "too much" rests with the child—only his reaction determines whether an approach was encouraging or not. The tone of voice, the inflection, and incidental implications may change the significance of a statement or an action. And again, the intentions may have been good and the method used perhaps effective in many cases, but the child may misinterpet the meaning and the effect may become detrimental.

Encouragement depends not so much on concrete actions as on underlying attitudes. It is an approach that is too subtle to be characterized by definite words or actions. It is not what one says and does, but how it is done. It is directed toward increasing the child's belief in himself. Therefore, it presupposes a positive evaluation of the child. Only one who has faith in a child, who can see the good in him as he is, can encourage. Too often the term "having faith in the child" is misused to imply that one has faith in his potentialities. Such a concept violates a fundamental respect for the child. *We must have faith in him now regardless of what he is going to do.*

The outward signs of such faith are kindness and praise. But one must keep in mind that love and commendation do not necessarily indicate faith. One can love a child dearly and still not believe in his abilities, in his strength, or even in his fundamental worth. For this reason, love by itself does not necessarily imply encouragement. On the contrary, it often means possessiveness, overprotection, indulgence, all of them lowering self-respect. Praise and commendation may be meted out as a grace, as a favor, implying condescension. This does not necessarily have the effect of encouragement.

Praise, necessary as it is, must be used with caution or it may lead to a dependency on approval. Overdone, it promotes insecurity as the child becomes frightened at the prospect of not being able to live up to expectations. More important is the child's realization that he has permanent value and that his value is recognized by his teacher regardless of what he is doing at the moment or where he may fail. Such an attitude of unlimited faith does not induce a child to neglect his duties or stop his effort. On the contrary, it opens the way for an unselfish desire to do his best.

Our present system of education does not make it easy for the teacher to encourage her pupils. In an atmosphere of competition no one child can be sure of his place in the group. The necessity to grade, the obligation to "show results," may induce the teacher to meet the situation in a way that is harmful and discouraging to the child involved. When mistakes are regarded as intolerable nonconformity, too much emphasis is placed on individual shortcomings and faults. Consequently, time and energy are wasted on efforts to remedy single deficiencies rather than to influence the whole child. In such mistake-centered efforts, the faulty behavior pattern or deficient function becomes further entrenched, and further discouragement is often inevitable.

We are fully aware today of our obligation to our children,

perhaps more so than ever before in the history of mankind. But our good intentions are not expressed in acts of encouragement, but rather in a kind of permissiveness which does not recognize the children's rights, but merely gives them the power of disregarding the rights of others. A child treated in the customary permissive way does not become self-confident; he only learns to become a tyrant. Permissiveness and encouragement, so often considered as similar, are actually opposites in their effects.

This situation is discouraging not only for the children, but for the teachers, who, defeated in their best efforts, become confused and lose confidence in their own ability to deal effectively with the child. A discouraged teacher cannot possibly be a source of encouragement. Only as the teacher becomes secure in her own knowledge and ability can she help the child to overcome his difficulties. Then, seeing more clearly the child's own strength and ability, she can convey her realistic and optimistic impressions to the child. This is encouragement.

The complex technique of encouragement needs special study. We are all only too well trained to discourage each other, partly in our efforts to gain self-esteem through degrading others. Few teachers have the ability of providing genuine encouragement to the child, although all would like to do it. But unfamiliar with the intricacy of the encouragement process, they believe that being nice is sufficient to provide encouragement and support to the child. It has been found, however, that the terms "supportive" and "threatening" are often misunderstood. When a child sincerely believes that he is stupid and the teacher equally sincerely knows that he is not and tells him so, she is not supportive or encouraging, but threatening. One has first to see the situation with the child's eyes to help him to a change in his own self-concept and self-evaluation. It is very important how the child interprets what is said or done to him.

Despite these complexities and difficulties in learning to encourage, it can be done. It merely requires the systematic training to which all teachers should be exposed.[1]

[1] Don Dinkmeyer and Rudolf Dreikurs, *Encouraging Children to Learn: The Encouragement Process*, Englewood Cliffs, N.J., Prentice-Hall, 1963.

INTERACTION BETWEEN
TEACHER AND CHILD

Although the child's personality, his goals, and his attitudes are well established when he enters school, the teacher inevitably encourages, provokes, and induces certain responses. Whatever the child does in school, in his academic progress, in his deportment, and even in his social relationships with other children, depends in part on the attitudes and actions of the teacher. The child's behavior, good or bad, is logical if seen in the totality of the situation. His method in dealing with the educator is a true reflection of the methods used on him.

Many educators are afraid license and anarchy will result if they do not "enforce" compliance. But countless difficulties result from such ill-advised efforts to press children into submission. Children become only more defiant, for their cooperation cannot be gained through humiliation and suppression. Without realizing it, the teacher becomes more interested in her own power and authority than in the welfare of the children. As soon as a teacher becomes resentful, frustrated, annoyed, she stops being a leader and an educator, and becomes just a fighting human being, fighting for her right, her position, prestige, and superiority. No psychological understanding or self-evaluation is then possible; the teacher is in no condition to recognize that her actions may be responsible for the child's behavior.

RECKONING WITH THE GROUP

With the development of democratic patterns, adult domination diminished and the peer group became increasingly important for the child. In the past the teacher and the family had the power to enforce conformity to their rules, and rebellion, which has always existed, could in most cases find only indirect and subtle expression. The group, accepting the standards of authority figures, reinforced conformity and submission. Today, in a democratic atmosphere, the group often supports rebellion. Moreover, the approval of the peers becomes more important than that of adults, parents, and teachers. The child is free to express his rebellion and defiance openly, both at home and in school. Individual power can no longer restrain a recalcitrant child; only group pressure can be mobilized for that purpose.

The impact of the group on the individual child can be observed whenever the child functions in a group setting. The use of the group to influence the child not only constitutes an effective way to teach and to exert corrective influences, but is imperative in our democratic atmosphere, where the authority of the group has replaced the authority of an individual adult. The group is the reality in which the child operates. It establishes and reinforces through a corrective feedback his attitudes and behavior. Strong peer-group loyalties reinforce the unwillingness of children to conform to the behavior patterns prescribed by parents and teachers.

The class can be of extraordinary help, or it can be a dangerous accomplice. Solicitation of group pressure is by and large a powerful and effective method. Some teachers who do not know this or who lack the skill to evoke group pressure in favor of the educational goals, permit a troublemaker to get the class on his side. The children who oppose the educational process and who are defiant and antagonistic have a superior ability to create group cohesiveness, which then is naturally directed against the teacher, particularly if she does not exert leadership and cannot establish a favorable teaching climate. Deficiencies in the usual method of teaching are often caused by the ineffective handling of group procedures.

THE TEACHER AS GROUP LEADER

Teachers usually consider their assignment to be teaching, influencing, and if necessary correcting individual children. For this reason she objects to a large class, because it restricts the attention she can give to each child. Little is the teacher aware that she does not teach twenty-five, thirty-five, or fifty children who happen to sit in one class; she teaches only one class, whether it be composed of twenty-five, thirty-five, or fifty children. She is a group leader without being aware of it. Some teachers have a natural ability to lead, but all teachers need to acquire this ability if they want to be successful. Unless she can utilize the group to her advantage, it becomes an obstacle. Whatever the child does, the way he functions in the class is part of his interaction with the other children and is not merely based on his relationship to the teacher.

A clear understanding of the subgroups which exist in every classroom enables the teacher to grasp fully the significance of a disturbing child who plays up to the gallery or of the defeatism of the isolate who sees no chance to establish himself in his peer group. Without this knowledge the teacher may unwittingly intensify existing detrimental intergroup relationships and fail to rearrange the subgroup structure to facilitate her influence on the class and on the individual child.

Without the use of sociometric methods a teacher does not know the constitution of the classroom and the nature and extent of subgroups. A sociogram alone will enable her both to diagnose the group structure and to proceed with corrective efforts to change it. In this way she may succeed in diminishing antagonistic forces in her class and strengthen the positive and cooperative elements so that isolates may be integrated and hostile leaders separated from their followers.

H. H. Jennings[2] has pointed out that without sociometric devices teachers are unaware of group relationships and often interfere with them. Good learning conditions may be destroyed or neutralized by wrong seating arrangements or assignment to work committees in disregard of the students' desires. Such errors may result in class disturbance that thwart social relationships.

The teacher as a leader has to lead and motivate his students. Some of the qualities of leadership are identical, whether the subject is an individual child or a group. It requires the ability to create interest and stimulate enthusiasm, to encourage and increase self-confidence, to promote cooperation and motivation to learn, and to remove obstacles to learning. The teacher needs to understand any

[2] An excellent short introduction to this field of applied group dynamics in the classroom is Helen Hall Jennings, *Sociometry in Group Relations: A Work Guide for Teachers*, Washington, D.C., American Council on Education, 1948.

misbehaving or deficient child; she may otherwise fortify his mistaken goals. In the classroom she needs to become aware not only of the child's immediate goal, but of the role he plays, either within the total classroom group or within a subgroup with which he identifies. It takes careful observation of the interaction between the children to provide the teacher with clues of the role the child plays. This presents to the teacher an assignment for which she is usually not prepared.

THE CLASSROOM ATMOSPHERE

Because teachers are inclined to think of the one-to-one relationship of teacher and pupil, they find it difficult to recognize certain aspects of group formation and group dynamics. Teachers have to learn how to work *with* groups instead of *against* them. Those who have success with individual children may try the same appeals and methods with the classroom group, and be disappointed. Actually, the relationship between a group and a teacher is different from the relationship between a teacher and an individual child. Classroom groups are, as a rule, not mere collections of individuals, but have personalities of their own.[3]

The teacher, regardless of what she is doing, creates a definite atmosphere in her class. This atmosphere is usually decisive in either creating a motivation to learn or in hampering it. The motivation toward learning is based on attitudes that are shaped by the norms and standards developed by the class. If the group finds problems interesting and worthwhile, its members develop attitudes that motivate attempts toward their solution. If the prevailing norm is cynicism or apathy, most students are inclined to resist positive learning. The progress of the class will depend on the extent to which group norms permit and encourage members to become involved. The problem of the teacher to develop norms which promote learning is a difficult one. The methods of traditional education make it impossible for the teacher to share much of her decision-making

[3] H. C. Lindgren, *Educational Psychology in the Classroom*, New York, John Wiley, 1956.

power with the classroom group, and group methods are new and untested on a large scale. Groups that are operating effectively probably have good morale. One of the chief factors of morale is optimism, a feeling that some positive outcome or some success will result, that the goals will be attained. Such morale involves the goals of the whole group. Good communication, cohesiveness, and morale are both causes and effects of satisfactory group activities. Groups that are discouraged, bored, or apathetic will resist the efforts of the teacher. Each class and each teacher have their own "climate zone." Although the climate is compounded of the personalities of the group and the teacher, it is the latter who is most responsible for the kind of climate that develops in the classroom.

Kurt Lewin,[4] in his Iowa experiment with Boys' Clubs, established three types of "social climate," established by the leaders in each group. The leader was autocratic, democratic, or anarchic. The effectiveness of the group under autocratic and democratic leadership was similar; the anarchic group only did not produce much. This should give educators much food for thought, because many think democracy means freedom for everyone to do as he pleases. They think that one can become democratic if one merely stops being autocratic. Of course this is a fallacy. One becomes only anarchic, a mistaken approach often found in so-called progressive education. One is not autocratic if one exerts positive leadership and strong influence. It is the kind of leadership which distinguishes the autocratic from the democratic teacher.

The main difference between the boys under autocratic leadership and those under democratic leadership was the behavior of the children when the leader was not present. The democratic group could function well without the leader, and the children were friendly to each other outside the group. In contrast, the autocratically led group immediately started to fight when the leader was absent and continued to do so outside of the group.

One aspect of Lewin's experiments is of tremendous cultural significance, and unfortunately is very little known. What happened

---

[4] K. Lewin, R. Lippitt, and R. K. White, "Patterns of Aggressive Behavior in Experimentally Created 'Social Climate,'" *Journal of Social Psychology*, Vol. 10, 1939.

when the democratic leader, on command, turned autocratic? Nothing happened. The children had confidence in him, went along with the new scheme, and before long acted in the way typical of autocratically led children. But what happened when the autocratic leader suddenly became democratic? Bedlam broke loose. It took a week or more before the children calmed down and settled into a democratic routine. We experience a similar phenomenon not only in the United States, but throughout the world. Wherever children move from an autocratic environment into a democratic setting, they tend to run wild, to abuse their freedom, because they have not learned to rely on their inner restraint when the outside pressure failed to force them into submission. For this reason we have the greatest difficulty in areas where the child has been controlled through domination and is now free to do as he chooses.

AUTOCRATIC OR DEMOCRATIC LEADERSHIP

If one would try to evaluate each teacher in regard to the social climate he creates, one would probably find what we so often observe—that our present educators are neither autocratic nor democratic, but always a peculiar mixture of both, tending toward one or the other. Even the most dictatorial teacher, living in a democracy, cannot be as brutal and forceful as her predecessors in another era. And many so-called democratic teachers are inclined toward anarchic permissiveness, with some lapses into traditional autocracy. The example of Kurt Lewin needs repetition. One should train teachers in all three approaches and then give them a preference. Their students should also be given a choice; it makes a tremendous impression on the children when they are exposed to autocratic and democratic leadership and then can choose which they prefer. Those utterly untrained in democratic living will prefer to be treated in an autocratic way because that is the only one which can keep them from mischief and dysfunction. And many other children will realize that the democratic approach may be preferable, even though it imposes on them a greater voluntary responsibility! The treatment by a boss may seem easier. But to accomplish all this, a very definite scale of autocratic and democratic leadership needs to be widely accepted and known. The following distinct approaches have proved valuable in training instructors to be good autocrats and good democrats. At least they eliminate the present vagueness and vacillation. This list is by no means complete. Many additional features will probably be added as teachers experiment with the proposed approaches.

The following are the two sets of approaches which seem to distinguish the autocratic leader from the democratic:

Autocratic	Democratic
Boss	Leader
Voice, sharp	Voice, friendly
Command	Invitation
Power	Influence
Pressure	Stimulation
Demanding cooperation	Winning cooperation
I tell you what you should do	I tell you what I will do
Imposing ideas	Selling ideas
Domination	Guidance
Criticism	Encouragement
Faultfinding	Acknowledgment of achievement
Punishing	Helping
I tell you	Discussion
I decide, you obey	I suggest and help you to decide
Sole responsibility of boss	Shared responsibility in team

What is the characteristic difference between the two columns? The left indicates pressure from without, the right stimulation from within. This is a fundamental difference which would permit every teacher interested in evaluating her own "democratic index" to examine every step she takes, every approach she uses. The difference is so obvious that one cannot miss seeing it if one wishes.

In this scheme punishment is clearly recognizable as an authoritarian method. Reward and punishment, constituting pressure from without, are effective only in an autocratic setting. But there they are the necessary means of compelling conformity. Today they are not only ineffective, but harmful. If the child gets a reward, he is not grateful to a benevolent authority; he considers a reward his right. And he is not willing to do anything unless another reward is forthcoming. The situation is even worse in regard to punishment. It is only effective with children who do not need it, with whom one could reason. Those the teacher wishes to impress with punishment, shrug it off as part of the fortune of war. Once one wins, once one loses. And this is exactly what happens. When the teacher punishes a child, his reaction is, "If the teacher [or parent] has the right to punish me, I have the same right to punish the adult." And our homes and classrooms are filled with acts of retaliation. Herbert Spencer, about one hundred years ago, pointed to the ineffectiveness of punishment in a democratic setting and distinguished between punishment and natural consequences. Piaget extended this concept by distinguishing between retributive justice, which is punishment, and distributive justice, which is the power and force of reality and of the social group and which affects all of us alike, adult and child. Yet the vast majority of our parents and teachers still expect good results from a method which at best brings temporary compliance, but does not influence behavior, does not "teach" anything. The child who may be afraid of punishment would also respond to less drastic forms of disapproval. In this light we may be compelled to reevaluate our grading system and its effectiveness. Usually grades impress the child only when they are good. Poor grades seldom improve the learning process. There are better ways to stimulate learning than through the fear of poor grades and failure. Even if they bring results, it is at the price of tension and waste of energy. Much more can be gained if the teacher is acquainted with the democratic procedures of stimulating rather than demanding performance.

Spencer first recognized natural consequences as a more effective alternative in a democratic setting. In our work with parents and teachers we are now very careful in suggesting the application of logical and natural consequences. It requires perceptivity and skill to arrange effective consequences. There is a fine line of distinction between punishment and consequences. The child quickly recognizes the difference. Natural consequences express a logical and immediate result of the transgression, not imposed on him by an authority, but by the situation itself, by reality. The teacher can maintain the role of a friendly bystander. Consequences are not arbitrary but self-evident.

However, if the teacher is involved in a power struggle, she cannot apply any logical consequences. Her mere tone of voice turns a good example of natural consequence into punitive retaliation.

The situation of the teacher is less difficult if she no longer considers herself alone responsible for what each child does. She can, and should, share the responsibility with the children. Unless a teacher can create a team spirit, she always is hampered by the division in her class, by the clash of interests and often by the tug of war between the "good" and "bad" students, between those who side with her and those who fight her, between the advanced and the slow learner.

UNIFICATION OF THE CLASS

The success of a teacher depends to a large extent on her ability to unite the class for a common purpose. Her ability to do so will often determine not only what the children learn, but how they develop and grow intellectually and socially. If she is primarily concerned with the few who excel or have the "proper motivation," then the success of a few will be at the expense of the many who fall by the wayside. Only by integrating all into one unit, can all be influenced and advanced, an effort which is rendered difficult by the existing opposing camps in her class. Instead of bridging the gap between them, many teachers almost deliberately accentuate the difference in order to win the support of one group against the other. In the end, all suffer. The morale is low, the atmosphere unfriendly, if not hostile, the learning of all, even of the so-called good student, is impaired.

The need for unification of the class is easily recognized; however, opinions differ on how that can be best accomplished. Lacking the skills to unify and cement any group with which they work, many educators advocate more homogeneous classes, separating the slow learners from the advanced students, the conformists from the disturbers. Segregation according to ability may make for peaceful classrooms, but it is destructive. It leads to hierarchy. The deviant children assume a minority status. In this way an elite of moral and intellectual snobs is fostered in our schools. However, the segregation does not solve the problem of unification. The teacher who is not capable of uniting her class will find similar antagonisms in her advanced or so-called homogeneous class; and if she knows how to integrate the class, then she can do so even with a highly diversified class population. (See example 61, page 233.)

What are the means available to the teacher? She can unite the class through creating interest, high morale, and a sense of purpose. Many teachers could make their classes more interesting if they merely would give it some thought. They are usually so involved in presenting the material and controlling the children that the aspects of fun, spontaneity, and creativity are simply overlooked.

Jennings suggested the establishment of long sociometric chains as a means of linking each child with every other, thereby creating a process of unification. She suggests that a teacher discover means to establish contact between different groups and develop a group spirit, fostering links and aiding information about groups, discover causes of separation and what curriculum content will aid in counteracting values inducing separation. Positive interaction in learning allows members of a group to complement one another's capacities and thus contribute to a greater total achievement.

Many teachers treat each child as individually responsible, assigning tasks according to his performance, viewing shortcomings as an individual matter. The child is thus systematically oriented to standing on his own feet, and rising and falling according to personal achievement only. He is not directed toward facing problems in a social context or developing plans for solving them with others. This emphasis on independent action has many harmful effects. The more a child succeeds in learning exclusively by and for himself, the greater is the loss to him as an individual.

COMPETITION VERSUS COOPERATION

A competitive atmosphere within a class prevents integration of each child into the group. In such a setting no one child can be sure of his place, a prerequisite for harmonious function within a group. The development of a competitive atmosphere does much to break down good group relations in classrooms and can break down the group spirit. Instead of providing a sense of worth and equality to each student, it makes one feel superior and the other inferior. Then no cooperation or team work is possible.

The differences in behavior of students working under cooperative conditions in contrast to a competitive atmosphere have been widely studied. When members of a class see themselves competing for their own individual superiority, cooperative efforts become impossible; communication of ideas, coordination of effort, friendliness, and pride in the group diminish and disappear.

Cooperation is a rather difficult complex of skills that cannot be easily obtained or used if competitive strife exists. Elimination of the latter in the classroom can be accomplished through group projects, which are an important means of integration. They stimulate cooperative efforts. The child does not serve selfish ends, but goals of the whole group if he participates in a group project. He can gain status and enjoy the significance of his contribution even if it is less impressive than that of his fellow students. Each can make his own significant contribution without any comparative evaluation with that of others.

Many objections are voiced to our suggestion that parents and teachers avoid competitive strife amongst the children. We are told that we should train our children in competitive efforts since they will have to live in a highly competitive society. This assumption is fallacious. The less competitive a person is, the better he can stand up under extreme competition. If he is merely content to do his job, then he is not disturbed by what his competitor may do or achieve. A competitive person can stand competition only if he succeeds.

CLASS DISCUSSIONS

Group discussion in the classroom is a necessary procedure in a democratic setting and serves many purposes.[5] First, it permits a

---

[5] "Neither teachers nor students know and share life and the interests of each other. The first and most primitive prerequisite is missing; the open discussion. Without such discussion, the teachers are discussed, criticized, condemned, behind their backs, as it happens in most schools. The students talk

complete integration of all children, because all participate and can express their opinion and learn about what others think. Second, in a free discussion, each student develops a sense of significance and responsibility, having the right to express his opinions and the obligation to listen to others. Third, children share the responsibility for finding solutions with the teacher. She can rely on the class to help her in solving their common problems.

Group discussions serve primarily three purposes. The first is that everybody has to learn to listen. At the present time nobody knows how the others feel. Teachers certainly are not accustomed to listen to children, and although children are forced to listen to her, they rarely know what she really feels, because of the front she usually displays.

The second function of the discussion is to help children to understand themselves and each other. To do so the teacher must be acquainted with a psychological understanding of the children, particularly of their goals. Our group discussions are centered around the goals of the child's behavior. This eliminates fault finding, preaching, and sitting in judgment, all against the spirit of free discussion. In the beginning the teacher may cite the problem of a child without mentioning a name. Soon the child will volunteer to identify himself. Children are extremely interested in such discussion and soon begin to ask personal and pertinent questions. They volunteer information about how they have tried to gain attention, show their power, get even, or give up in discouragement, although prior to the discussion they may not have realized what they were doing.

The third goal of class discussions is to stimulate each child to help the other. It is no longer the teacher, with her authority and superiority, who "instructs"; the children assist each other in finding better responses to their problems. Thus, the discussion turns the class into a cohesive group. The children feel how much they have in common.

---

at any rate, but without control, immature, without a sense of responsibility. Such talks cease as soon as provisions are made that the pupil can express himself openly. In this way, a public opinion is formed which counteracts the unreasonable scolding and criticism. Such public opinion can only develop when the whole student body can express itself, listens to itself and becomes conscious of itself." So wrote Wyneken in 1910 (*Schule und Jugendkultur*, Jena, Diederich). His words are as revolutionary today as they were then.

The spirit of competition becomes replaced by an atmosphere of mutual sympathy and help. The weaker one, who previously was an object of scorn and contempt, now becomes a challenger for assistance. The fortunate child who succeeds socially and academically can no longer bask in the glory of his excellence, but realizes his responsibility for service to others.

Such discussions give the child the opportunity to air his misgivings. They help him to clarify his attitudes toward school and teacher and also toward members of his family. His dealing with his siblings at home, with whom he is in competition, may appear in a new light. Mistaken doubts about his own abilities and erroneous concepts of others can become obvious.

In this way group discussions are more effective than individual instruction in changing behavior. Something happens in a group discussion that has more potent effect on behavior than lecturing or personal help. Children learn more from each other than from what the teacher says. In many cases, particularly in dealing with older and more defiant students, group discussion is the only way that they can be reached. Classroom discussions can even counteract delinquent tendencies. They reflect a value system on which these children operate and to which the values of adult society are opposed. Values can only be changed in a group, since every group is a value forming agent. In this way, with the help of the rest of the students, the teacher can bring for discussion the ideas and values of every member of the class for scrutiny and reconsideration. However, this can only be done if the teacher refrains from preaching and prevents other children from moralizing and humiliating.

There is hardly any teacher who does not have discussion with her students. But these discussions, dealing mostly with class projects or disturbances, have little bearing on either understanding or improvement of the student. Most teachers use such a "discussion" to express their own ideas, to explain and to preach, and to get some confirming remarks from the members of the class. Others conduct their discussion as a free-for-all, in an unrestrained and unstructured way, letting every child express himself as he wishes, without taking any leadership. And when leadership becomes imperative because of the ensuing anarchy, it is often autocratic.

To be a leader of a group discussion requires considerable self-assurance, spontaneity, and inner freedom. These qualities permit a teacher to function without fear, without concern for her own prestige or distrust of what the children may say. It is important not to jump into finding a solution before teacher and children investigate why something went wrong. A good way of keeping the discussion alive and bringing out new ideas is the question, "What do you think about this?" Then the children venture some ideas about causes and possible solutions. This gives the teacher a chance to follow those remarks which are more conducive to solutions.

The average teacher can be safely encouraged to experiment with this kind of discussion. There are safeguards. As long as the teacher uses common sense, induces the children to express themselves freely, and make psychological interpretations only about possible goals rather than causes, she is on safe ground. Some interpretations may be wrong, but they cannot do much harm. The beneficial effects of building morale, providing a feeling of togetherness, and considering difficulties as projects for understanding and improvement, rather than as objects of scorn, outweigh any possible harm.

It is evident that without group discussions in which all participate equally, the gap between the good and the bad, the advanced and the slow, the conforming and the defiant cannot be bridged, and therefore a unified class group cannot be attained.

DEMOCRATIC CLASSROOM ORGANIZATION

A democratic atmosphere does not imply anarchy and permissiveness, as is often assumed. The democratic group requires order and discipline; but its order cannot be established by the authority of a dominant adult.

Our children have become immune to adult domination in the process of a democratic evolution which provided them with a sense of equality. They became free—but they have not yet learned to take on full responsibility for themselves. This lack of responsibility, often evident in our homes and schools, is primarily due to the fact that all responsibility still rests with the adults, the parents and teachers, who do not know how to lead children toward democratic living in freedom but with responsibility. In an autocratic society freedom and order were mutually exclusive; in a democratic setting we need freedom and order, otherwise we have anarchy. This requires new approaches on the part of the teachers and an increasing degree of self-government by the students.

The question has been raised whether students should be given the right to decide whether or not they will learn and what they will learn. Unfortunately, it is no longer the question whether it is wise to let them decide; they are already in a position to arrogate this decision for themselves, and we are in no position to force an unwilling student to learn.

We underestimate greatly the ability of children, their intelligence and their capacity for responsibility. Since we can no longer dominate them, we have to win them as equal partners in all activities which we conduct with them. Planning and decision making cannot be left to the teacher or her allies in the class. The defiant, those who presently negate the educational goals set by society and the school administration, have to be drawn in. The leadership of the educator will be needed to unite the current antagonistic elements among youth for a common purpose, beneficial to all and to society.

Children can be expected to develop effective group action. But this requires that the teacher be able to trust the student's decisions, and that the children, in turn, learn to trust each other and adults. Pupils can participate in the planning of activities which meet both the needs of the curriculum and of the students. At any age they can work creatively on all school projects, provided they know that they have the respect, cooperation, and support of their teachers. We have examples of students sharing in determining curriculum content, methods of teaching, and school management.

The crucial point is the inclusion of every member of the class and of all classes within the school to participate in the planning of the whole educational process. Many school systems have student councils; but their activities are usually restricted, often charged with the obligation to impose penalties for violation of adult standards, contrary to democratic principles. If planning is involved, it usually concerns very minor and extracurricular activities. The students who need most to become involved in the school program, because they are either indifferent or openly opposed to the educational process, are usually excluded from representation. Without their active participation, both the school administration and the community are seriously hampered in reaching their educational goals.

The schools can greatly help in bridging the present gap between youth and adults. They can provide a forum where students, teachers, and parents can meet regularly to discuss their common problems. They can learn to listen to and to understand each other, before they reach the point where problem solving becomes possible. In this way, youth can even help solve community problems, if they are given the opportunity to express themselves and the community can respect their ideas.

If youth is not given a respectable place in our schools and in the community, its determination to be independent and to claim its right as equals may well express itself in useless, often highly objectionable and even harmful ways.

Part II

PRACTICAL APPLICATION

CHAPTER 5

Encouragement

T HE APPLICATION of the psychological principles outlined in Part I can be either general or specific. Some principles are applicable to any situation; others require an understanding and evaluation of a specific situation or an individual child, his makeup, and difficulty.

Encouragement has been described as a basic requirement for any corrective approach. While it is true that it can and must be generally applied whenever improvement is sought, encouragement is also a *specific* form of corrective effort for the disturbed child whose actions are based on complete discouragement (goal four). Thus, encouragement can be considered as either a general or a specific method.

One of the characteristic differences between methods which are generally applicable and those which are designed for a certain situation may be seen by their effects. Only methods designed to meet the specific needs of a situation or a child can bring lasting results; nonspecific approaches procure a generally improved atmosphere in which cooperation is facilitated. In this sense, the use of encouragement will help every child; in children pursuing goal four, encouragement will have lasting effects.

An encouraging attitude on the part of the teacher should be as all-pervasive as kindness and warmth. However, techniques of encouragement require special discussion and experimentation since their characteristics are not as well known or as well understood as the meaning and practice of kindness.

The examples that follow in this chapter and throughout the remainder of the book were submitted by students in classes for teachers at Indiana and at Northwestern University. They form the basis for the class discussions of teaching methods which are referred to from time to time in the following chapters. In order to keep distinctions clear, these students, the majority of whom are practicing teachers themselves, are referred to here as teacher-students.

Example 1

Fred attends a sight-saving class and comes to me for science each day, along with a fifth-grade class. At the beginning of the year, and for most of the first semester, he felt unable to finish his work with others in his class and seemed to be too discouraged to care. When I distributed notebooks to the class, he told me that his sight-saving teacher did not want him to write in a notebook. When the others read in their science textbooks, Fred either looked at the pictures or left the book unopened. The experiments, which different groups carried out as demonstrations for the class, apparently had no interest for him.

I did not urge him to take part, but left the way open so that any time he wanted to have a share in the class activities he would feel wanted.

Gradually he began to show signs of wanting to take part, and he suggested jobs in the room which he might do to be helpful. *I was pleased with his sudden interest and showed my gratitude for all his helpfulness.* One day he asked if he might have a notebook, saying that Mrs. M had said he might write now. From this time on he has written his observations of the experiments and seems to be proud of himself in being able to do the same things others are doing. Now when reading assignments are made, he has asked that I permit some boy in the class to read to him, since his eye difficulty makes it hard for him to read print. His sight-saving teacher tells me that Fred talks a great deal about the science class and is getting some valuable experiences.

C O M M E N T . Fred's discouragement was twofold: he doubted that he could do the work because of his poor sight and he felt different from the others, inferior and left out. The teacher apparently succeeded in giving him a feeling of being welcome. She ignored his deficiency and, therefore, did not accentuate it. It is often difficult to refrain from being impressed or provoked by a child's deficiency.

Nevertheless, it is essential for exerting an encouraging influence. This was the teacher's first accomplishment. In minimizing Fred's deficiency, she opened the door to his feeling of belonging in the class. And as his interest in what went on around him increased, he himself moved into active participation. Again the teacher showed wise restraint in not pushing him ahead, but letting him move at his own speed. Only after he made the first decisive move did she respond, and to the fullest extent. It is worth noticing the subtlety of her response. She was not only pleased but showed her "gratitude." This absence of haughtiness, this humility and friendliness, is evident in all the lines of the report. It probably was an essential part in bringing the boy around to participation. His experience in the science class exceeded learning science; he learned to feel a part of the group despite his sight handicap. It was an important step toward the social adjustment of this boy within the world of the nonhandicapped.

Example 2

A discouraged-looking boy in my second-grade class was dragging his feet past me on his way for lunch.

"Miss P," he said, "I don't think I'll ever learn to read." "What makes you think you'll never learn to read?" I replied. "Oh, I'm just too dumb, I guess."

I reached into my filing drawer and pulled out a large folder. I said, "You know, Johnny, I know for sure that you aren't dumb. When you first came to this school, a teacher had you answer a lot of questions. You did such a good job on these questions that we know that you are not dumb."

COMMENT. This is an excellent example of a teacher who immediately sensed the boy's main problem and went to great lengths to provide him with impressive proof that he was not dumb. Such an approach cannot fail to bring results.

Example 3

Mary, age 8, with the IQ of 106, did not make very good progress in reading in either the first or second grade. She was attentive and cooperative during class periods, but she displayed helplessness when she was given seat work to do. Mary was not promoted since it was thought she needed to get a better foundation in reading. Once, Mary cried during a period when craftwork was being done, saying that all the other kids could make the article except her. She was given a little assistance and was able to complete the project.

COMMENT. Mary could only complete her craftwork project with help, after tears. This was undue service, and not encouragement.

But later this faulty method was replaced by a more constructive one.

For seat work the class cut a letter from colored paper, wrote a jingle, and drew a picture illustrating the jingle. Mary was observed twice asking the girl sitting behind her to cut the letter out for her. After the second time I gave Mary two more pieces of paper and told her I thought she could make a good letter, and I would like her to make one for me for a chart. She cut out both letters, and happily and proudly laid the one she made for me on my desk.

COMMENT. This is a fine example of proper encouragement. The teacher gave Mary an incentive to overcome her disbelief in her own ability which induced her to rely on others. The added glamour of doing something for teacher motivated Mary to do her work.

The most important implication of this second effort is the fact that the teacher—far from scolding Mary for her transgression in asking another girl to do her work, and thereby discouraging her further—used her imagination to stimulate the child's efforts.

Example 4

Tommy, age 7, is left-handed. When school began, his writing was almost illegible, and he messed up his papers with scratchy lines. I told him that some left-handed people became good writers, and that I thought he had learned well how to make his letters. One day I asked him to put an assignment on the board so that I could see how he was coming along with his writing. There was quite an improvement. Today I called him up to the front of the room and had him read from his tablet. His writing was beautifully done, and his tablet was neat. I had not given him instruction in writing.

COMMENT. This approach was well planned and well executed. All this boy needed was encouragement. Apparently he had already given up hope of learning to write properly. Any additional "instruction" would only have discouraged him further—although the temptation might have been great to show him how to write and to correct him if he messed things up. Tommy's discouragement was counteracted first by telling him that left-handed people can become good writers, then by finding some point of achievement, namely, his ability to write letters well, and finally by giving him a chance to show his accomplishment in front of the class.

Example 5

Joseph came late to school at least three times a week. When we were selecting new monitors, I noticed Joseph had his hand up—wanting to be captain-slip monitor. I gave him the job. It is his function to bring the captain slips from the office to the first-hour teacher. Thus far he has not been tardy.

COMMENT. Nothing was *said* to encourage the child. Still, the action taken gave him status and an opportunity to function in the very area in which he was deficient. He had a responsibility which made it worthwhile for him to be in school on time. Without any information about the psychological reasons for his being tardy, the teacher seized upon an opportunity to counteract whatever motivations prompted the boy's reluctance to come on time. It is obvious how much damage scolding and punishment would have done. Nor would merely ignoring the child's transgressions have helped. She did not give Joseph the job conditionally, reminding him of his obligation. She merely showed her trust in him—and he responded. This is encouragement.

Example 6

Robert, a junior in high school, had troubles in the bookkeeping class. He could not add up columns of figures. I had seen Robert using the adding machine in his father's store and knew he could operate it. I made the school adding machine available during the class and told the students they could use it if they wished. Robert was the only student who knew how, so I asked him to help the other students with it. His work in adding columns improved a great deal, and it also became neater. Since Robert was behind his age group and was much aware of it, this experience gave him a chance to show his importance to the rest of the class by operating the machine and teaching it to others. His increased pride in his work improved his total efficiency in class.

C O M M E N T . Robert was moved from a minus to a plus position. Instead of remaining deficient, he became efficient in his classwork, with all the implications of greater self-confidence.

Example 7

Ray, a sixth-grade student, was continuously involved in fights on the playground. Once he did a good job of subduing Ronny, one of the most popular boys in the class. Ronny came to me in tears, with a big scratch on his chest. After drying his tears and administering first aid, we talked over Ray's belligerent attitude on the playground. We decided that he probably felt that the other boys didn't like him, since they never chose him to be the leader in any of the games. Ronny agreed that he would talk to the other boys and persuade them to be nice to Ray.

The next week new officers were elected for our room, and Ray was elected treasurer. The duties of the treasurer consist of collecting the lunch money, taking it to the director of the lunch room, and advising her of the number of people from our room who wish a hot lunch that day.

This encouragement from the entire group has made a different boy of Ray. He has not been involved in any fight for several weeks. He takes a greater interest in the classroom work than he has shown the whole year. He makes an honest effort to contribute something to our discussions. Most important, the other children treat him with more respect, and when he does something commendable, someone, or more than one, will praise him for it. The first time that he had his math assignment completed, it was such a surprise that the whole class applauded. Ray did not seem embarrassed by the applause; he seemed to love it.

C O M M E N T . The teacher succeeded in providing Ray not merely with one encouraging experience but with a chain reaction of them.

It was a brilliant idea to win the support of the leader of the class. Most important, this incident again shows how a minus situation can be used to help establish a plus situation, if the teacher grasps the opportunity. In the very moment when Ronny was hurt and humiliated, the teacher appealed to him and succeeded in soliciting his help. Instead of siding with a good one against the bad one, and thereby intensifying the group antagonism to Ray, as she might have felt tempted to do, she seized upon this opportunity to instill sympathy in Ronny. And he in turn became sold on a common classroom project, which apparently was carried out excellently. We can assume that the teacher, by her attitude and constant encouragement, continued to exert some influence in the right direction, not only improving Ray's behavior but stimulating more adequate social attitudes in the others.

Example 8

Robert comes from a bad home situation. He lives across the street from the school so that the children can see the broken windows, the unkept yard, and the dirt on the inside. The family has a reputation for dishonesty, since several of the older brothers have been to a reform school. All this made Robert feel a social outcast among his classmates. He did not attempt to mix with them, never made any effort at joining in class recitation or projects. Occasionally he would torment a child smaller than he.

I tried to figure out how I could raise the boy's personal morale and help the group to think of him in a different manner. The answer came to me quite spontaneously. One day as the roll was called I asked Robert, "Where is your oldest sister teaching?" Several of his classmates looked up. Robert himself showed a spark of interest.

A subtle change began that day. The boy started to make an effort to recite. Occasionally a classmate would include him in free talk periods. As the year went on his attendance and participation improved.

COMMENT. We can be sure that it was not this one incident alone that brought about the change. Rather it was the teacher's determination to use every opportunity to show respect for Robert, something he had probably never before experienced. This is true encouragement.

Example 9

Danny, an 8-year-old of average intelligence, is still in first grade. He has been a bad disciplinary problem, bullying, talking out of turn, not paying attention. He can read, but not well enough to be promoted. His background is one of changing from one school to the other. He did not stay in any school long enough to become adjusted. There was also a lot of illness in the family which was responsible for frequent absences.

I tried to encourage Danny by telling the children that they should turn to him whenever they needed help and I was busy. I explained Danny's background to them so that they could understand why he still was in first grade. I also put Danny in charge of some reading groups. I call on him to help the weaker children. He seems to have thrived on his new position. The children, too, have a new respect for him. And, most important, the discipline problem has diminished. I gave him a lot of responsibility in order to give him a sense of belonging and make him feel an important member of the class.

C O M M E N T . It takes empathy and understanding to see the humiliated boy behind the overt provocative behavior. The significance of this example lies in the teacher's ability to spot the one advantage Danny possessed: his age and size, and probably a certain amount of experience due to his constant change in environment, experience which he had previously used only in a negative way. The teacher did not take too many chances by giving him some authority; nothing would have been lost if it did not work. But it did work, because she succeeded in giving him status. This counteracted the boy's understandable feeling of social humiliation.

Example 10

Leonard, a restless boy in fifth grade, seemingly not interested in anything, came to me one day and wanted to work on a project which was limited to the next grade. When I told him it was too difficult for him to do, he left with his head hanging. I called him back into my office and told him I had changed my mind and decided to let him try it.

He wanted to make a lanyard; and within the first two hours he made only one mistake in it. I praised him for the fine job he had done and told him that I was proud of him. All that day and the following he worked on the project and finished nearly three-quarters of it.

The following day he brought it into my office at recess. I told him how beautifully it was done, and that if it looked as nice when it was finished, I would let him give it to the principal for Christmas. Just then his classroom teacher came into the office, pulled him out by his hair, and told him never to come into my office to bother me. She asked him to stop working on the lanyard in class, because it was too difficult a project.

Why had she been so against the lanyard project? It had kept him quiet in class and—as the teacher told me later—he had not been running around the room as he was accustomed to do. Actually, the teacher admits she could not do anything with him.

At any rate, twenty-five minutes later, at recess, he came back into my office and showed me the lanyard, all finished, neat and accurate. I praised him and told him it could be given to the principal. He said, "Gee, I like you, Miss F. If I am quiet in class from now on, will you give me something to make for my mother?" I had never told him he had to be quiet in order to work on the project, but since then he has been very conforming in class.

COMMENT. Frequently a teacher who uses the proper psychological approach clashes with another who is moralistic. This example shows that the constructive effort of one teacher is not necessarily destroyed by the faulty approach of another who has no faith in the child. An encouraging attitude in one person can offset many discouraging experiences to which the child is still exposed.

Actually, what did the teacher do? A boy with an apparently bad record wanted to do something supposed to be beyond his reach. The teacher, sensitive to the need of a noncontributing child for accomplishment, gave him this chance. She followed up this decision with repeated appreciation, and became his ally in a hostile school situation. He felt her confidence in him, and lived up to it.

Example 11

One teacher gave us examples of encouragement through the use of the report card. In each case she noted the improvement in the very area where the child had difficulty. Her statements were always true, but she did not emphasize deficiencies.

One report card reads, "William is well liked by his classmates. They elected him room captain and he did a fine job. He was also chosen to be room representative to the student council. He started the discussion at the future teacher's club and gave excellent reasons for wanting to be a teacher. He is working hard. I hope he soon will be able to be in another reading group."

Background. Actually, William is three years behind in reading. His IQ is 75. I did not mention his constant talking aloud while studying or while others are reciting.

Another: "Dorothy is helping at school by serving on lunchroom duty and on patrol. She is very good in reciting poems on the stage. I am proud of the way she is overcoming her shyness in the room. She is kind to others and is making many friends. She helps me a great deal. She is good in reading and improving in arithmetic."

Background. Dorothy is fourteen years old with an IQ of 60. She has had two stepmothers and has been in an institution. She is now living with an aunt who wanted to put her in the state home for the feeble-minded at the advice of a social agency. I said that I did not believe the IQ finding and hoped I could keep her in my room for one semester at least. The aunt was willing. She now is reading fourth-grade material and can add one-digit numbers.

Another: "Marjie does above grade-level work in all subjects. She has gained a great deal of valuable experience in dealing with people through her experience as office helper. She is always willing to do anything she is asked."

Background. Marjie in 6A and with an IQ of 113 has a reading of 9.7, vocabulary of 10.3 and arithmetic of 7.6. She is mature but never gets elected to anything. She seldom volunteers. When she was given the job of organizing the girl's patrol she failed. Nevertheless, everything said on her report card was true—and encouraging, I hope.

COMMENT. This way of writing report cards may be questioned oy some. Can a child ever improve if his deficiencies are *not* pointed out to him? Does not a "good" report card delude the parents and give them the impression that everything is well when it is not? Naturally, it would be objectionable if the report card contained false statements. But the teacher made sure that the good points she reported were accurate. This is all that counts: what can the child do well and how is he progressing? *Deficiencies are not eliminated by being emphasized.* One cannot build on weakness, only on strengths. Improved self-confidence leads to an overall improvement in functioning, and necessarily includes improvement in areas of deficiency. It is possible that this improvement will not be spectacular or even sufficient. But emphasizing the deficiency in a report card will do little to remedy it, despite the pressure which parents may exert. This is particularly true when the child is already discouraged.

Example 12

I do my grading with pictures—a smiling face and a frowning one. The poor students do not feel upset and rejected by this type of grading as they do by a D or F. They smile instead, and show their neighbors their pictures. Before, the slow child often was tempted to hide his paper and feel defeated.

C O M M E N T . The last two examples show the wide range of possibilities of grading and evaluating in an encouraging way, by using imagination.

Example 13

Joe is a 12-year-old boy with an IQ of 102, whose reading grade placement is 4.1. The discrepancy between the IQ and the reading level seemed to indicate that Joe had received some poor reading instruction in the past or had failed to do his class work in the previous grades and thus had fallen behind in reading.

During the first week of school, I tried to give him direct verbal encouragement to get him to participate in the class and group reading activities. But this method failed, for he continued to do nothing in the class but sit.

It was during the second week that I discussed Joe's activity with the teacher he had had the previous year. I found out that he had behaved in the same way, and that the teacher was unsuccessful in getting him to do any classroom work, although he had the ability to do it.

During the next two weeks, I said nothing to him about doing his class work, and just let him sit there and do as he pleased.

After two weeks of inactivity, Joe finally came to me during the class period and asked if he could read at the table in the rear of the room on which the supplemental readers were stacked. I told Joe that it was up to him, he could read at the table if he wished, or he could continue to do nothing, for it made no difference to me. Joe decided to read.

C O M M E N T. Apparently it worked. This means that the teacher's guess—that Joe's nonreading was an effort to defeat him—was correct. And the teacher, seeing the beginning of some good results, continued by emphasizing his personal noninvolvement. Actually, this example so far is more one of natural consequences than of encouragement. But let us see what happened.

Joe, at first, would look at the pictures in the books and later began reading the easy readers. Before long, he joined the class and caught up with his reading.

C O M M E N T. The teacher submitted this report as an example of encouragement but then added, as an afterthought, "through natural consequences." He concludes his report with his own analysis of what happened.

Whether this was the best method of dealing with Joe, I do not know; but since I did not press him to get him to read, he soon became bored doing nothing in class, and asked if he could read. Even more important was that I, as the teacher, did not behave as he had expected. And since it seemed to Joe that I was not disturbed by his doing nothing, he decided to do some reading. It could also be that having failed to get attention from the teacher, he changed his tactics.

C O M M E N T. One of the rationales for the teacher's actions was his effort to do the opposite of what the child expected, a generally effective procedure. The teacher's analysis was valid except for the last sentence. If Joe's behavior had been motivated by the desire to get attention, he would have kept the teacher busy. It was obviously a power contest, and, peculiarly, this power contest was almost restricted to class work and reading.

Example 14

Johnny is a repeating second-grader. His spelling was poor, and his interest in spelling even poorer. One day I gave Johnny a job of writing the spelling words for the day on the chalk board—a job I usually gave to the better spellers. Johnny was thrilled. His interest in spelling immediately went up, as did his spelling score.

COMMENT. There is not much to add to explain the beneficial effect of this excellent example of encouragement. What is more important, however, is the teacher's frank admission that she participated in one of the most devastating practices in our school systems and in our general pattern of dealing with children. The encouragement implied in honors is only given to those who need it least, to those who are already excellent. Those who most need appreciation and experiences of significance generally receive none.

Example 15

I had a reading group of eight children who had difficulty in the pre-primer reading books. The supervisor did not advise introducing a new set of books because they might confuse the children. Therefore, I needed a reason to repeat the material to strengthen the basic vocabulary. I decided to take each story as a play situation. As the children reviewed the vocabulary of each story, they developed a play. When they had successfully completed a story, they gave the play for the remainder of the room. They also gave one of their plays for another first-grade group in the building. They felt greatly encouraged because their efforts were successful and accepted by other groups.

I believe I accomplished two things through this procedure. The children had a real reason to review their material, and they also felt that they read well enough to perform a special activity.

COMMENT. The teacher used her imagination to make a dull job interesting; and what is even more important, she gave the learning situation a useful function. In this way she avoided the pitfalls so often found in remedial reading work: boredom, lack of stimulation, uselessness, and so forth. Learning can be fun—it should always be fun.

CHAPTER 6

Natural Consequences

LETTING THE NATURAL CONSEQUENCES of a transgression take place does not require any investigation or understanding of the psychological causes for the child's misbehavior or deficiency. Proper evaluation of the incident and sufficient resourcefulness suggest the natural consequence inherent in a given situation; they impress the child with the disadvantage of continuing his nonconformity, disregard for order, and other forms of noncooperation. Natural consequences are not the only form of corrective influence; and many transgressions are not of such a nature that natural consequences can be applied. Yet in the hands of a trained and resourceful teacher they are applicable in many situations.

Comprehending the dynamics of natural consequences seems to be more difficult for many teachers than understanding the mechanisms of encouragement. This difficulty is reflected in some of the following student-teacher's examples. It is evident that many confuse encouragement with reward; similarly, many are inclined to confuse natural consequences with punishment. Encouragement is not identical with reward, although praise, which can be used as a means of encouragement, may take on the aspects of a reward. But encouragement goes further than reward; it expresses confidence and faith at a time when the child is failing.

Similarly, a teacher's action in permitting the natural consequences to take place may be identical in some regards to a punitive measure. But the similarity is superficial; upon closer scrutiny this action has none of the retaliatory qualities of punishment nor—if properly applied—does it emphasize the personal power and superiority of the teacher characteristic of punishment. Natural consequences express the power of the social order and not of a person. Although it is the teacher who is responsible for what is taking place, she acts not as a powerful authority but as a representative of an order which affects all alike.

Example 16

Safety on the playground has always been an important rule for me. Before I took my class of first-graders outdoors for recess, at the beginning of the semester, I had a simple and vivid discussion on safety on the playground. We discussed the equipment the children could play on, what playground they could use (we have three), and above all, the articles or toys they could play with. After we discussed these points, we stressed not playing with sticks, guns, glass, and throwing stones. Then the children were asked to make a list of the rules they made and to decide what should be done if these rules were disobeyed. They decided that the "naughty child" should stay in the room and sit in his seat for one week while the others were outdoors playing. They all agreed to this, and we have followed through with this consequence, and the only accident we have had was skinned knees from falling.

COMMENT. The procedure was partially good. The teacher started off on the right track. First she won the children's interest and cooperation. She made it clear why certain rules exist and that she was fully prepared to hold to these rules. This was probably the reason for her effectiveness. But when she tried to implement natural consequences, she failed because she was not yet sufficiently familiar with the dynamics and the application. It might be fine to let the children decide what should be done with those who disobeyed the rules. But children are not yet trained in the democratic procedure; they are just as autocratic as their elders. The children's answer to the teacher's question offered a wonderful opportunity to impress them with the need for mutual respect and for a more democratic procedure in maintaining order. But the teacher seemed not to object to calling the child who disobeyed orders "naughty," and thus she missed her chance to tell the children that there are no "naughty" children, although each child sometimes behaves in a naughty way.

And we do not have to punish them for that, but rather should help them to learn how to behave better.

How can we achieve this end in such a situation? As soon as a child disobeys the rules, he naturally will have to leave the playground, because apparently he has not yet learned how to behave there; but next day—or the next time—he should have another chance. If he continues to misbehave, he may have to wait more than a day before he can join. And if he still does not catch on, he may have to be excused for a whole week. "But we can be pretty sure," the teacher could have told the children, "that each one of you will learn quickly so that we do not have to miss too much."

This is the spirit of natural consequences. The decision "that the naughty child should stay in the room and sit in his seat for one week" is punishment, unadulterated retaliation. "You have done wrong, I will show you what happens to bad children." It is not less a punishment because the whole group of children agreed to it.

This subtle distinction between punishment and natural consequences is all-important. The use of natural consequences permits the maintenance of order without humiliating the child. And its effects on the child go much deeper since it does not imply submission and, therefore, does not create a latent hostility in the child, who, if humiliated, would wait for the first moment to retaliate.

Example 17

Ernie is a first-grader who is happiest when he is the center of attention. From the first day of school he rocked back and forth in his chair—usually catching himself just before he tipped back far enough to fall. His teacher pointed out the hazards of this activity, but Ernie continued rocking. One day there was a mighty crash—Ernie had rocked too far. He got up, rubbed himself—and sat down quietly. The children paid no attention, and the teacher continued with the reading group. She appeared not to notice.

I believe this is a situation of natural consequences because Ernie suffered the results of his behavior. Also, he did not gain any desired attention from the group. At present, Ernie uses the chair to sit on rather than as a piece of gymnastic equipment.

COMMENT. The falling down was a natural consequence, but one with which the teacher had little to do. It was good that she ignored the incident; the natural consequences would not have taken place had she indulged in preaching or other forms of distracting the boy from the consequences he had brought on himself.

But the teacher could have applied natural consequences earlier, and did not. Instead of pointing out to Ernie the hazards of his activity, as if he had not known them himself, she could have moved into action by suggesting in a friendly way that his chair would be removed if he did not use it properly.

The teacher is in a much less favorable situation than parents as far as consequences are concerned which might involve some danger. Mothers can take a chance where teachers cannot. For this reason it is inadvisable to let a child, in the first grade particularly, rock his chair until the natural consequence of falling down occurs; discretion advises stepping in much earlier and arranging for another "natural" consequence, namely, the removal of the chair. However, this alternative must be presented in a friendly way; otherwise it implies a punitive retaliation.

Example 18

A few weeks ago one of the boys in the classroom was constantly getting out of his seat, leaning on his desk, and doing his work from a half-standing position. This was repeated several times. I finally asked him whether he would rather stand or sit while doing his work. It made no difference to me which way he preferred. The boy stated that he would prefer standing. I explained to him that he would then no longer need a seat and we could therefore take the chair out of the room—which we did, allowing the boy to stand up for the rest of the day.

The following day, at the beginning of the period I asked the boy whether he would like standing or sitting. This time he preferred sitting. We no longer had any difficulty with him about his half-standing position.

COMMENT. This is a good example of a natural consequence properly carried out. It was proper to give the boy a choice each day and let him decide which he preferred.

Example 19

Amy is an only child. Her mother devotes much time and effort to her training and tries to give her all possible opportunities for advancement. In September of her first grade, Amy and her mother came to me and asked that the girl be excused an hour early each Friday to attend dancing class. I explained that it was the policy of the school to refuse such requests, as it would be a hardship on pupils, teachers, and school to grant such special favors to all. The mother admitted the wisdom of this policy, but still felt that Amy should be given special permission since she was such a good dancer and so interested in dancing. Since I did not yield, she took her problem to the principal and was finally given permission.

Later in the year, it happened that on three successive Fridays the class had a party, a program, and a movie. The third week Amy and her mother came and asked that the hour of the movie be changed so that Amy would not miss it. I said this was quite impossible without inconveniencing the schedule of several rooms. Then they decided they would skip the dancing class. I told them they had made their decision that the last hour on Friday was of more value to Amy in dancing than in school and they would have to abide by this decision and not let Amy choose the activity that appealed to her most on any particular day.

COMMENT. Here is an example of how a teacher tried to influence both a child and her mother. It is interesting because it indicates the difficulty in distinguishing between retaliatory punishment and natural consequences. Some might consider it "pure and simple retaliation," and feel that a quiet acceptance of the change would have been more graceful and effective. Others may feel that the teacher applied natural consequences firmly and quietly, and probably with beneficial effects to both mother and daughter— letting the situation and the established order take care of themselves merely by not yielding to undue demands. It was the mother's determination to substitute the dancing lesson for the class hour. All the teacher did was to stick to this agreement between the mother and the school authorities. But did she do so perhaps because she resented that the mother had disregarded her decision and gotten a contrary decision from the principal?

Example 20

Jim had been late coming in after recess. This happened several times, and caused him to miss the explanation of his seat work, which is given immediately following the recess period. Jim was told that it was not fair to the other children for the teacher to take time from the class to go over this work again just because he, Jimmy, wanted a little extra play time.

The next time Jimmy came in late, he was not given the explanation; therefore, he could not do the work. When he asked what to do he was told that he would be given the explanation as soon as the others were dismissed. Then he had to finish the work before he left. He has not been late since.

COMMENT. An excellent example of natural consequences which shows the difference between this approach and punishment. The teacher simply refused to give the boy special service during the class hour, so the boy had to adjust himself to the situation. And he knew beforehand what the situation was, so that what happened was entirely up to him.

Example 21

The following form of natural consequences sounded rather daring when the first teacher-student reported his experience. But others tried it out also, with the same results. Here are the incidents:

One day the group of twenty-two seventh-grade slow learners was particularly restless, and several boys talked out in rather defiant bossiness every time I started to explain the lesson. Finally I said, "I'll be in the library reading a good book. When you are ready for the lesson, come and get me." I sat in the library with my book and some misgivings, wondering what I'd do next if they never came to get me. However, in about eight minutes, a delegation of two serious-faced youngsters came in and said, "We're ready now—if you will come back." Later, whenever the group got noisy and I showed my disapproval, someone would say to the restless ones, "Be careful, we'll lose our teacher again." The experience proved a great help.

❄

I told my sixth-graders we would have no art that day until they were ready to quiet down. But the talking continued. I left the room, and told them to call me when they were ready for art. The room quieted down as soon as I left and they came for me. We had a fine art lesson.

The bell rang, but the class continued to talk. I stood before the class and asked that they become quiet since the bell had rung. The talking continued. I still waited. Finally, after a minute or so I declared, "I am not going to teach such a noisy class." I took my briefcase, and as I left the room I said "When you are ready let me know. I will be next door." I left the room and went to the teacher's room next door. Three or four minutes later, two boys came in for me, saying that the class was ready. As I walked into the room, there was a complete silence. It was so quiet, I had a hard time keeping a straight face.

We were changing activities in the room. I felt I had given these fourth-graders plenty of time to collect their materials and get ready for the next activity. I stood at the blackboard, ready to start the introduction of our new work. Usually, just standing and waiting is enough of a cue for quiet, but they kept on chattering. I tapped the blackboard with a ruler that I use as a pointer. They went on chattering. I tapped the board harder and said, "I guess, the class doesn't want to work. I am here to prepare you for your reading lesson, but apparently you don't need a teacher. I think I'll just go out into the teacher's room [next door] and sit down. When you are ready for your reading lesson, send someone out to get me, and I will be glad to come back."

After I sat in the teacher's room for a minute or two, Ann came to tell me that the class was ready for the reading lesson and they wanted me to come back. I came through the cloakroom entrance, not even opening the main door. You could have heard a pin drop! (I almost burst out laughing—such angelic faces.)

C O M M E N T . This approach is using a big gun. One cannot do it too often, and should not try it for minor incidents where other methods would prove adequate. It seems advisable to size up the situation first. If the class is already too much in defiance or has too strong anti-teacher leadership, one must be careful and make sure that the majority of the class is on the teacher's side. But if that is the case, one can take a chance.[1]

Example 22

Tom, age 5, is in first grade. He is an alert, intelligent boy who demands much attention. One morning he entered class with his hat, coat, boots and gloves on, and joined the group for the opening activity. (The children have lockers in the hall and remove garments before entering class.) He was asked to go to his locker and hang up his outer garments. Next day, during the science period, we had a discussion on clothing and why we remove it indoors. (Tom suggested many reasons for removing outer garments indoors.) Nevertheless, for the next three days he would come to class fully clothed, and had to be asked each time to go to his locker. The fifth time he did this, I said nothing but let him remain fully clothed. About an hour later he became uncomfortable and wanted to go to the locker. I told him he would have to wait until the end of the class period, which was about forty minutes later. He has not since entered class wearing outer garments.

C O M M E N T . The teacher was correct in explaining Tom's behavior as a bid for attention; he did not do what he was supposed to do until he was told. (If it had been power and defiance, he would not have obeyed so quickly.)

It was also correct not to waste words at the moment of the transgression, but to have a discussion the next day at the proper period. However, the teacher was mistaken if she assumed that Tom did not know what he was supposed to do with his clothes and why. It was obvious that he knew all the good reasons for removing his clothes first, but this knowledge did not prevent him from doing the opposite.

[1] It is interesting to note that no teacher-students in our class objected to this procedure, and several tried it out after it was first reported. In contrast, some of my co-workers with whom this was discussed expressed grave doubts about the feasibility of such an approach, particularly without first checking with the principal. They were alarmed at the thought of what would happen if the teacher was not called back, situations which allegedly had occurred. Frankly, I do not share their apprehension beyond the caution expressed above. A great deal seems to depend on the self-confidence of the teacher. Some can do things and get by where others would not have dared and would have failed.

The final solution was excellent. If the teacher had known at the outset how to cope effectively with a child when he wants undue attention, she probably would not have waited for the fifth time to think about possible natural consequences. However, it was better to wait until she found a proper approach than to respond in a wrong way through scolding, preaching, threatening, and the like. There are many natural consequences applicable to such a situation, such as waiting to begin the class until everybody is ready, asking Tom to leave the class until he is ready—which is different from asking him to go out to "remove his wraps." However, the teacher seems to have found one of the most effective approaches since it required no words at all; this is always advisable if conditions permit it.

Example 23

Teaching physical education on the elementary level (upper fourth, fifth, sixth grades), I have organized several sport teams during the first semester and intend to organize more in the second. I considered it wise to establish the rule that only those who attended the practice session could play at the scheduled games, regardless of their abilities.

During the football season several of the good players were conspicuous by their absence during practice; they just showed up for the games. For me as a coach it was bad not to use the better players even if they didn't practice, bad for the morale of the team and for its reputation and prestige. As a consequence of our rule, the boys who practiced did the playing, and the better players were relegated to sitting on the bench, where they criticized and griped. The season's record was not as good as it might have been, but I think I won my point. Now, during the basketball season, I have had no trouble with the players showing up for the weekly practice sessions.

C O M M E N T . It would have been easy for the coach to weaken and give in, thereby condoning the breaking of the established order. The teacher was right; he gained much by not taking the easy way. *Order is too precious a thing to be sacrificed to expediency.* Natural consequences may sometimes be hard, both on the child and on the teacher. It may be easier to scold, preach—or punish. But the results show that it pays to have patience and even to sacrifice immediate benefits for the sake of establishing and maintaining order through practical experience. Only in this way can the genuine and lasting cooperation of the children be obtained. The conformity achieved through threat and pressure means submission and is in most cases short-lived.

Example 24

A junior high school student had refused to prepare a written contribution requested for that day's English assignment. I told him to have the paper the following day, or not come to class. The next day when he was asked to read his contribution, he had one, which he read. It was concerning a disagreement between a student and a teacher in which conversation the student referred to the teacher as "an old heifer." It was quite evident that this pupil was referring to me. Upon reading the contribution he started to leave the class, anticipating that I would expel him anyhow. But I merely asked him to be seated, since he had written the composition requested of him.

After that incident, the student's attitude in class and toward me changed. He not only became a good student, but remained a friend— an older sister told me that her brother had said he would always be ashamed of what he did.

C O M M E N T . The end of the story and its good effect somewhat obscure the element of natural consequences. The teacher herself gave this report as an example of "seeing the pupil's expectations and then doing the opposite." And she was right; this is the most impressive part of her report. It is a good example of one of the techniques available in situations where one does not know what to do.

However, this example is deliberately included here because it shows an important implication of natural consequences. The original problem was the student's refusal to bring his written assignment. In this situation the teacher applied the natural consequences. "Don't come to class tomorrow unless you have your assignment." This is a pretty good approach; and the student conformed—but not without hitting back. The principle, which the teacher apparently guessed, is *not to fall for a side issue if you want to impress a child with the natural consequences of his behavior.* If you want to impress him with the necessity for bringing the assignment, nothing else counts at that time; otherwise, you let the child divert you and lose all sight of the original problem. This the teacher refused to do by openly declaring that she was satisfied because— after all—he had brought the paper. This refusal to be dragged into another issue, linked with the principle of doing the opposite of what the child expected, made the procedure effective.

Example 25

While we were reciting our lesson in my fourth-grade class, Nancy and Viola, who were sitting close together, were having a private conversation, using sign language. I tried to attract their attention by simply looking in their direction, but they were so busy they didn't see me. Finally, I said, "Nancy and Viola, you seem to have something important to say to each other, something that can't wait until class is dismissed. You two may go out in the hall and tell each other what you want to say—and when you are through, you may come back."

As they started out, Viola said, "I wasn't talking." I said, "I know you weren't, but your hands were."

The two children went out, but returned in a few minutes and joined our oral discussion. After school Viola came to me and asked me if I would change her seat the next day. I did.

C O M M E N T . This episode contains a number of important points. The teacher did not talk unnecessarily. She first tried to stop the girls by merely looking at them. Sometimes it is sufficient in such a situation to call their names. This would probably have stopped the girls, at least for a while. But the teacher thought that more should be done—and she did it, nicely invoking the natural consequences. It is important that the teacher succeeded in making the logic of the consequences clear to the child. And she did not let herself be sidetracked by the child's attempt to make an issue about "talking."

The whole incident took only a few minutes; the children returned and everything was resolved. This smooth and calm handling of the immediate disturbance had an effect on the real cause. It stimulated the child to resolve a situation fraught with potential new transgressions. During the whole incident the teacher was firm and at the same time friendly and understanding.

Example 26

Peter fiddled during arithmetic period: "You could do it now or you can do it after school," I told him. Peter didn't say much but continued to fiddle, waste time, and glance about the room. After the arithmetic period ended, Peter turned his paper in with only one problem on it— and this did not have the right answer. I told him he must stay after school to complete his work. He didn't say anything. After school I returned Peter's paper and told him to finish his work. He said he couldn't stay, that he had to go uptown. "I am sorry, but you know your work must be done," I told him. "But I have to go home," he insisted. "You can leave as soon as your work is done." Peter took the paper to his seat, and after a minute burst into tears and cried violently. "I know how you feel, Peter; I would like to go home too, but when work isn't finished, I must stay until it is done." Peter continued to cry. I noticed he would raise his head now and then to look up at me. After a while he stopped crying, and in a relatively short time, he completed his problems with every answer right except one.

COMMENT. The natural consequence of letting a child make up his work deficiency after school is so well established that alone it would not deserve discussion. However, this incident merits consideration because there was one moment when the teacher turned what could easily have impressed the boy as a punishment into a truly natural consequence. That was her remark about understanding how he felt, identifying him with herself: she too would like to go home, but had to finish her work first. These were crucial words in a crucial moment. They removed her from the position of an authority and established order as the authority above both the boy and herself. They implied a humbleness which did not diminish her firmness.

This example shows the kind of relationship which the teacher develops when the child is kept after school, and which may differ from the one she has with him during school hours. A joke illustrates this well: Johnny was kept after school to finish his work. He was so nice and well behaved that the teacher, surprised, commented on his good behavior: "I can't understand why during the class you are so mean, disturbing, and unpleasant, and now you are so friendly, pleasant, and cooperative." The boy looked up and said: "I was just thinking the same about you."

Example 27

The following example of natural consequences introduces an interesting aspect which may be disputed by some.

Students in my mathematics class had a tendency to ask each other for help, both in daily work and even on tests. One day I told them that as far as I could see there was nothing wrong with it; however, if it took two people to get the correct answers, they would each get half the score. Some stopped the practice that day; some had to see it in practice to realize what it did to their grades before they gave up the procedure.

C O M M E N T . This example will arouse opposition from any teacher who holds with the tradition that in a test no credit should be given if the work cannot be done alone. Yet it is exactly the rather unconventional attitude of the teacher toward this essential problem that makes the example interesting.

The real problem is *cheating*. And on this point the teacher took a remarkable stand. She realized that mutual help is not objectionable as such. Students are inclined to help each other; some teachers frown upon this altogether, others overlook it, and still others may accept it. A spirit of mutual help is inevitable in any well-organized class. It is discouraged in a competitive atmosphere and intensified in a hostile class where the children help each other against the teacher. It cannot be expected that in the moment of a test the relationship between the children should suddenly change. No talk about an honor system, no threat of punishment, will alter this fact. Consequently, there will be cheating as long as a punitive authority tries to impose its will on a reluctant and often rebellious class. Cheating has been considered by some as the first step toward delinquency. Actually, it is understandable and human. If teachers can cope with it without making too much fuss, they can deal with it effectively.

In this light the example is significant. The teacher did not put on a cloak of moral indignation, she was not disgusted and outraged—on the contrary, she even stated clearly that as far as she could see "there was nothing wrong with it." Her reasoning that each should get only half the score if it takes two people to get the correct answer does not reflect retaliation by an infuriated authority; it makes light of the situation, and adds an almost humorous touch. Although 50 is a failing grade, it is based on a more logical rationale than the practice of giving no credit for work that has not been done alone. The sad part of dealing with cheating is the usual punitive approach toward it.

If tests have any meaning—and there are some doubts about their value and their need—it seems advisable to make the consequence of cheating not punitive but natural. In this sense, the example has made a healthy contribution.

CHAPTER 7

Understanding the Child's Life Style

T HE AIM OF PSYCHOLOGICAL training for teachers is twofold. The teacher must learn to understand the child's immediate goals, the motivation behind his overt actions. This is an elementary prerequisite for any effort to deal effectively with a child and to exert corrective influences. A teacher who is not aware of the goals toward which the child's behavior is directed will fall victim to the child's unconscious schemes, and fortify the tendencies she is attempting to curb. To the trained educator, however, the child's immediate goals are so obvious that they can be ascertained through observation.

The second and more complex aim of psychological training is directed toward the ability to understand the child's basic concepts and tendencies, his life style. A clear understanding of a child's life style requires more than accurate observation; the teacher must also be able to gather detailed information about his development, his family constellation, his relationships to parents and siblings, his training, and so forth. This requires intense preparation and training, and complex exploratory procedures that cannot always be carried out in the classroom.

The following is an example of the methods by which a child's life style and goals can be ascertained by trained investigators. The interview and its follow-up were conducted by the instructor as a demonstration before a class of teacher-students.

Example 28

Bob, age 7, came for the interview with his mother and his teacher. While the child is generally kept outside of the room when the mother is interviewed, it was decided in this case to keep him sitting in the back of the room to observe him while mother and teacher discussed his problem.

The mother gave the following background: Bob is the older of two; his brother Dick is 1½ years younger. Bob walked at 9 months, began to speak at 1 year, and was toilet trained at 16 months. However, his speech did not develop at all, while his physical development was normal. He said only a few words at rare occasions, and made his wants known by motions.

Outside of this deficiency he was well adjusted. He was no feeding problem, but still did not dress himself completely. He could accomplish things well that did not require language, and appeared to be a happy child. The teacher reported that Bob was cooperative, but he seemed not to hear what was spoken and could not speak at all. The teacher assumed that he did not learn to read since he could not express himself orally, and made him repeat the first grade. She assumed a hearing deficiency since he often did not hear even when his name was called. The mother agreed with her because Bob often did not hear when he was called for meals.

Bob had been sent to a speech therapist who was also inclined to believe that there was something physically wrong with his speech and hearing.

Dick, the younger brother, was independent, talked a great deal, and did not conform too readily. He whined and cried easily. Bob provoked him sometimes, and he lost his temper when he felt frustrated and could not ask for what he wanted.

At this point no definite diagnosis was made, although it seemed obvious that Bob used his lack of ability to talk to demand service. The mother apparently did for both children what they could do for themselves, and still dressed Bob when he could already do it. It was quite improbable that he could hear only at times; and the assumption of an emotional disturbance rather than a physical one was supported by the lack of any pathological finding during previous examinations. It was pointed out to the teacher that she should not have decided that Bob could not read merely by his inability to express himself verbally. There are other ways by which his reading ability could have been tested, through simple written requests, and so forth; but apparently such tests were not attempted.

When mother and teacher left the room, Bob was asked to come to the front of the room. He had been observed by some of the surrounding teacher-students who reported his facial expressions when he was discussed. He seemed to be interested in the discussion. When asked to come in front he sat there quietly as if he did not hear anything. As the invitation was repeated, with some explanations about his probable understanding of what went on, he squirmed, covered his face with his hand, in such a way that he could see with one eye and not miss what went on around him. As the long-distance discussion continued and his behavior was explained to the students as one of pretending not to hear so that he could defeat our pressure, he began to smile in the characteristic form of the recognition reflex. Whereupon one of the students tried to bring him to the front. At this point Bob resisted actively, struggling to free himself, and had to be carried to the front against his strenuous efforts. Then the diagnosis was no longer in doubt.

As soon as he was placed on a chair close to the interviewer he calmed down and became "cooperative." He answered all questions he wished to answer with the signs of yes or no, or with a shrug of his shoulders. Most of the time he had his face half covered. A rather lively discussion, nonverbal on his part, followed. Among other things, he did not know what he wanted to be when he grew up (shrug of the shoulders) and refused any answer when asked whether he wanted to grow up. This point was then discussed with the group, with Bob listening in. Maybe he didn't want to grow up, but wanted to be taken care of by others? He did not respond, but apparently did not like it. He shook his head each time when he was asked whether he liked his mother, father, brother, or teacher. Whether it was only on the spur of the moment or actually true, he indicated that he did not like any of them. When asked whether he could read, he did not indicate either yes or no, but rather made a motion which could be interpreted that he did not want to say anything about it. Then he was asked whether he would like to know why he covered his face and eyes with his hands. He shook his head emphatically; he did not want to know. Despite his negative reply, this question was discussed and it was pointed out that perhaps he was waiting for somebody to take his hands from his face. He also wanted to show that he could do as he pleased, and he wasn't even here. Whereupon he immediately removed his hands, indicating thereby that he recognized the validity of our assumption.

Then mother and teacher came in. As soon as they entered Bob put his hands in front of his face again, whereupon the mother immediately pushed them aside (responding to his bid for service).

It was explained to the mother and teacher why Bob behaved as he did and why he did not talk. He not only wanted attention and service, but defeated the demands of all authorities. He was the boss in a passive way. Typical were his fight against being brought in front of the room, and the hands in front of his face. It was explained that he was dethroned at 1½ years of age and succeeded in keeping his mother's attention and service, despite the birth of his younger brother. He did not oppose the powerful mother openly, but in a passive way. By refusing to speak he not only defeated her power and pressure but gained service. He actually was not as cooperative as he appeared to be. He certainly understood everything that was said, and probably could talk well if he only wanted to.

Both mother and teacher were skeptical, the teacher even more than the mother. The mother could not believe that her obedient, cooperative son would try to defeat her, and the teacher was sure that there was something wrong with his hearing and that he really could not talk.

Definite recommendations were given to the mother. She should not repeat what she said or call him more than once for meals. She should not assume that he did not understand. Instead she should play with and show affection to both children. When Bob lost his temper she should leave the room. The teacher likewise was asked to proceed "as if" Bob could understand and talk, and make no fuss if he didn't.

Both mother and teacher came back after two weeks. Their skepticism was gone. The mother had become aware of the amount of service which Bob had demanded. She refused it, and Bob dressed himself and took care of himself. After he missed one meal by not coming at the first call, he always "heard" when she called him. She finally became convinced of the psychological reasons as they were explained to her, when a few days later Bob's cousin came for a visit and she heard them talk freely and aloud upstairs, when Bob thought nobody could hear. Since then, she had ignored completely his pointing and motioning. A few weeks later Bob's talk was almost normal.

The remainder of this chapter contains a series of brief reports submitted by teacher-students in the process of learning how to explore a child's life style. In each case, a problem is stated, along with some background information, an analysis of the situation, and recommendations for corrective procedures. Since beginning students are naturally less familiar with techniques of psychological exploration than those who have had some previous training in this approach, the reports are uneven in their sophistication.

The case studies are discussed in teaching class in a manner similar to that used in this chapter. Comments by instructor and fellow-students center around correct or incorrect interpretation, adequate or insufficient information, pertinent missing data without which a reliable evaluation of the individual child is impossible. Some of the initial reports are later made the subject of research projects of the sort discussed in Chapter 11.

These case studies show various stages of incompleteness and inaccuracy. They are not used for a final analysis of the child but for a clarification of the underlying dynamic processes and the problems involved. In other words, they serve merely didactic purposes. No clinical certainty or definiteness in regard to corrective measures is implied or attempted. The tentative character of all statements must be kept in mind, although it may not always be obvious in the flow of the discussion.

One aspect of the following discussions may require clarification, since this technique is based on theoretical assumptions with which many may not be familiar. An attempt is made to fill in the gap left by incomplete information through a process of speculative exploration of possible data about background and past experiences. We can only guess, but our guesses are more than simple hunches: they are based on certain scientific premises.

Since human behavior, as we understand it, is goal directed, and since individual "qualities" are not lodged within the personality but are expressions of movement and interaction, every report about a child, his personality, and particularly his actions indicates more than merely what the child *is* and what he is *doing*. Nothing happens in a vacuum. His character and personality traits reflect his interaction with his family, his behavior in class expresses his interaction with his teacher and classmates. For this reason we can, in many cases, visualize the counterparts of the child at home and in school. The reporting student may not have given any information about them, but we can guess possibilities. We cannot be certain, to be sure, and since we have no follow-up of these case studies, we never will be certain. But "guessing in the right direction," as Adler called it, is an intricate part of promoting understanding. In practice, these guesses can be and are tested by any additional information that can be obtained. In our artificial didactic setting we have to be satisfied with establishing probabilities without verification. For this reason, our conclusions can only be tentative. However, it is our experience that our "guesses" are more often verified than unsupported, if the situation can be further explored.

Characteristic examples of such tentative assumptions are the personalities of siblings, the way the child was treated by his parents, and similar factors which can be assumed if we take the child's personality and behavior as an expression of interaction. A child who smiles readily and exhibits considerable charm proves the effectiveness of such approaches in his family. Whether the teacher has information on it or not, we can be fairly sure that important members of his family respond to them. Without having experienced affection at home, he would not have learned to evoke affectionate responses in others. Our conclusions from the description of the child may permit us either to assume what we do not know or to contradict what seems to have been assumed by the reporter.

It is relatively unimportant, at this stage, whether our guesses and assumptions are correct in each case. It is better to make a wrong guess than not to guess at all. One can always correct a wrong guess; but if one makes no guess, one does not get a better understanding. It is of utmost importance that the teacher-student acquaint himself with this form of thinking and exploration. He has to learn to see the child in his total life situation, not as an isolated particle. Our emphasis on a further exploration of the people around him and his interaction with them serves this purpose.

Example 29

Ten-year-old Tom was chosen for study because of extreme nervousness and because he had a severe speech defect.

C O M M E N T . To choose such a child is rather daring. Nervousness and a severe speech defect are serious disturbances; their psychological analysis requires careful study and skill. This is a report by a beginning student who, despite her master's degree, could hardly be expected to be proficient with the psychological approach.

Interviews were held with the school nurse, school physician, teachers, classmates, parents, and the school psychologist.

C O M M E N T . The student went thoroughly about getting her information. She went to all the sources. Was she prepared to get the pertinent data?

Tom was seen by the school nurse who indicated that vision in both eyes was normal, but that he was slightly underweight.

C O M M E N T . The normal vision has little apparent significance at this point. Inclusion of such details may be less objectionable if it is certain that all important data are provided. But can we expect that from a short report? The teacher must keep in mind the relative significance of each piece of information. If he does not do that, he ends up with a large amount of information which means little or nothing, and misses what he ought to know.

The school physician stated that Tom's general condition was good. He has bronchial asthma and a nasal obstruction. He should not be put under pressure, according to the physician. The mother stated that Tom is under the care of an allergy specialist, whom he sees twice a week. She also said that his appetite is about fair; there are many foods he does not like.

C O M M E N T . Here are some important data: Tom's bronchial asthma and allergy. Such conditions indicate over-sensitivity. In this light, the nurse's reference to his underweight condition and the mother's report that he does not like many foods become significant. He is much concerned with what he likes and what not; and he probably cannot stand what he does not like. He was—and still is—a food problem. This fact indicates a characteristic mother-child relationship.

The family occupies a six-room apartment in an average neighborhood. The front lawn is well kept, the home extremely neat. On the floor are white throw rugs which are immaculate. However, the home does not have the appearance of being designed for comfort and enjoyment. It seems to be a home that Mrs. R takes much pride in keeping immaculately clean and in perfect order.

C O M M E N T . Here again is an abundance of insignificant data from a psychological point of view. It would have been sufficient if the student had merely stated the impression expressed in the last sentence of this paragraph. The mother is overambitious and probably a perfectionist; this is important for understanding the child.

The father is employed in the steel mills, the mother works as a secretary. She went to work when Tom was 8 months old. She is aware that he is nervous and stutters. She has noticed that at meal time he cannot sit still; he is in constant motion.

C O M M E N T . This is, so far, the first important clue to an understanding of Tom. We know that food is a problem; he does not eat what he should. And his restlessness is pronounced at meal times. Apparently, this restlessness is part of a struggle, probably primarily with his mother. Both his dislike for food and his restlessness may have the same goal: to defeat his mother in a passive way, not in open rebellion, and at the same time to keep her busy and anxious.

The mother stated that the children worry her. The father thinks that she annoys the children because she yells at them constantly. She explained that she tries to give the children everything that money will buy. But when she comes home from work, she is tired and the children "get on her nerves."

C O M M E N T . Here is considerable insight on the total family situation. First of all, the mother herself is a "nervous type"; the children worry her and get on her nerves. Could it be that Tom imitates her? The mother is a fighter; yet she does not do her fighting openly, but through her concern. Her yelling is, in her own opinion, only for the benefit of the children. She probably does not realize the extent to which she fights everyone, and assumes that the others are fighting her. She and the father do not see eye to eye. We can imagine how unfairly she feels he treats her when she tries so hard to do everything she can for the children.

Tom is the second child; he has an older brother.

C O M M E N T . It is unfortunate that the student does not say more about the brother. He would be a key figure in understanding Tom. We would like to know how much older he is and—most important —what kind of a boy he is. Since the first and second child in each family are generally different in character and personality, more so the more competitive the family is, we can imagine what Tom's brother is like. Tom plays weak, therefore his brother is probably independent and "strong." Tom fights mother in a passive way; his brother is probably openly rebellious in an active way. All this would be important to know. The relationship to the older brother could well have significance for Tom's development.

Tom seems to get along well with his peers. He seems relaxed in their presence, and is able to talk and play with other children in a relaxed manner. His difficulty seems to appear in his relationship with adults. The mother does not allow his friends to come to the house because "they tear it up" and make too much noise.

C O M M E N T . Here we see Tom's good social adjustment. He is a good boy—again probably like his mother, who is what one would call a "fine person." With his peers, Tom is among equals; no special demands are made. But apparently it is difficult for him to deal with "superiors." This quality of superiority may characterize the adults with whom he appears to be nervous. He may be as overambitious as his mother, and therefore afraid of not being able to live up to her high standards. These standards are also revealed in her reluctance to have his friends over. As long as nothing is expected from Tom he can relax; but not if he has to live up to a certain level of performance.

Mrs. R was seen alone in order to determine the relationship between the parents.

C O M M E N T . It would have been better to say "to get further details" about the relationship; because we have already seen that the relationship is not a good one, since the mother reported the father's critical comment about her.

Mrs. R explained that her husband drinks too much. He often comes home and begins to fight. She and her husband have been separated on numerous occasions. She always took the children, or—if he left—the children remained with her.

COMMENT. It is quite possible that Mrs. R is a typical "drunkard's wife." Such women are so good that nobody can live up to their standards. Consequently, the husband feels his deficiency more and more, and then either finds consolation in liquor or uses it to gain the strength to fight back. His drinking is both an expression of discouragement and of rebellion. And Mrs. R, like a typical wife of a drunkard, always gives in again and takes him back. She is too "good" to let him down completely, but she constantly pushes him down a little bit.

We can assume that Tom is siding with her against his father— and his brother probably sides with the latter. Tom has learned how important it is to be good; otherwise, one is just as bad as a no-good father—or brother.

Tom was seen by the school psychologist and classified as high average—(IQ 114). His teachers seem to agree that he tries hard and wants to conform in class. His nervousness prevents his remaining seated quietly for an hour. It seems necessary for him to move about often. When asked to recite, he often becomes excited and cannot talk. When asked to contribute orally, he becomes nervous.

COMMENT. We can now understand Tom's behavior. He becomes excited and nervous when he has to perform; he is never sure that he is good enough or will do well enough. Therefore, at times he cannot even talk. This same fear of not expressing himself well and clearly enough is probably the reason for his speech difficulty. That in turn increases his feeling of inadequacy, which is unbearable to an overambitious "good" child. The harder he tries, the less he accomplishes; he only gets further discouraged in the process.

Now the question arises: why is he so restless and unable to sit quietly? His "nervousness" is not an explanation. He appears nervous because he does not want to sit quietly. But for what reason?

There is only one clear clue, his restlessness at the dinner table. We have assumed that he used it both to rebel against his mother's demands and to keep her busy with him. This is the mechanism generally found in poor eaters. They exasperate the parents, but in turn force their mother to cook special food, to coax, remind, and threaten. Mrs. R is the kind of mother who would easily get involved in such a struggle with a child. Her exaggerated sense of duty and responsibility cannot permit her to stand by quietly when the child does not eat enough. So she makes herself a victim of the child's demands while trying to subdue him at the same time.

It is probable that Tom has succeeded in forcing his teachers into the same kind of relationship. He forces them to remind him, correct him, talk to him, encourage and urge him, while he seems to be so good. In other words, he has learned to conceal his hostility and rebellion behind a display of good intentions. This is the typical mechanism of neurosis and nervousness.[1] Tom, being creative and resourceful, operates with a wide range of purposes. At times he is probably seeking attention, at others he is involved in a subtle power contest, and at others he displays his inability to accomplish a task at all, driven by his overambition and exaggerated fear of failure.

Despite insufficient information, we get a pretty good picture of the boy and the dynamics of his difficulties. Now let us see how the teacher evaluated this case and what recommendations she made.

Evaluation—recommendation. Tom has had little feeling of security, because his mother has been employed since he was about 8 months of age, which indicates that he was left with strangers and did not receive from his parents the love and affection which is necessary for emotional security. Parents perhaps gave many material things to make up for the limited time they were able to spend with their children. Both parents should try to spend more time with Tom.

COMMENT. It is obvious that the teacher did not understand Tom's difficulties and the reason for them. She is probably right that Tom does not have a strong feeling of security, but such a statement is meaningless. Every child who misbehaves feels insecure. Insecurity as such does not explain why Tom behaves as he does. Furthermore, the term "discouraged" is preferable to "insecure." Discouragement

---

[1] The teleological interpretation of psychopathological conditions is characteristic of Alfred Adler's Individual Psychology, the frame of reference used in this book

is a general term which applies to all forms of deficiencies and misbehavior. However, the difference in terminology is more than a play on words. It opens different perspectives. Security is something one gets from somewhere or someone—or fails to get. Courage, on the other hand, is something which one has within oneself; one cannot get it from the outside, although the environment may stimulate or prevent its development. The feeling of security comes from within, from courage, from the realization of one's own strength and ability to cope with whatever life may have in store.

If the teacher had recognized Tom as a discouraged child, she would not have assumed that the mother's employment was the cause of his troubles. A mother's absence as such cannot "discourage" a child; but her relationship with him may have such an effect, particularly if she feels sorry for him and tries to compensate for her "neglect" with overprotection. Why should a mother's employment indicate that Tom did not receive love and affection from his parents? It is not the *amount* of time a mother spends with a child that counts, but the *quality* of the time spent together. Giving love and affection does not require much time; it can be expressed in a few seconds, and can permeate all experiences which the child has with his parents. No, it is the *kind* of relationship which existed in the family and particularly between the mother and Tom that induced Tom to develop his concepts of himself and of life and to act accordingly.

It is felt that Tom reacts to adults as he does to his parents; they are authoritative, demanding, and inconsistent. He seems to become nervous and tense in the presence of adults. Tom should be allowed to have his friends come to his home. Having friends who accept him may make him more secure.

COMMENT. It is true that Tom's relationship with his parents is carried over to his relationship with other adults; but we would suspect that this is true only with adults like teachers who demand and expect something from him, while he may have a good and relaxed relationship with other adults. Our student makes the common mistake of considering all parents and adults as authority figures, who in Tom create tension. This is a mechanistic and inadequate explanation. Prior discussion pointed to the dynamic interaction taking place between Tom and his mother, and similarly between him and his teachers. There is more to it than the parent's authoritative demanding and inconsistent behavior, which, by the way, is not obvious from the report.

Tom should be allowed to have his friends come to his home. But here again the reasons for such a recommendation are different from what the student has in mind. His friends will not "make him more secure." He feels secure with them; and his good relationship with them does not carry over to his relationship with adults. No, having his friends at home would have a quite different corrective implication. It might induce his mother to be less perfectionist, to learn to take children as they are, instead of being annoyed with their shortcomings. This she needs to learn in regard to other children as well as to Tom. And this would change their relationship and give Tom an opportunity to have more of the necessary "courage to be imperfect" than he ever learned from his perfectionistic mother.

Tom may make a better adjustment to a small special class. He may get to know the teacher better and also have a closer relationship with the students.

COMMENT. This recommendation is based on a lack of dynamic understanding and a search for a mechanistic form of solution. Tom needs to understand his own mistaken concepts and to change his methods of dealing with adults and their demands. Such training can be achieved in a large class or be lacking in a small one; it does not depend on the size of the class but on the psychological understanding and the ability of the teacher. Tom must learn to believe in himself *as he is*, stop trying to be so good, and no longer fear mistakes. Then he will no longer need special attention, nor rebel against the demands and expectations of certain adults. Teachers and his mother can help him toward the necessary reorientation, provided that they begin to understand the situation and act accordingly. The mother in this case is the problem and would need help and guidance.

Example 30

Marty, age 9, will not work. He will not do anything constructive. His lessons are never done, and he doesn't care. If I ask him to read such and such a page, he will blankly refuse. When the children go out on the playground for games, he will not join in, but would rather fight with the gang of boys. His conduct is a little on the silly side, always saying silly things and getting the class to laugh at him. When the teacher is talking or trying to explain a problem, he may be wrestling with someone or doing silly tricks. He certainly does get enough attention. The only situation in which he will cooperate is one which has been organized by him. He gets angry if he cannot be the first in line, and he shows his irritation. He is a rough, husky-looking boy.

C O M M E N T . We can see the boy in action—and his teacher, too. Every line of her report shows her feeling of defeat. This is a typical power contest. Characteristically, neither the boy nor his teacher is aware of it. If the teacher knew it, she would not be such a ready partner. He is apparently successful in mobilizing the whole class on his side; for this reason he acts "silly" or uses some other kind of attention-getting device when she is talking or trying to explain a problem. His evident overambition is unfortunately mostly expressed uselessly. He is concerned with his power and superiority, wanting to be the first one in line, organizing situations, and showing his temper if he does not have his own way. So far we know nothing about the reasons for his behavior. But the teacher has fortunately added one other piece of information.

His brother is very, very quiet. He gets all A's. He works with groups, takes part in organization, and does not like to get reprimanded for anything.

C O M M E N T . It is not clear whether the brother is older or younger, but the first is likely. He, too, is overambitious, but—in contrast to Marty—operating on the useful side. It is certain that his achievements have some bearing on Marty's difficulties: Marty is discouraged by his more successful brother. On the other hand, we can assume that the brother, the "good" boy, is likely to be physically weaker, depending on the approval of others, while Marty can stand up for himself and feels strong enough to tackle the whole world singlehanded. He is not easily intimidated, and apparently is a good fighter. Such children can be won and switched to the useful side if the teacher gives them opportunities to show their prowess by contributing to the benefit of the class. To do so, the teacher would first have to stop responding in kind and fighting with the boy, as he fights with her.

The term "switching to the useful side" may require some clarification. Many are accustomed to regard children like Marty as being possessed by some inner hostility which has to come out. They may be inclined to ask: Would such a switch to the useful side mean that he would stop fighting? Or would he become a fighter in the "good" sense? Would he displace or repress or sublimate his hostility? Would it help to buy him a punching bag or give him a cap pistol so that he could get rid of his hostility without exhibiting it in class?

These are not the answers; hostility is not a force or energy within a child which can be discharged or let out like gas from an overfilled balloon. Marty's hostility is part of his attempt to gain status, to find a place for himself in the group. He does so by fighting with the teacher. In a way, he successfully challenges the teacher's leadership in the group. He is not "full of hostility," but uses his hostile emotions to his advantage, to be more forceful and to succeed. He is not fighting merely because he wants to fight and needs this outlet; he fights to show his superiority, to win and to "succeed" in a masculine way.

In this light, switching to the useful side means merely a change of approach toward having status in the group. He would not fight against the teacher and what she stands for if he could expect to gain status through her. This is what she will have to accomplish, giving him a chance to feel important by contributing and helping instead of by fighting and opposing. Marty's basic motivation seems to be his desire to be important, to be first. He will eventually have to change it to become adjusted, but for the time being his desire can be utilized and channeled into useful contributions.

Example 31

Dick, 6½ years old, is quiet, passive, and inattentive in school. He misses much of the class work. He does what he is told to do, is always busy, but alone, playing with little cars, drawing, looking at a book. He causes no disturbance. He follows school routine when he hears. Such things as his class being called, or instruction for seat work, have to be repeated often, for he does not listen. He plays well with other children, and has one particular friend, a neighbor boy his own age.

C O M M E N T . Dick is not too disturbing in school, but rather annoying. This, and his need to be repeatedly called, would indicate that he is seeking attention, and apparently getting it. Even his isolated play makes him conspicuous.

Family Constellation. Dick has three sisters, three, six, and eight years older than he. The father is a quiet man, the mother a busy housewife, much engrossed in the activities of her teen-age daughters. The three girls are industrious and share all household tasks. Dick is too little to work. Besides, he is a boy and not suited to work about the house. The conversation about the dinner table and at other times concerns the problems of the girls. The family gets along well together; there is much love and harmony. The mother does not come to school for programs, parties, etc., and was grocery shopping when the class went to Dick's house to call, as we do to each home.

Impression. Dick has come into this older female setting—nothing is expected of him. All his wants are taken care of. He has trained himself not to listen to the conversation about him, but has retreated into a world of his own. There is no service he can render the family that is acceptable. Nothing concerning him is considered important

He really wants to listen to class instruction, and has the mental ability to do well; but the habit of inattention is so well developed that even though interested, he falls back into the dream world of his own making.

C O M M E N T . The family constellation is well described, the little boy in a matriarchal family of four much older females. One may point out that the father is also quiet, the two men apparently do not count too much. Dick has two handicaps. First, he is the baby, too little to work; and besides he is a man—what can you expect from a man!

So far, so good. But it does not seem to be adequate to attribute his behavior solely to the "habit of inattention." This does not answer why he "has trained himself not to listen to the conversation about him." For what purpose has he retreated into a world of his own? This is the important question which the teacher has not attempted to answer. If she had done so, she might have found that it is questionable whether Dick "really wants to listen to class instruction." His passive and "inattentive" behavior is not merely withdrawal but a form of seeking his place within the group. He cannot find his place in his family through any service and contribution *he* can render, as the teacher has so correctly pointed out; he can find his place only by doing what he likes and letting others take care of him. To get attention and service is the goal of his behavior.

In an interview with his mother, I asked her if this neglect of Dick was not the situation. She admitted that it was, but had not realized that she was not doing justice to Dick, who is so good and so quiet.

COMMENT. There is no doubt that Dick is somewhat left out and neglected, but that is only part of the picture. In talking with the mother, the teacher could have explored any undue service which Dick may get in his family, in dressing, eating, and so forth. She missed this point and, therefore, neither found out nor made the mother aware of any special service she and some of the sisters may be rendering.

I asked that the mother and the girls give Dick some home duty for which he was entirely responsible, and refrain from helping him with it. I also asked that the mother give Dick at least one chance each meal to tell something that had happened in his school day, and ask the girls to let him have a part in the conversation. I asked the mother to make more effort to attend school functions for Dick as she does for the older girls.

COMMENT. All these recommendations seem excellent, particularly the advice that Dick should not be helped when he assumes some duties. But it will take more effort and supervision to permit the women to carry this out. It would be important to know which of the four women would be most inclined to continue her undue help.

In other words, while the teacher is right to suggest that more should be done for Dick, she neglected to see that less should be done for him also. And her blind spot may be due to the fact that she is not aware how much undue attention she herself has paid to Dick.

Example 32

The problem. Tony, age 7, isolates himself from the group. He wants to correct everyone and refuses to do what he is asked. He hits anyone who says anything that sounds like making fun of him. He falls and slides as he walks, and is nervous. If any teacher or classmate urges, commands, or corrects him, he tightens himself and tries to do the opposite of what they say. If he does not get his way he leaves the group. He does not complete jobs in reasonable time. He cannot wait for his turn.

C O M M E N T. This description gives a rather complex picture of the boy. There is much hostility and defensiveness, drive and discouragement, the desire for power and superiority, defiance and resistance. Let us see whether the teacher can bring some order into this chaos.

Analysis. Tony is the only child of older than average parents. They expect perfection from him. They criticize anything that is less than exceptional behavior. Tony wants to have a place in the class, but thinks he can have it only by being perfect or exceptional; therefore, he feels that everyone is criticizing him when he is not perfect or when he does not get special attention. Negative criticism is unbearable, and he revolts against it. He does not finish work, because he wants to show that he does not have to do what someone tells him, and because he wants to show that he can be different. Instead of finishing something, he does some small part of the assignment in an attractive, unusual way. Often the work itself is too easy to challenge him.

C O M M E N T. Tony's being the only child of overambitious parents explains a great deal. He is spoiled and wants his own way. He probably is convinced that he is special, different from anyone else, and whoever does not give him a special place is unfair to him. There is a certain amount of vengefulness in his behavior; he is not sure that he has a place and, therefore, not sure that he is liked and accepted. The teacher is probably correct in assuming that his exaggerated assumption of the necessity of being important and exceptional increases his feeling of deficiency and his fear of it. In whatever he is doing he is still exceptional, although not always in a useful way. But he makes sure that he is different from the others. This explains the first impression of unusual complexity in behavior.

Tony is far above average intelligence. He responds to encouragement and kindness. His whole being seems to go into a "thank you" for a compliment, and he is eager to please anyone who seems to like him.

C O M M E N T . This seems to confirm the earlier impression. An only child, he is overdependent on the opinion of others; he can gain status only through others, not through his own strength, which will never match that of his parents, the only other members of the early family group in which he has tried to establish himself. His eagerness to please indicates that he has not yet given up hope of being liked and accepted, although he is not sure he will be. Every unfavorable remark evokes this danger.

Possible corrective procedure. I can stop reminding Tony. I can be a friend to him and not make him feel that his work is more important than he is. I can recognize his good work and behavior more often, and give him more positive than negative criticism. I can try to use natural consequences and stop trying to force him. I can, at times, give him more challenging work to do.

C O M M E N T . All these suggestions are excellent. Most important seems to be the realization that Tony should feel acceptable, irrespective of his work and accomplishments. Because he is overambitious, he thinks he is not good enough unless he does exceptional work. Therefore, he must learn that he has a place even if he is not so good. Efforts to accomplish that may conflict with the recognition of good work and behavior. Such recognition can be helpful; but one has to be careful not to exaggerate the significance of good work to Tony or he is induced again to maintain his mistaken assumption of the need for excellence. It is essential that he not be forced; he is well trained to defy force, and has probably defeated his parents innumerable times. But appealing to his ambition to accomplish challenging work might be effective, provided that one avoids any indication of his being exceptional in accomplishing it.

Example 33

The little girl of this study is the youngest of three. The oldest, a girl, is 22, the brother is 20, and Ann is 6 years old. She was conceived and born during the war while her father was in camp. She was not exactly wanted, and certainly arrived at an inopportune time. The mother had to give up her job, although she needed the money to supplement the family income.

COMMENT. The teacher is right: Ann has had many strikes against her from the beginning. However, her greatest handicap is probably the tremendous age difference. She is a super-baby, an only child, with many fathers and mothers. This seems to be more important for her development than the peculiar circumstances surrounding her birth. Whatever feeling her mother may have had at her birth could have changed afterward, but her inappropriate smallness in a family of grown-ups has remained during her formative years. (In this regard various schools of thought may differ.)

Ann was born small and not too healthy. Both of the other children had been robust. The mother gave the child every physical and emotional care that she could. The sister was then 16 and the brother 14 years old, and both became willing slaves for the little weak baby.

COMMENT. The teacher herself has apparently given up the assumption of an early rejection by the mother. It is now obvious that the age discrepancy between Ann and her siblings is of considerable importance.

At the time I first met the family, Ann was 2 years old and not yet walking or talking. The mother had consulted the doctor who told her there was nothing physically wrong with the child. Ann got around in a part crawl and drag manner. She made only unrecognizable sounds. The father had returned at the time, and not only was also a willing slave for the child but opposed any attempt to let her be more independent. He felt she should be treated in a special manner.

C O M M E N T . This case shows the factors that may lead to the slow development of a child. It illustrates clearly the tremendous social significance a child can obtain merely by being deficient and doing nothing.

The brother was the only member of the family who showed any desire to encourage Ann and to help her become independent. When he was left alone with her, he would not get her what she wanted, but would encourage her to take a step or two to get things for herself. He also tried to get her to say words and name objects. He discovered that she could say simple words plainly if she wanted to. But when the rest of the family was around, Ann reverted to her usual behavior. Mother and brother got together and talked over the situation. After this talk, the mother tried out the brother's method.

C O M M E N T . This is an interesting situation, fraught with considerable dynamite. After all, who is the man of the house, the father or the brother? And to whom should the mother listen? But it is evident that Ann's deficiency could not survive if the brother's approach was maintained.

The family lived in a neighborhood where there were children Ann's age. The mother encouraged other children to come to her house with or without their parents. Soon she noticed that Ann became lost in play with the others. From time to time she would see her attempt a step and hear her attempt words. More and more the mother began trying to treat Ann the way she treated her other children when they were Ann's age. She found herself gently but firmly refusing "to fetch and carry" for her. Soon the child was taking more and more steps. By the age of 4, Ann could walk well and run well. She still prattled, saying only a few words.

C O M M E N T . The mother apparently slowly learned to extricate herself from Ann's demands, to free herself from the child's domination. It was a slow process, however—Ann still got along without speaking clearly.

The other children in the neighborhood attended nursery school. The father firmly refused to allow Ann to go. When she reached kindergarten age she was entered in a school near her home. At first, the mother took her, but soon Ann made known her desire to walk there with the other children. The mother sent her with an older girl. The neighborhood children had learned to understand much of her prattle and played well with her. She fell more often than others and cried more often, but soon learned to make a satisfactory playmate. The father worked much of the time; and since the mother tried to "push her out," Ann had many chances to play with others. The mother made herself stay indoors as much as possible on these occasions.

COMMENT. There can be no doubt that the mother had the right attitude. However, we have no information about the details of events taking place at home, about Ann's dressing herself, coming when called to meals, her table manners and food habits, and other incidents which would demonstrate the extent to which the mother continued undue service, probably driven into submission by the overprotective father and Ann's persistence.

Ann's first school experience was not satisfactory; the teacher felt sorry for her and taught or allowed the other children to "baby" her, to put on her clothes, and so forth. Ann was permitted to impose on others without anyone letting her experience the consequence of her acts.

COMMENT. This is a wonderful example of the scarcely believable power of the "weak" over the strong. Ann put her teacher and the whole class into her service. It was not without Ann's active participation that the teacher and the other children did all these things for her. *There is a subtle interplay in the impressive helplessness of a child who waits in order that something will be done for her.*

This situation also warrants another explanation of a dynamic process unfortunately unknown to many teachers and parents. It is the effect that sympathy has on a child. Any adult who feels sorry for a child, regardless of how justified this sympathy may be, is doing harm to the child. In many cases the harm done through pity exceeds the effects of serious mishaps. A child who senses that others feel sorry for him feels justified in feeling sorry for himself. And nobody feels as low and miserable as one who feels sorry for himself. Feeling sorry for a child has the most detrimental consequences. If adults knew what harm they were doing through pity, even when most understandable, they would stop and reconsider. What the child needs is neither pity nor sympathy but empathy. We can express to a child our understanding about how he feels without necessarily feeling sorry for him. In Ann's case the teacher felt sorry for her, as did her father; Ann paid the price for it.

Ann is now repeating kindergarten. Her teacher is not so easily "taken in." Another advantage is the fact that most of the children in her class did not know Ann before; therefore, she must try to talk to get things and have a place in the class. She is now able to dress herself, can talk in sentences, draw pictures, run, skip, and so forth. She is making fair progress.

C O M M E N T . One might perhaps think that just one year of growth is responsible for this improvement. However, considering the total situation, one must agree that probably the understanding teacher, who influenced Ann's classmates, is responsible for her progress.

The child's progress at home is not as good as in school, because of the father's attitude and because of occasional relapses on the mother's part. The older sister who always was very easy on her, has left home. The brother is still firm with her and plays a big part in her development.

C O M M E N T . Progress or lack of it depends on the situation in which Ann finds herself. The mother has probably never come to realize completely the amount of overprotection and service she has offered; and the father lacks any insight in the role he has played. It is interesting to note the extent to which Ann has been a focal point for opposing forces within the family, father and sister siding against mother and brother, probably in more ways than in their attitudes toward Ann.

I think this child exhibited a passive-destructive form of demanding attention. She was allowed to become so because she lived with too many adults. Her weakness encouraged the adults to baby her too much and too long. The brother either saw through her behavior or became tired of waiting on her. He was instrumental in changing the attitude and behavior of the mother toward the child and thus changing the child.

C O M M E N T . Little need be added to this summary. It is still not certain to what extent this child may be mentally retarded. We have no psychological findings. However, it seems probable that the child's intelligence is not below average, and may even be above.

Ann now seems to be fast changing to an active-constructive behavior; she seems eager to do things. When I visited her home a few days ago, I was greeted with a friendly hello. She not only answered all my questions about Christmas but volunteered some remarks in whole sentences. She offered me some cake and insisted upon bringing it to me.

No comment necessary.

CHAPTER 8

Toward Changing the Child's Goals

T HE PREVIOUS CHAPTER was concerned with the teacher's efforts to gain an understanding of the child's motivation, to analyze the goals and purposes which the child has set for himself, both in life and in a given situation. This chapter presents methods of dealing with the child when his goal has been recognized. Different approaches are indicated for each goal. It is not the overt behavior itself, nor the type of deficiency, but its underlying purpose that warrants a specific response. For example, there is no set rule for dealing with a lazy child. If his laziness is a means of getting attention, it requires entirely different responses from the teacher than when laziness is being used to defeat authority and, therefore, is part of a contest for power. On the other hand, the great variety of behavior patterns used to get service and attention require similar reactions. The approach based on the recognition of a specific goal behind the child's disturbance or deficiency will bring the best results, although, as has been pointed out before, nonspecific methods can also be effective.

The short reports in this chapter are presented in four groups, each dealing with one of the four goals. Each illustrates the limited purpose of this chapter: after recognizing the child's goals, to determine which methods are adequate and which detrimental in dealing with a specific purpose. No effort is made here to deal with the more elaborate corrective measures available to the trained teacher in the classroom situation.

The question of the therapeutic effectiveness of this procedure may arise. There can be no doubt that the child will not give up his established goal merely because the teacher was able, on one or the other occasion, to make his efforts unprofitable. Nevertheless, if the teacher is able to convince the child by similar and persistent experiences of the futility of his goal, he is likely to reconsider and change it. It is important that in his reconsideration the child turn to a more constructive direction. For this reason, the specific response to a mistaken goal should be a part of a more generalized corrective effort in which encouragement plays an indispensable part.

By way of introduction, it may be useful to examine what happens when the teacher tries to jump an essential step, as in the following example.

Example 34

Here are the facts. What is the solution? Peter, age 10, in fifth grade, is a natural leader, well liked by classmates. He dislikes all subjects, but loves to entertain. He refuses to take part in any activity he does not organize. He distracts the attention of all who sit near him. Whatever he does as far as school work is concerned is done because of pressure or fear. He does not hesitate to lie or cheat to get any person in authority to let him alone momentarily.

How should one cope with this situation?

C O M M E N T . The teacher seems to be looking for a solution before she has understood the facts she reports; she does not make any attempt to analyze first.

Peter's behavior is not difficult to understand. He is obviously involved in a personal feud with any authority, and with his teacher in particular. He is leader of his peers; all his activities are directed "to the gallery." He defeats the teacher's efforts to win the attention of the class. He gives in only when he has to, if the pressure or unpleasant consequences become too strong. But, as in any war, all means are permissible to defeat the enemy; thus he does not hesitate to lie and cheat and to use any tricks to bring about the defeat of the teacher.

If the teacher had realized the full implication of this situation, she would have avoided doing anything that would intensify the warfare, and tried everything to remove herself from the power contest and win Peter to her side. But what did she do?

I have tried everything in the books. I tried motivation and organization of lessons so that they would become interesting. I tried talking to Peter, reasoning with him, giving him special duties so that he would gradually feel more important.

C O M M E N T . With exception of the last, all her efforts were in vain. Making the lessons more interesting can be of no avail as long as Peter is not interested in the school procedure. And the nature of her talking and reasoning can be easily visualized from her emotional reaction to Peter, which is revealed in her report. She probably preached, explained, coaxed, and in general told him things which he already knew, and that in a rather superior way. That is the way such discussions generally go, and is the reason why they are so futile. Trying to give him special duties to make him feel important is a good approach in general, but it is easy to see why it did not work with Peter. The teacher may have presented his special assignments with the same air of superiority exhibited in all her contacts with him, thus confirming Peter even more in his determination to defeat her. The teacher's idea of turning the recognition which Peter got through his destructive behavior into useful channels was good; but not knowing the purpose of Peter's behavior she did not know how to redirect it.

Finally, in order to bring about some sort of solution, I went to him, shook him until his shirt tore, and told him that he knew what had to be done in class and that every class had to have organization and that he would have to cooperate.

C O M M E N T . Here the teacher openly declared her bankruptcy, but probably without knowing it. She thought that she was acting "to bring about a solution," while actually she was showing Peter that she had no idea what to do with him. It is one thing to tell a boy that he *has* to cooperate, and another to induce him. What did she accomplish?

Peter went home, and his mother came to class the next day very angry, and said she was going to send the father up to take care of the matter. But I told her that I must have her cooperation, and that if thirty-one papers were handed in each day, why couldn't one of the thirty-one be her son's? She has promised to cooperate.

COMMENT. It is not surprising that the teacher found it easier to get the mother's cooperation than the boy's. After all, they both had to contend with his rebellion, and the mother understood what the teacher had to put up with in Peter. While it was probably the mother's and father's fault that Peter was what he was, it was not their fault that the child did not bring his assignment. It was up to the teacher to induce him to do so; and she could have accomplished it, provided she knew the proper methods. Shaking him and tearing his shirt coupled with empty talk certainly do not belong among the effective methods. However, we can sympathize with her feeling of frustration and desperation.

This example demonstrates how the response of the teacher is part of an interaction taking place between her and the child. In this interaction the child's goal comes into play. The teacher is on the receiving end of a well-planned, effectively executed, although unconscious, strategy. Her countermeasures must take it into consideration; otherwise, she is no match for him.

1. ATTENTION GETTING

Example 35

Pat, a pampered first-grader who lives with his grandparents, had a unique response to my suggestion that each time he required my attention without justifiable cause I would number the times I had to call his name before the class. (As, "Pat, get back to your seat—that is the fifth time I have had to call your name this afternoon.") Pat loved every minute of this "game" and responded with "Mrs. S, Mrs. S, watch me, that is number twenty-three."

COMMENT. The example seems to suggest that this method of dealing with children who demand too frequent attention may backfire and, therefore, may not be adequate. But does it prove it?
This is a fine example of how much depends on the way a certain

procedure is executed. It was recommended (see page 48) that the teacher make "a deal" with the child as to the number of times he thought he would require some special attention during the next hour. And then the teacher should merely call his name: "Pat, number one," "Pat, number ten," and so on. This the teacher did not do; it would have stopped the child, for he wanted more attention than that. What she did was to make a fuss, giving him a long lecture each time, and thus playing into his hands. After the discussion concerning her faulty technique, the teacher reported again.

I then tried this method with Ben, an only child, from a home with a great deal of pressure, who cried daily when first brought into the classroom (first grade). At that time he also had to be reminded to keep busy. Now he needs few reminders; numbering the times he requires attention has reduced them to a minimum.

Example 36

Ralph, age 10½, in fourth grade, displays a puzzled and pleading look. His eyes beg for service and attention, yet he never seems to understand exactly what is expected of him.

C O M M E N T . The "yet" does not make sense. Is he not asking for service when he seems not to understand what he should do? Does not the teacher's description imply that she feels compelled to "explain" again?

One day, Ralph's class was working with words and with pictures which were to be pasted on construction paper. Ralph brought one which had been passed to him, and showed me that it had come unpasted. He seemed concerned and anxious for me to do something about the matter. I asked him what *he* was going to do about it. He went to his seat, held the two papers in his hands and looked forlorn and helpless. I waited at some distance behind him, so he turned and watched me, still pleading with his eyes for assistance. Then he began talking to himself. I asked him what he was saying; he answered, but in such a soft voice I didn't hear what he said. As I came closer to him, I heard him say, "I could fix this if I had some scotch tape." He was sitting five feet from an open jar of paste which he knew he was free to use. I asked him what he could use instead of scotch tape, and I received a helpless look. Several of his classmates became interested and wanted to help him, but I quieted them down.

Ralph sat and continued to look pleading at all of us. Then I said, "Ralph, you are waiting for me to tell you what to do; but I am waiting for you to remember that you are 10½ years old and in the fourth grade, and that you do not need any help on this job." Immediately, the infantile expression left and he began studying me seriously. By then the class had become interested, so I told them, "Boys and girls, let us all watch the clock and see how long it will take Ralph to decide that he can do that job alone." As we all looked toward the clock, Ralph jumped up and went directly to the paste jar and pasted the papers. In all the time I have taught Ralph I have never seen him move as quickly or do a job in such a self-assured manner.

As an afterthought—or as an explanation?—the teacher added: "Ralph is the oldest of four, and the only boy."

C O M M E N T . This is a good example of a child who wants attention and service. And the teacher probably gives the correct reason for Ralph's behavior: the only boy with three sisters and a mother who probably all serve him. (Perhaps his next younger sister is as capable as the mother so that he has neither need nor chance to exert himself.) But did the teacher actually refrain from giving him service and undue attention? She refused to help him and to tell him what to do; but while she refused this demand, she nevertheless kept busy with him. It was a good idea to invite the whole class to watch and see how long it would take him. But before she moved into action, there was a great deal of conversation between her and Ralph, even though he spoke—as she realized—only with his eyes and facial expression. In other words, she fell for his trick and demands although she thought she was resisting them. He did not mind her preaching as long as she kept addressing herself to him. This example shows how careful one must be if one wants to avoid falling for the child's designs.

Example 37

Gene, age 5, is in my morning kindergarten class. He is—most of the time—a normal, happy child. But sometimes he hangs back. For example: Some mornings he will take at least fifteen minutes to take off his coat and get his rug. Then he will stand by the door, waiting for me to notice him. When I do, he walks slowly into the room, almost as if he wants me to say, "Hurry up!" or help him sit down.

Since I am now learning that this is just an attention-getting device, I simply call attention to someone else who is already seated and ready to start. By the time I look at Gene again—he is sitting down too.

COMMENT. Apparently the teacher had in the early stages continued to look at Gene. Even though she may not have said what was on her lips, she gave him sufficient attention for Gene to wait even longer. Only when she stopped responding to his hesitation did he find it useless to continue it.

One day I looked over at Gene and found him lying on the floor and kicking his feet up in the air. Since we were beginning a game the children love, I said, "The one I choose to start will be someone who is sitting nicely." Gene flipped back up again. I managed not to choose Gene at this time, but maneuvered so that he did get chosen by the children.

COMMENT. This was nicely done. The teacher ignored what Gene did, but took action which impressed him. No direct notice, no word of reminding, none of the usual superfluous admonitions.

When I first saw Gene doing these tricks, I had a talk with his mother. She was not surprised, since he had done such things at home too. I suggested to her that he might be doing it to get our attention; and maybe if we ignored his "tricks" of babyishness and "funny behavior" he might give them up. He has a brother, two years younger, and I suggested to the mother that Gene and his brother might vie for her attention. She thought that could be possible and she would watch for it and be careful not to fall for it.

Now, a few months later, Gene has almost given up the process of acting up. He does draw well, and has been getting along fairly well with the other children. He takes a much greater interest in playing, painting, and games than he did at first. I have been encouraging Gene to try activities and his success in doing them seemingly has added to his enjoyment.

The teacher concludes by asking whether she has understood and treated this case correctly.

COMMENT. One could not have approached the situation more adequately. Not only did the teacher understand Gene well and eventually find out what to do with him, but apparently she was able to communicate the same understanding to his mother and suggest to her the proper approach. Still, this way of perceiving and doing things must have been so new to her that she was not quite sure of it Or was she seeking approval?

Example 38

Mary, age 6, is the oldest of three; her brother is 3 and her sister, 2 months old. When Mary entered school in September, she was a shy, dependent, charming little girl. The smallest child in the class, she was regarded by the others as the baby in the group, rather than as another classmate. Displaying much shyness, Mary accepted this role of the baby, and soon had her classmates doing for her things she felt she could not (or would not) do, as well as things she could do.

COMMENT. Being the smallest child in the group helped; but it was not really the reason that the children chose her as "baby." This shows the subtle, but effective, interaction which takes place when one member of the group is pushed—or lets himself be pushed —into a certain position. It is hard to say who started such a development, although it is generally the "victim" who, consciously or unconsciously, induces his peers as well as his teacher to treat him as he expects to be treated. Mary certainly displayed considerable prowess in inducing all the other children in her group to be her self-appointed slaves.

Then a conference with her mother was held. It was found out that Mary's parents were separated, that she lived with an aunt during the school week, and spent the weekends with her mother. Both women babied her. Mary had no independent tasks to perform, never dressed herself, never had to put her toys away, and seldom misbehaved. She was considered a very good child, in contrast to the three-year-old younger brother who was "always getting into something." Her passive but pleasant behavior made her the center of attention in the home, and was being carried over into the classroom.

C O M M E N T . These few facts "explain" Mary's behavior sufficiently. Both her aunt and her mother fell for her charm and passivity. What role the father played in inducing these two women to overprotect the children is not quite clear. The brother probably showed the same tendency to keep them busy, only with opposite, namely, active, means, perhaps following the masculine guiding lines established in this family. One might classify Mary's behavior as a passive-constructive form of getting attention, since she succeeded in giving all those who babied her considerable satisfaction and pleasure, while her brother displayed an active-destructive AGM.

Sometimes Mary would stand by her clothes locker, looking sad, and on two occasions crying, until someone would help her take off her coat and hang it up. At play time she would stand off by herself until a classmate would ask her to come and play. When asked by the teacher to tell about a picture at reading time, she put her finger in her mouth and smiled sweetly.

Mary was soon selected to be a table helper in class, in an effort to remove her from the receiving end. It was her responsibility this morning to get out the supplies, i.e., paper, pencils, scissors, and books. She took much delight in this task. After a time she began to go to her locker without hesitation, hang up her coat, and hurry to the room to do her work. She began to take more *active* interest in the children and in her paper work.

C O M M E N T . This was an excellent approach. Without saying anything about Mary's deficiency, the teacher succeeded in giving her recognition and a place where she got attention through doing. It was the satisfaction Mary experienced through this "doing" that made it possible for her to give up the satisfaction previously obtained through passive provocation.

Mary's passive attention-getting behavior began to change. On her birthday (as is the routine in our classroom) she sat in the "birthday chair," and beamed all over when the children sang Happy Birthday to her. She volunteered to tell them what she had received for her birthday, and about the plans for her party. Still occupying the "birthday chair" at story time, Mary asked if she could tell a story. Upon finishing it, she was delighted with the way the group enjoyed it. She has since become an active member in her reading group, and works independently at her table.

COMMENT. These highlights confirm the teacher's reference to the change. The beaming over the children's singing to her was a passive form of reaction to the attention she received. Her volunteering to tell them about her gifts and plans was a more active form of maintaining the limelight. Her asking to tell a story was entirely active-constructive. And the last remarks of the teacher indicate that the girl even moved toward full participation without any attention, the desirable end result. One wonders whether all this has been accomplished merely by classroom experiences stimulated by the teacher, or whether the teacher had succeeded in instituting a different routine for Mary at home also. The teacher finishes with a summary:

I feel that when Mary discovered she could be accepted, be a part of the group and get attention by doing, she gradually moved out of her passive-constructive behavior and is now showing more and more evidence of an active-constructive approach.

We may add—even without a bid for attention.

These examples have brought out the main principles that characterize the recommended approach to a child whose behavior is recognized as an AGM, a bid for attention. These same principles hold true for all forms of behavior with the same dynamic pattern. The main endeavor is directed toward changing destructive behavior into constructive, passive into active.

In the teacher's effort to recognize the purpose of the child's action without succumbing to it, the bid for attention can either be ignored or answered in a manner the child does not expect. The scheme of the child, directed against the teacher and the class, can be channeled thereby into a procedure arranged by the teacher as part of an educational experience. This makes the undue attention a legitimate one and thus takes the satisfaction out of the child's mistaken endeavors. And without continued satisfaction with his pattern of disturbing behavior, which the child derives from the reaction of teachers who do not understand his purpose, no reason remains for continuing it.

Two forms of attention-getting which have come up in these reports may require a few comments. One is the role of overambition leading to a bid for attention (Example 32). It does not always have to be an active-destructive AGM, although it always requires recognition by others. Our formulation of "attention-getting" implies the demand for attention from the teacher. Striving for special status in the group, however, which is often the cause of overambition, may not necessarily consist of a demand for undue attention from the teacher. When it does, it is because the child does not yet believe in his ability to gain his place among his peers without active support from an adult—this is then expressed in his dependence on special attention. It is also evident that overambition plays an important part in the development of goal four (Example 33). This will become even clearer later on in the discussion.

The other point which may need clarification is the child's desire to get service. This is *always* an AGM. The child is not primarily concerned with *what* the parent or teacher actually does for him. He just wants them to do something for him, as a means of belonging, of getting something, of being noticed; and he capitalizes on anything that seems to justify his request for undue assistance and help, which is service.

2. POWER CONTEST

The situation is quite different when the teacher is confronted with a child who challenges her power. The main principle in counteracting such a tendency is to *extricate oneself from the power contest so that the child's efforts become futile.* It is like *taking the sail out of his winds.* Only then it is possible to redirect the child's efforts into more constructive channels. If this desire for power is part of an overall overambition to be somebody and to feel important, then the method of redirection is similiar to the one effective with an overambitious AGM. Nobody has to fight with a child if he does not want to.

Example 39

Al is a bright 8-year-old who has just started fourth grade. The regular classroom work is not challenging enough for him. He does not complete his assignments, and demands a great deal of attention by coming to the teacher's desk frequently. He is critical of everyone. As an example, I wrote a problem on the board: "Write four hundred seven in figures." He came up to tell me that I left out the word "and." He said it should be written "four hundred *and* seven."

COMMENT. Al still has some characteristics of a child who wants attention; but his display of critical superiority, even over the teacher, indicates a beginning struggle for power, although it may be limited for the present to the intellectual sphere. If this is not recognized and the response is faulty, the child may then extend his contest for power into the behavioral area.

Each day I place five problems on the board which are to be done as soon as the children come into the room. While I am checking their papers, they continue another assignment in their books. If I find, in grading the papers, that a child has made an error, I ask him to put the correct answer on the board. Usually the error is due to carelessness and not a lack of knowledge. Only if the child has difficulty in writing the correct answer do I help him to find out where the difficulty lies. Later I give each child his grade. If one error is made, I give an S. Every problem has to be correct in order to get an E.

When I gave Al his grade, an S, he said. "You graded my paper wrong; you gave me an S and I should get an E." I remembered which problem he had missed, and told him what was on his paper. I would have sent him to the blackboard to work the problem out, but just before Al another child had had the same error, and it had already been worked out. He still insisted that he had the correct answer to the problem, an addition, with 48 as the correct answer; he had put down 47 on his paper. I said: "Maybe I did grade your paper incorrectly; come to my desk and we will check your paper together." We found his paper. We both looked at it—I looked at him—he looked at me—he had 47 on the paper. He said, "I thought I had written a 48." No more was said.

COMMENT. It is obvious that Al tried to get the teacher involved in an argument, for he has probably learned to defeat people by arguing with them. He was persistent and obstinate. Instead of arguing with him, the teacher invited him to look at his paper. The most important part of her report is her ending of the paragraph: "No more was said." It would have been so easy to take advantage of this moment of victory over Al to preach and impress him with his incorrect behavior, but any such victory would have intensified his determination to win the next time. The teacher did not let herself get involved in the contest.

Recently I forgot to tell the boys and girls to look for the eclipse of the moon. I felt that here I had an opportunity to direct Al into a constructive channel. I called his home and told him to watch the eclipse and to report to the class the next day. I thought this would also give him a chance to contribute to the class on the useful side, thus giving him status within his group. He does not feel a part of his group; he complains that the children will not play with him.

The next day Al was quite excited about giving his report to the class. He brought his source of information, a little booklet about the solar system which he had in his collection of books. His report and his presentation were excellent. We decided to put Al's report in the newspaper which we publish monthly, and put his name under it.

C O M M E N T . In redirecting the child's motivations it is important to seize on opportune occasions such as this. It requires alertness, imagination, and—first of all—awareness of the problem.

Example 40

Earl, age 8, had been in another school system last year. He was not promoted. Generally I am able to maintain a good relationship with him; but sometimes I am surprised how easily defiance, destructiveness, and a drive for power can be aroused in him.

He is doing good class work, but has manifested destructiveness particularly in his art work and seat work. The other day he plainly refused to do his seat work. He was talking to another boy while I talked to the class. I moved his seat and continued. He became defiant, saying, "This is just where I want to sit." I smiled and said, "O.K."

C O M M E N T . The teacher demonstrated how she "maintained good relations" with him. She simply acted and didn't talk. And when he challenged her by pretending that she had done what he wanted to do, she did not get provoked but with a knowing smile let him pretend to be victorious.

After school I detained him and gave him a piece of paper to put down the lesson he had not done in class. He said he had already done the first four sentences and, therefore, would just do the last two. When he had finished the last two, I looked at his paper and said, "Good." He looked at me flabbergasted. Then I told him to take his book to the board and fill in the first four sentences at the board. He seemed most eager to do that.

COMMENT. How did the teacher make him do what he first had so staunchly refused to do? She did not make any fuss over the situation, and praised him for what he had done well, without talking about his deficiency. The boy was not used to such treatment by a teacher (as can be assumed from his previous failing). She proved to be his friend and did not let herself get involved in the power contest. As a consequence he cooperated with her.

The next day I noticed him working hard on a similar assignment. At recess he brought his tablet to me, of his own volition, to show me that he had done his work. I told him that I had noticed how well he worked.

COMMENT. She could not have succeeded in "making him work"; but she succeeded in stimulating him to do his work. That is the main difference to keep in mind when a child provokes a contest for power.

Example 41

Ned, aged 8, special class, reads "word—word—word" without any sense of the meaning of a sentence. When he stopped in the middle of a sentence to talk of something else, I said, "Oh, now you stopped in the middle! You'll have to go back and start over."

He said, "I won't do it. I read those first words, and I am not going to read them again."

"All right," I answered. "But let's stop and talk about why I asked you to do that. Suppose I were reading the sentence, "See the bird on the limb of the tree.""

"See the bird—do you think it's going to rain? It is really a lovely day—on the limb—that's a pretty picture you made, I like it—of the tree." "There! Does that make any sense?" Ned laughed and said, "You are funny!" I agreed with him and laughed too.

"You see," I explained, "you've been reading like that and I don't wonder you hate reading. It would be very tiresome reading just by the word, but when you can read whole sentences, they make sense and it's like talking. Now, would you like to read the whole sentence and see if it makes sense?"

He did, and read the rest of his lesson in sentences. I felt that he had attained a completely new concept of the process of reading, and I told him that I thought he had made a big stride in his progress on this day.

COMMENT. This is a typical example of the lengths to which children will go when they pretend to read but actually refuse to do so. Interrupting his sentence showed Ned's effort to defeat the teacher, and he showed his open defiance by refusing to read again.

How did the teacher extricate herself from the situation? First, by not falling for the provocation. She sidetracked the issue in two ways. She showed him in a mirror technique how silly his actions were, and then she used humor and made him laugh. This alone would merely have relieved the situation and helped Ned to continue in a cooperative spirit. But she did more than that. She showed sympathy for the fact that he hated reading. She motivated him to read the whole sentence, and thereby removed the block based on Ned's assumption that reading makes no sense and is merely submission. It also removed his assumption that he could not read.

Example 42

The teacher starts his report with the following remarks: "This report will reveal my confusion and mistakes in the application of the principles and ideas we have studied and discussed; I hope I have made some progress in my approach."

Charles, age 15½, is a student in my seventh-grade class. He is small and slight, and almost three years older than the other students. He comes from a large family with several older married children. A sister, one year younger, is in the same class with him, and there is a baby, a recent addition to the family.

COMMENT. This information about Charles' family does not provide too much insight. It seems that he and his younger sister are close together. While she has managed to catch up with him somehow, she has not surpassed him; therefore she must be slow too. Both of them are the youngest in a large family with much older siblings. This is probably the most important detail of the information so far.

I was assigned to this class four months ago, following a substitute. At that time Charles was uncooperative, wanted to wander around the room at will, and speak out when he wished. Frequently he ignored my request to return to his seat and work at assigned tasks. When he did mind, he did so swaggeringly and soon was up again. He frequently disturbed the activities of his group by throwing things and punching others as he passed them. Although he was not the only one who disrupted the group in the unbroken 2½-hour period, Charles was more arrogant and vicious than the others.

COMMENT. From the description of Charles' behavior, he belongs to the group of children who contest the power of authority, although there is an element of revenge in his viciousness and punching. Nevertheless, the exhibition of power seems to be in the foreground.

Not understanding the situation, I did little to begin with, but kept an eye on him, trying to be friendly and courteous as I tried to draw him back into line. All other rooms used the paddle to enforce discipline, and it was suggested that I start right off with one which was furnished to me. I declined the paddle, although Charles was quite a challenge and gave me great concern.

COMMENT. Without "understanding" much of the specific dynamics of this case, the teacher had a correct attitude and some sensitivity. The general use of the paddle probably contributed to the disturbances with which the group was beset. We can appreciate the teacher's decision to do little, as long as he did not know what to do.

Attempts to use the class as a judging body sometimes resulted in considerable confusion, noisy accusations, and counter-accusations from all angles. I was a little apprehensive about the two-way public address system through which the office had fingertip contact with each and every room. Group discussions on order and discipline were sometimes interrupted by demands for silence from the office.

COMMENT. The technique of group discussion will be explored in a later chapter. Apparently, the teacher did not know how to keep an orderly discussion going.

I noticed that Charles sought the company of the larger and more rugged boys, trading punches with them at every opportunity. Once he exhibited a knife, a switchblade, and I calmly told him to keep it out of my sight or I should have to ask him to give it up to me. He agreed not to bring it to school, a promise which I do not think he always kept, although he kept the knife out of sight.

COMMENT. Charles obviously was affected by a prevalent masculine ideal. Being tough meant being a man, being somebody, having a place. The teacher dealt rather effectively with him, it seems. The secret of his apparent success in inducing Charles to conform to certain rules was his calmness and firmness. There was no doubt in anyone's mind that he would have appropriated the knife had he seen it again. The statement that he would take it was not a threat, nor was it a provocation daring the boy to exhibit the knife. And the boy responded to this calm but firm approach.

Once, exasperated after many courteous but firm reminders day after day, I asked Charles what he was doing out of his seat again. He said he had lost his book and was looking for it. The assignment in the book had been made fifteen minutes before. Firmly, wishing not to browbeat him, I said: "Well, perhaps you'd better sit down before you lose your seat." The class laughed, and Charles returned to his seat sullenly and resentfully. Unsolicited, the class suggested the use of the paddle: "Everyone else does." Charles mumbled that nobody had better lay a paddle on him.

COMMENT. At first the teacher was not so successful. He has told us why, although he is not aware of doing so. Regardless of how courteous reminders may be, they are no good if they are repeated day by day. His approach was bound to fail because he was exasperated, convinced of his failure and inability to do anything about the situation. That is exactly what the boy wanted him to feel. It was the boy who called the turns, and the teacher merely obeyed orders—until he decided to move into action. He could have stopped the class until Charles was seated; or he could have declared his defeat openly, without resentment, letting Charles look for the book. He chose to use humor—and it worked. The teacher at least got the class on his side, if not Charles, and this helped the situation. Solicitation of group pressure is by and large a powerful and effective method. Some teachers who do not know it permit the troublemaker to get the class *on his side*; then the laughter is at the expense of the teacher. Naturally, it is better if all can laugh together.

On another occasion I took Charles outside the room and tried to reason with him about his actions; I scolded him. He cried and said I was always saying something to make the class laugh. I thought this was a rather pertinent comment, and after thinking it over to determine whether the criticism was justified, I said that perhaps he misunderstood; it was not my intention to make the class laugh at him or at anybody. I merely wanted Charles to join the group activities without being disagreeable about it. If he thought I was trying to make fun of him, I would apologize. Charles said, "Oh, that's all right. I was in the wrong."

COMMENT. This is an interesting piece of conversation, effective even though its dynamics are not so obvious.

First of all, using the class to make fun of Charles had proved useful. The boy admitted his defeat; the tough guy cried. And it was at this point that the teacher took full advantage of his strategic position. Instead of pursuing his attack further, he beat a strategic retreat. First he denied that it was his intention to make the class laugh at Charles. Of course, this was not true; he had done that very thing, whether intentionally or not. However, it was kind to say that he did not want to hurt Charles but wanted him to join. And it was humble to offer an apology. This took the wind out of Charles' sail. He reciprocated with the open admission that he was wrong.

It has to be emphasized time and again that no simple incident like this can have lasting effects, particularly when the boy is already

15½ years old. But each step is a step in the right direction, establishing a relationship of equality and friendly understanding without which no real help is possible.

At every opportunity I recognized Charles' work well done and his improvement and cooperativeness. But at times he still provoked troubles with other members of the class.

C O M M E N T . Did the teacher expect him to become perfect all of a sudden? Or was the teacher himself overambitious?

In another class Charles was struck by a teacher with a paddle so hard that he cried before the class. He claimed he was struck in the spine, and only the threat of examination before witnesses made him drop the claim.

C O M M E N T . Charles has to contend with other people, and not all of them exert the same beneficial influence.

From observation it seemed to me that Charles' size bothered him, and he was attempting brave compensations. Occasionally he bragged openly of friction with the police, and acted tough all the time. He said he liked Ken because Ken wasn't afraid of anything.

C O M M E N T . The teacher is probably right. It would require considerably more thorough study to reach the psychological basis; the masculine compensation, so obvious in Charles, is often based on a family trend imbedded in certain cultural patterns. It could also be that his smallness was particularly distasteful to him because it reminded him that he was only a baby in the family. The assumption of a compensatory drive is justified.

In a brief talk with Charles, I once mentioned casually that if size were the only measure of a man, then an ape was a better man than any of us. He guessed I was right, and I encouraged him to take advantage of his brains because he was quite intelligent.

C O M M E N T . Again a step in the right direction.

Charles continued to improve. His attempts to provoke me became more infrequent. However, the class complained that I indulged Charles for things that I reprimanded in someone else. I gave Charles chores which he did agreeably.

COMMENT. Although the teacher had won the cooperation of Charles, he had apparently failed to keep the cooperation of the class. At one time he used the support of the class against Charles and was promptly called down by the boy. Maybe he actually switched to the other side and showed preferential treatment. It is not possible to cope effectively with any child in the class unless one succeeds in winning the whole class, to solve the problems of the total situation.

Twice during my first two months in this class, I received a reprimand from the office for poor discipline: once for an attempt to employ natural consequences, giving a student a choice of standing outside the door until he felt he could work with his group, and the other time for giving my class a "break" in the middle of the 2½-hour period. When the principal walked in, one pupil had reached into his desk and pulled out a banana. The principal said, "Recess?"—and walked out. The next day I was notified that I should tighten down and I would accomplish more.

COMMENT. At a time when the whole educational system is undergoing drastic changes as part of what one may call an "educational revolution," differences in methods, approaches, and standards are inevitable. Such differences exist not only between school systems but often within the same school system and even within the same school faculty. Methods reflecting a democratic trend in education are naturally ill-suited for a school system where paddling is not only possible but even required. It takes courage, conviction, and stamina for a teacher to apply methods contrary to prevailing and often outdated traditional procedures. It requires considerable inner security to let one's professional security be endangered by the application of "new ideas."

After these two months, I resorted—reluctantly, regretfully—to the paddle, attempting to solve my treason by making its use the natural consequence of two warnings. Word had gotten around that in my room everyone was safe from the paddle. Eventually, I was caught in my own trap. The second time I used it, Charles had provoked trouble by twice engaging in a wrestling match with a large girl. With some misgivings I approached my task, since Charles, understandably, bristled under the touch of a teacher. I asked him who should be first, he or the girl. Charles asked, "Where are you going to hit her?" "Across the palm of the left hand, as usual." "Where are you going to hit me?"

"On the backside, as usual." "How many?" "One." "Oh, no," Charles said, "you are not going to touch me." He went back to his seat.

Not wanting to enter into a power contest, I let him go. Someone murmured, "Go ahead, Charles, I took it." One said, "He is yellow." That brought Charles to his feet, fighting mad and fists doubled, with tears in his eyes. He was going to bust the boy's jaw.

I told the class to return to its work. This was no longer their business, I said. If it were merely an issue of courage, Charles had as much as any boy in the class. When Charles was ready to accept the natural consequence of his behavior, which he knew was wrong, he would come to me.

Charles subsided, the class resumed its work. In two minutes, Charles came and said he was ready, if I would take him outside into the hall. He came back quite proud, one may assume, because he felt he was a man and now a member of the "fraternity of the flogged."

C O M M E N T . This was a difficult situation wonderfully handled, provided one can accept the teacher's decision to use the paddle as an inevitable submission to the pattern of the school. Naturally, paddling can never be a "natural consequence," but the teacher presented his case to the boy in such a way as to eliminate almost any trace of a personal contest for power, which could have so easily ensued. He was able to reach an agreement with the boy; he even let him name his own terms—outside the room—to emphasize that he was not using his power over the boy. The way the teacher broke up the incipient conflict between Charles and the class was also noteworthy. The teacher was on the spot, but found a good way out. He used sensitivity and imagination—and accomplished what he decided to do without outward conflict. If anyone had said before that a boy like Charles would be willing to take such punishment in his stride, it would not have been believed.

On the surface Charles bore no resentment. His participation again improved. He even turned to criticizing his sister for not paying attention and for talking. On one occasion he asked to get a paddling which I declined to give him.

C O M M E N T . There is certainly a change going on; the boy is giving up the masculine ideal of toughness and replacing it with a concern for cooperation. The question naturally arises of how deep this change is. His offer to get paddled seems to indicate that deep down he still thinks he is a bad boy. He has not yet accepted himself in a respectable position within society.

In another room, Charles was paddled by a six-foot-four woman teacher, and she says he gives her no trouble any more.

COMMENT. The question is because of or despite the paddling? His improvement under the influence of our teacher may have to be taken into consideration also.

However, one incident indicates what is going on in Charles. I suggested free themes one day, like things that make me happy or unhappy, what I would like to be when I grow up. Charles spoke up, "Shucks, I don't have to write it. I can tell you. I want to be the worst outlaw in the country. I'd like to have a dozen guns, two dozen knives, and shoot everybody up clear across the country." The question, "Why, Charles?" was asked, but lost in the discussion.

COMMENT. Quite an ambition for a baby boy! It is interesting to note how Charles on this occasion almost deliberately exaggerated. The way he said it would indicate that he was beginning to recognize what he was doing. The old pattern is still here, but not so deeply entrenched any longer. His statement, almost humorous, was more bravado than sincere desire.

Frequently in the past during oral reports, Charles told of escapes from police and floorwalkers. He has a record of delinquency. In school he was in an "opportunity class." Once he confided that his father had killed a "nigger" in the South before they came up here.

COMMENT. It is now becoming clear what the masculine ideal in this family is.

But Charles was no longer rebellious when conformity to the classroom procedures was requested from him. I felt I was making considerable progress in a room with many other behavior problems and an IQ median of about 80.

On his report card in April I graded Charles as steadily growing in all areas, because he had improved considerably in assuming responsibility and completing assignments, even though he sometimes tried to cheat (to copy from another boy) to finish on time. But when it came to behavior patterns, I had some misgivings. I graded him as needing help—or self-effort—in two areas: active concern for the welfare of his group, and attitude toward self.

COMMENT. The teacher is certainly making headway. It is not quite clear, however, whether he understands why Charles is cheating to finish on time. This is another indication of his considerable ambition. But the teacher is right that Charles has not yet integrated himself into society; he does not yet consider himself a worthwhile member, although he has diminished his fight against the representatives of society.

A remark was required for all grades under average. I hesitated a long time before I finally decided to sink or swim, and asked another teacher (one who thinks the paddle is overused) if he thought I was treading in an area in which I was not competent to meddle. He came in contact with Charles only once every other day for forty-five minutes during an activity period. He was the one Charles claimed had struck him in the spine, although I think Charles did not resent him much. Charles had done a good piece of work for him for which he was complimented. This teacher, after careful consideration, thought I was not transgressing. I thought it over for another two days before I wrote on the back of his card under "comments," after explaining that Charles was improving in all ways scholastically: "Charles' poor attitude toward the welfare of his group comes perhaps from his poor attitude toward himself. He seems to think that he is not important enough. We consider Charles an important person, as important as anyone else in the class, because he is *Charles* and not because he can be tough and uncooperative at times." When Charles read this as he left class he said, "Who wrote this on my card?" I said, "I guess I did, Charles." He left without further comment and has not mentioned it since.

COMMENT. In line with his other sensitive approaches to a ticklish situation this teacher managed to couch a critical remark behind encouraging and revealing words. Psychologically he is entirely correct. The way he said it and the occasion he used to say it cannot fail to make an impression. If Charles can fully understand what the teacher meant, and if he can change his mistaken concept of himself, he will really be rehabilitated.

Recently Charles entered somewhat of a power contest with a woman teacher, Mrs. D. Another boy was being scolded in the hall and made a face. Charles laughed. The teacher grabbed him, intending to crack his head with that of the other boy. A struggle ensued between the two. Charles told her she was not going to crack his head against the wall or anybody else's head. She didn't have the right to do it. The teacher insisted she did have the right, and continued "those are mighty big words for a little boy." Charles tore loose from her grasp, and she pursued him into my room where the struggle continued. Both were furious. I was afraid the struggle was going to have tragic consequences. I quietly told Charles to calm down, and put my hand on his shoulder. He quit struggling and Mrs. D loosed her grip on his coat collar. When Charles was calmer I suggested that he return with the teacher to her room and try to adjust their difficulty without losing his temper. After I dismissed my class, I went to the other room. The struggle was on again. Charles insisted that she was not going to make him miss his bus; she insisted that she had the right. He knocked over a desk and threatened to fight his way out. Again I interceded, calmed him down, and told him he would not miss his bus if he'd behave himself. Otherwise, someone would have to drive him home. He didn't want that. He quieted down, and I told him to go and get his bus and think things over before he came back next day.

The next morning Charles was in a defiant mood. He was unwilling to admit that he had provoked the trouble. He told me he hadn't been laughing at the teacher, but at the other boy for making the face. That didn't give her the right to swat him. She wasn't going to lay a hand on him. "If she does, she'd be sorry."

Before I could make Charles understand his share of the trouble, Mrs. D appeared. She asked me what Charles had decided. I took her aside and told her that Charles was still defiant, that he did not feel laughing at the other boy warranted the kind of punishment she had in mind. Mrs. D admitted that she had been angry, that perhaps she shouldn't have grabbed him as she did, or said what she did about his size. But she had talked it over with her husband and they both agreed that Charles should not be allowed to escape punishment; otherwise he might feel that he had gotten away with something. She was sending him to the principal's office.

Charles was called to the office, the paddle was used on him, and he was told to apologize to Mrs. D. He asked her if he might apologize in the hall outside her room. She insisted that he do it in her class, and he mumbled something to her in front of her class and left. He returned to my room tearful and furious, mumbling to a friend that he still should not have taken it.

COMMENT. This is another example of how children who need encouragement the most get the least, how *those who need most urgently to be treated with respect get pushed around the worst.* If Charles had had a *good* reputation in school and had laughed at the face the other boy made, the teacher would probably have asked him what was the matter with him, but not proceeded in the way she did. On the other hand, if Charles had been a well-adjusted boy he would have reacted differently to her provocation, would probably have apologized, and everything would have been settled. Here is the clash between a power-drunk boy and a power-drunk teacher.

Our teacher again proved effective in mitigating a bad situation, although he was unable to prevent the harm done to the dignity and self-respect of the boy. He was unable to buck a whole system, but under the circumstances he fought a brave rearguard action.

The next day in my room Charles was almost back where he started, uncooperative, rebellious. He left his seat frequently, and did only half of his work. He rolled dice in front of me, but gave them up when I asked him to. During a boastful oral report on his activities he toyed with a knife. In the art class of Mrs. D where he goes twice a week, he drew a picture of a woman and then put a slight goatee in the shape of her initial. She returned the picture to him as unacceptable.

It would seem to me that Charles's pattern of behavior has passed the power stage and is deteriorating into a revenge pattern. Would it be a mistake to assume that Charles feels sorry for himself?

COMMENT. The teacher is right in stating that Charles is on the verge of directing his main activities toward revenge against a society and its representatives by whom he feels mistreated. It is also true that he is inclined to feel sorry for himself. Many children involved in an intense power contest have at least at times the tendency to be vengeful. They consider it unfair if others do not give in to them but try instead to make them submit to their demands. A great deal of the mutual warfare consists of retaliation and mutual punishment, which comes close to a display of revenge.

However, this case is a typical example of a power contest. Charles provokes teachers to get involved in such a contest with him, and he responds vigorously to anyone who tries to show him power and authority.

There is no reason why our teacher should be discouraged about his own contribution to Charles' development. Naturally, the boy is exposed to many unfavorable influences and experiences similar to the last episode with Mrs. D. But we can assume that the thoughtful teacher's influence has made the boy receptive to other kinds of relationships. Even when Charles was at the peak of his hostility, the day after his defeat by the other teacher, he gave up the dice when asked to do so. The good relationship was not destroyed; probably it was even more firmly cemented by the mediating role which the teacher played throughout the course of the struggle. It is possible that Charles was merely testing his relationship the next day in class. Unfortunately, we have no detailed report about the teacher's reaction to Charles' relapse into his previous behavior. Maybe the teacher did not pass the test, because his last remarks sound rather discouraged. Maybe this discouragement of a person who should be a source of encouragement for the child was only temporary. But we can assume that the kind of relationship which the teacher had established throughout the year would bear fruit in the development of the boy.

At the end of his report the teacher added a footnote in pen:

This report need not end on such a sour note. After a talk with Charles I have hopes he will "come around" again.

3. REVENGE

It becomes obvious that it is not always easy to distingush between an intense power contest and the desire for revenge. Both may be present simultaneously in children who have assumed a hostile attitude toward society as a whole, or at least toward school. In many cases, the contest for power may only at times be replaced by vengeful retaliation when the child is forcefully subjugated.

It is primarily the intensity of hostility and viciousness which distinguishes revenge from the power conflict. In the power contest the child merely wants to win or at least to defeat the teacher's power; in revenge he wants to hurt where it hurts most.

As to corrective measures, in a situation where the child is driven only by the desire for revenge, little can be done constructively except waiting for the proper psychological moment to win the child. The fundamental mistake of such a child is his assumption that he cannot be loved or accepted. Any action—words are generally not too effective unless very well chosen—which can convey to the child a different self-evaluation will be helpful. By and large, it takes considerable effort, time, and stamina to convince such a child that he has a chance. Such efforts are generally not only counteracted by the child himself, who does not believe in the teacher's sincere concern, but also by other adults who are more concerned with their own defeated authority than with the welfare of the child. To make it worse, even the most persistent and skillful people cannot reach all children of this type. In many instances, months of constant effort may show no tangible results. However, the experience of having saved one child from an inevitable fate of crime and misery provides such gratification that it compensates for all other disappointments.

Waiting for the right moment when the child can be reached is fraught with continuous provocation. It is necessary to prevent danger and damage, to protect other children, and to maintain order with a minimum of restraint and a maximum of calm, friendly firmness. It is important to realize that retaliations, regardless of how understandable they are as impulsive reactions to the child's provocations, must be avoided. They are ineffective and—worst of all—they fortify the child in his mistaken convictions. The teacher needs the group to help her with such children. Often the group is antagonistic and hinders constructive steps unless the teacher has won the cooperation of the group or at least of some other students. Open discussions about such problems are often quite effective.

Example 43

Peter, 6 years old, was in my first-grade class last year. He was born in Europe and has a brother two years younger. He spent his mornings in the kindergarten to become acquainted with our schools, learn English, and become ready for the first grade. The afternoons he spent in my class. He seemed alert and quick in learning, so it was assumed that he could pick up first-grade work along with his readiness in kindergarten.

He came to school untidy, but was not physically weaker or smaller than the other children. He continued with the set program without any noticeable incident, until one day when the principal came to inform me that Peter had rebuked the kindergarten teacher and had kicked her in the ribs, cracking one of them. The principal and the kindergarten teacher had decided that he was too old for kindergarten and should be "tried" all day in the first grade. I had not been conscious of such behavior and accepted him just as I would any other child.

I think I treated Peter like the others. I helped him when he asked for help, and chose him to be a group leader, as I did the others. I must have slipped somewhere, though, because things began to take a turn.

One day I had taken the class out for recess. After a few minutes a little boy came crying to me saying that Peter had thrown sand in his face and on his clothes. I immediately called Peter. We had a discussion trying to get from the two boys a picture of the incident. They blamed it on each other, but both admitted that they had defied one rule, namely, how to use the sandbox. Therefore, they were told to sit on the step and watch how the others made use of the sandbox. Both were sitting there, when all of a sudden Peter got up and ran past me, screaming that he didn't like me and wouldn't stay in school. He ran right out of the playground and headed straight for home. This had never happened to me before, and I couldn't leave my class and chase him, so I sent a youngster for the principal. I wanted it reported just in case something happened to Peter on the way home. About an hour later, Peter came back to school with his father and stepmother. They had already spoken to the principal, and Peter had decided that he was wrong and wanted to apologize. I accepted the apology and pushed aside the incident.

COMMENT. So far we do not know whether Peter got involved in a power contest if he could not have his own way or acted with revenge in mind when he felt frustrated. One can appreciate the teacher's suspicion that she may have slipped when something went wrong, although it may not have been her fault at all. Factors outside the classroom may be responsible for a child's getting upset and becoming disruptive. However, it is good policy to ponder carefully what one may have contributed if a child suddenly causes trouble. Only too often the teacher is not aware of the role he has played, blaming increasing difficulties on the child or on others.

The boy's work was good, but a little untidy. He read well and seemed to enjoy the first grade. But once again things became unpleasant. Once he scratched a boy's face because the boy told him to stay in his seat until I returned to the room. On another occasion he marked up the papers of other boys and girls while they were in their reading groups. It seemed to me that he was trying to hurt others, so I discussed him with the principal.

The home visitor made a call to his parents, and I wrote a note asking them to come and see me. In conference with them I learned that neither parent wanted Peter. They had placed him several times in foster homes, but he was so naughty that they always had to bring him back. His stepmother told me that she just didn't care for him, but she did adore his younger brother who was also her stepson. She was tired of trying to keep Peter neat, because he always came home with a dirty shirt. I tried to explain to her that quite a few of my other boys went home looking like that, but she just gave me a wave of the hand. She did not love Peter, and she let him know it too. With this information I took a different outlook to the boy, knowing that what he wanted was love, affection, and the feeling of security.

C O M M E N T . It was a wise step to find out more about the boy when he behaved in an unusual way in the school, apparently displaying unprovoked hostility. And what the teacher found was important. We can see how the boy was defeated by the younger brother, who not only dethroned but actually overwhelmed him by winning the affection of his parents—probably through charm, and perhaps by good behavior also. Since Peter was hostile and defiant, we can assume that his brother was just the opposite.

I still treated Peter the same, and yet in some ways tried to reach or approach him a little differently. I let him stay after school, when he wanted to help clean the blackboard and straighten the worktable. During these short visits he told me more about himself and how unwanted he felt by his father and mother. He spoke much about his younger brother, how they played together and came over to the playground. This helped me understand the boy much better, but yet I did not permit myself to show him too much affection.

COMMENT. This is the right approach to a child who feels unwanted and left out. It is not clear what his relationship to his younger brother was. Was he, being two years older, the leader and was this the reason why he enjoyed playing with him? There is something peculiar about his relationship to a favored younger sibling.

Things ran smoothly for a while, and he told the class several times about the things he and his brother did. But again things began to turn; and it seemed that he was getting meaner and meaner. Whenever he behaved in this way, I could never get him to listen to me or to talk to me. One time he didn't like the art work he was doing; so he tore it up and stamped over to the wastepaper basket. I went over to him to ask him about it and also to see if he wouldn't try it in a different way. He was tense and screamed out, "no." *I called him down for it* [author's italics], and he began to cry and ran over to grab his coat, and then headed for the door. I got there first and asked him where he was going. He said, "Home." I attempted to put a stop to it, but he kicked me and scratched me and called me names and told me to "shut up." I struggled with him, determined not to give in this time. We struggled so that my arms were shaking when I let go of him to see if he wouldn't settle down, thinking that I might have the power this time. But I did not leave the door because I knew he would run out. Instead I just stood there looking at him.

Well, we were doing this for a few minutes when he got up, ran over to the wastepaper baskets, threw them on the floor, scattered the papers all over the room, and then stood there screaming. Still standing there watching him, I sent a youngster upstairs to get the principal so she could see the things just the way he had scattered them. She came down and tried to talk to him, but he turned his face. Finally, she took him out of the room, while the rest of us were going about our work. He was upstairs until the last part of the hour. Then he came downstairs and told me he had done wrong and wanted to apologize and stay in my class. He called it "giving me another chance."

COMMENT. This is a rather interesting aspect of the teacher's effort to understand and help Peter. What had happened to her?

What made her get involved in a power struggle with him for no good reason? All the boy had done was tear up his paper and throw it in a basket. Then things began to pop because she went after him and "called him down for it." This was a crucial moment in Peter's life; but the teacher did not know it.

At closer scrutiny, the situation was not so difficult. She could have known by then that Peter's hostility was expressed in a temper. Nobody is reasonable in a temper; the best—and the only possible approach—is to leave such a child alone for the moment. He will get out of it before long, and *then* one can talk with him. From her experiences with Peter she should have known how far he would go once he was angry.

This simple piece of information was evidently unknown to the teacher, and her ignorance about the proper way to cope with a child in a temper apparently was responsible for the deterioration in their relationship. She attributed it to something that went on *within* the boy: "He would get meaner and meaner." Although she gave the reasons for this development, she was unaware of the connection. She stated that "whenever he behaved in this way, I could never get him to listen to me or to talk to me." She obviously did not know that in such a situation she should never have tried to talk to him. But she did more than that; she tried to make him talk to her. One can sense the high tension between them. No wonder he got meaner and meaner—so did she.

What else could she have done? Some may say that she *had* to "call him down" so that he would not give a bad example to others, which might happen if she let him "get by with it." This can be avoided if the teacher keeps cool. It may require tact and poise, with such a child in a room, to maintain interest and a calm atmosphere, but it can be done. Some friendly, understanding words can go a long way. After all, there was a moment when she knew why Peter behaved in this way, and felt compassion. She could exhibit such a feeling, and the class, far from being provoked by Peter, could have become a friendly group stretching its hand to a poor boy who had never felt that he belonged anywhere.

Instead of exerting a corrective influence on Peter, she succumbed to his efforts to prove that nobody could like him. Without determination to help him, no one should attempt to come to the aid of a child who feels that he never will be loved. It is worse to instill hope in the child and then let him down, than never to try to come close to him. Unless one is prepared to watch for every discouragement in oneself, for every provocation on the part of the child to prove how impossible it is to be his friend, one should avoid involvement.

Once again we had a nice room and we went about learning. Peter stayed in my room knowing that if there was another outburst he would be taken out once and for all.

C O M M E N T. Did the teacher really believe that this kind of pressure would convey to Peter the feeling of being accepted, and that no temper outburst would occur again? Instead of helping the child to get over his temper by minimizing it and depriving it, therefore, of its effectiveness, she made it an important factor which could break up the whole relationship. It is too bad for Peter that she did not know more about psychology at that time.

During the winter months, Peter carried his lunch to school. In a short time the children came to me and said that Peter was eating their cakes and fruit. I asked if they had given him the food, and they said yes, because he asked for it. I spoke to Peter about it and he told me that he liked that food and never had it in his lunch. I felt it necessary to talk to his stepmother about this because I did not want this practice to continue. She informed me that Peter never wanted anything but sandwiches. I told her what he was doing and asked whether she could not try a few times to give him a piece of cake or fruit. Well, this never happened, and Peter continued to eat the lunch of the other children; he even went between classes to someone's locker and took out their food. One day he had thrown his lunch away and told me that he did not have any. I thought it over and then pretended that I did not know what he had done and asked him if he would like to go out and eat with me. (I thought this might perhaps give him a feeling that someone liked him.) We had a very enjoyable lunch; he ordered hamburger, french fries, and chocolate soda, things any other youngster would have ordered. After we went back to school and had just started the afternoon, Peter acted up again. I had gone to tell the principal about our lunch; and when I came back I was told by the class that

Peter had hit two girls over the head with a book and one little boy with one of our little reading chairs. By this time I just didn't know what to think and do but to carry out the consequences that had been threatened. I took him upstairs to the principal and told her the story.

COMMENT. That's what happens when the teacher does not understand a child. She was so close to understanding Peter, and then went astray. It is obvious that Peter could not believe that anyone would really care for him. Therefore, just after she took him for lunch, he left almost honor-bound to tell her—not by words, but through his actions—that he was no good. She did not understand that and fell for his convincing evidence. That happens to most adults when confronted with such a child. Instead of correcting the child's wrong concepts of himself, the teacher is convinced by the child and drops her assumption that he could be helped—and liked.

If she had understood the situation, she would have expected something like that to happen just after she made a grand gesture of being his friend. And when it happened she would not have been so surprised. Then she could have explained to Peter what he did not know, that he was trying to prove to her how bad he was. But this sequence of events had begun much earlier. She let him down when she fought with him about the discarded drawing. She threatened to remove him if he ever had an outburst. That was not the action of a friend he could trust. Her handling of the lunch situation was another misguided step. There was neither a need to feel sorry for him because he did not get cakes and fruit nor any sense in appealing to his stepmother, who was not going to coddle him anyhow. The teacher does not report what she did to stop him from taking the other children's lunch and going into their lockers. From the preceding we may assume that she did not handle this too well either, probably preaching, scolding, and threatening. Then, to invite him for lunch when he had just lied to her was also not a good idea. She thought she could pretend that she did not know he had thrown his lunch away, but you cannot easily fool a smart and suspicious boy like Peter. She could have been reasonably sure that he knew the situation. This lunch as a "reward" for what he had done speaks of neither sincerity nor trustworthiness. So he tested her, and she failed.

Any teacher with no insight into Peter's problems would have acted as she did.

After this incident, Peter's parents were called in for another conference, to which the school psychologist was also invited. It was decided to take Peter out of my class and keep him at home with a home teacher. This seemed to work for a while, but then they found that he had too much time to get into mischief. The welfare agency was called in to the case and took it over from there.

COMMENT. This was the worst that could have been done for Peter: to let him stay home all the time, in an environment which was responsible for his maladjustment and not interested in a possible change of attitudes.

He was re-enrolled in school in September in the second grade and then taken out again. He was then sent to a parochial school. Recently I sat in a court session with the representatives of the welfare department and Peter's parents. All I say is simply that this youngster wanted to hurt and to be hateful to those who were nice to him because of the mistreatment and hatred shown to him by his father and stepmother.

COMMENT. It is easy and perhaps comfortable to see what the others have done wrong. Unfortunately, this teacher, well-meaning, sincere, full of the best intentions, and originally full of sympathy for the boy, almost succeeded in winning him and giving him a new chance in life, perhaps changing the whole course of his future, and failed because she did not know what to do with children like Peter. Her fault was not deep-seated emotional inadequacy but simply ignorance. And the principal to whom she constantly ran for help and protection knew as little as she about how to help such a child.

Example 44

Hal was the older of two children. I first met him in my English class. He had seldom made any preparation in his assignment, took little interest in class discussions, and was habitually truant. His parents were divorced when he was 11. The mother then supported the family by working from 4 to 12 P.M. Thus the two boys were left on their own.

Hal and two classmates were caught robbing a home and succeeded in getting many articles from other homes. Hal had been the leader of the trio. All were put on probation.

In school he was nervous, irritable, and disrespectful. He assumed that everybody was against him. For instance, once during an examination, I happened to look at him; he immediately remarked, "What are you watching me for?"

COMMENT. This defensive attitude is characteristic for a boy who is ready to jump at the slightest provocation, ready to get even with anyone who might hurt him—or oppose him, which to him means the same. This attitude is understandable in a child who is pushed around a great deal and who expects this treatment, and thereby provokes it. Revenge is the motive for all his actions, revenge against a society in which he has no place, and against its representatives who hurt him.

When we were studying drama, I asked Hal to read the part of a certain character. He did it—and did it very well. I commented on how well he had read, and suggested that he try out for a part in the junior class play. He tried out for every male character in the play, and did each part better than any other boy. Of course, I gave him a leading part, with the understanding that he was to keep up all his class work and not miss a single rehearsal.

COMMENT. Hal was ambitious and capable. Both qualities were evident in his criminal activities; but here they were displayed in a cooperative venture, within the framework of society, not against it. However, the boy could not have been too deeply set in his antisocial attitude or the prerequisites demanded by the teacher would not have been acceptable. She took a chance on that. Generally, it defeats the purpose if a child who has already been discouraged and antisocial is accepted only conditionally. After he is integrated, the conditions can be met without pressure and threat.

Needless to say, on the night of the performance he was the outstanding player and was recognized as such. During the remainder of the school year, he cooperated. He took an interest in his studies and was never truant. Even his personality changed and he became rather likeable. The superintendent, the principal, and the students commented on the great change in Hal.

COMMENT. It is improbable that this one act of letting him participate in the play was solely responsible for the fundamental change in the boy. One can assume a great deal of friendly inter-action with an understanding and encouraging teacher. There was more to it than she related. One can also assume that the antisocial activities of the boy might have been stimulated by the kind of asso-ciations he had developed, which he might have dropped after associ-ating with the students who participated in the play. It is likely that this one event made him a part of a group by which he had not been accepted until that time. He wanted recognition badly and previously had been able to find it only among the outcasts. All this is mere conjecture, but with some reasonable probability. It would explain the rather quick and complete change.

I had been advised by the principal against using Hal in the play. I'll admit that I was apprehensive and afraid that I was taking a big risk.

C O M M E N T . This is an illustration of the teacher's courage and daring, qualities necessary to cope with children of this kind. Although this report sounds too good to be true and too simple to be convincing, it indicates the kind of corrective efforts which are sometimes necessary.

Example 45

Margie, age 12, is in my seventh-grade home room. Last year everyone gave her up. She stole frequently, fought with the teachers and pupils, and failed all her classes. She started this year in her old pattern, stealing three times in two weeks and fighting constantly.
   She is a middle child, the older being a boy.

C O M M E N T . This is important information. A middle child often feels left out and unfairly treated. Perhaps Margie's behavior is her reaction to this situation, which would be even more understandable if we found out that the mother was siding with the two others. We would like to know what kind of a child the brother is. But it is significant that the teacher tried to find out more about Margie's background.
   Some comment about the teacher and this report is necessary. She had decided to write this case up as a "short report." Being an advanced student she knew all the implications of her short state-

ment; but one with less training would not understand what is meant. For her it was sufficient to point to Margie's position as the middle child. The same assumption that everybody would know what she means characterizes some of her following remarks.

Some time ago the neighbors called the school to inform us that Margie was distributing cigarettes to groups of pupils on the street. The next day we had a home room discussion about the purposes such an action may have. No names were mentioned.

The next day she behaved differently. Became more friendly. She took hold of my hand when she asked a question and was much more cooperative than ever. She began to talk about herself, told all the "bad" things that happened to her, the tests she failed, the times teachers sent her out of the room; but she never mentioned the days when she was the only one in the room who had a math assignment entirely correct, something I only found out later.

I have had two short private talks with her and visited her home. We talked a little about taking things, expressing the idea that many children sometimes do that, but as they become more sure of themselves it always stops.

COMMENT. Note the reaction of the teacher when she was officially informed that the girl distributed cigarettes to other pupils on the street. All she did was to have a discussion about the purposes of such action. She refrained even from naming the culprit. Such a restraint presupposes considerable psychological sensitivity. One could easily have been tempted to take the opportunity to preach, admonish, and threaten—and certainly make it clear to all who the culprit was. But she could be sure that Margie would catch on just as well despite not being mentioned by name, or perhaps even more so because of it.

The second important detail is the kind of discussion the teacher stimulated. She did not discuss the moral merits of the case, why it was objectionable to distribute cigarettes, what people would think, that the school is responsible, and similar aspects which would impress many teachers. She discussed the *purposes* of such behavior. Unfortunately, she has not reported the content of this discussion. She probably considered many possibilities, or better still, directed the trend of thought among the children to explore various possibilities which would include defiance, provoking retaliation, punishment with a consequent feeling of injustice, and the like. It is regrettable that no transcript of this discussion is available.

The change which took place in the girl is not surprising. She believed her teacher to be her friend, and opened up. The teacher reveals her sensitivity by mentioning the significant gesture of the girl when she took hold of her hand to ask a question. And one can see the trend in the teacher's effort when she investigated the possibility of positive accomplishments—and found evidence of them.

Again, the teacher mentions the two private talks but does not discuss their content. She describes them only by inference, emphasizing the things they did *not* talk about, which probably would have been the main topics for a less-trained educator. Even when they talked about taking things, it was not in a derogatory but in an encouraging way. And finally, she linked transgressions with a lack of self-confidence, touching the main point in the girl's maladjustment.

I have tried to have a warm relationship with her. I was invited to her piano recital and attended it. Again, I expressed my appreciation and mentioned casually in the class next day what a fine job Margie had done.

For seven weeks there has been no stealing. Her report card last week showed passing grades in all subjects. Her attitude toward teachers and pupils has improved greatly.

COMMENT. The teacher had succeeded in restoring Margie's confidence in herself and others. One can imagine what would have happened if the teacher had resorted to lecturing and punishing because stealing and lying are wrong; or had not been able to establish a warm relationship and get the child to talk freely about her problems; or, most important, had not had the ability to give her insight in an acceptable manner.

4. INADEQUACY AS EXCUSE

This goal, like demanding attention, striving for power, and seeking revenge, may not always characterize *all* the actions of a child. In some cases it is a total pattern; in others it appears only under certain circumstances and in specific situations. The discouragement leading to the assumption of deficiency may be limited to certain functions; but it may also engulf the child in all his activities. Disability as an excuse is used to avoid activities which are judged in terms of good or bad, excellence or failure. Academic subjects provide activities which are constantly judged. Therefore, they lend themselves easily to feelings of inadequacy in the child, who may reach the point where he becomes so convinced of his inadequacy that he makes no further effort. It is irrelevant whether this inadequacy is real or imagined; *for the child it is always real,* and always based on his comparison of himself with others.

While encouragement is a prerequisite for all corrective measures, it is the specific counteragent against the conviction of inability. The difficulty for the teacher is that it is easier for such a child to convince the teacher of his utter inability than to become convinced of his capability. The teacher's success requires considerable faith in the child's ability to fight his own defeatism. The demands are too great for a discouraged teacher; the effort also spells defeat for a teacher concerned with his own success and prestige. However, one who is humble enough to try his modest best and who believes in the innate human capacity so underdeveloped in all of us, may just plod ahead; he may finally succeed where he himself never expected to get results.

Example 46

Bessie is a repeater in the third grade. Her learning rate is probably low. In arithmetic, for instance, she might put down anything for an answer, or she might copy the problems but put down no answers at all. She seemed to be afraid to recite.

C O M M E N T . The child is obviously deeply discouraged and functions on a lower level than her ability would warrant. Any child can recite, unless there is a speech difficulty, for which we have no indications here.

I had some short talks with the class about being good listeners. We decided that the person who was called upon would be given a fair chance to recite, and only when he really needed help would we give it to him. We agreed that if all children put up their hands it might sometimes keep the reader from trying as hard as he could. Therefore, it would be better to keep hands down until the teacher asked the class for help.

After this discussion the class stopped putting their hands up as soon as I called on Bessie to recite. If she was slow in giving an answer we waited for her to figure it out. Slowly, she began to gain confidence, and started in turn to put her hand up if somebody else needed help.

C O M M E N T . This was a fine way to induce the whole class to give Bessie encouragement and moral support. It was particularly good to help Bessie through a *general* discussion.

When the five arithmetic problems were placed on the board, Bessie generally required more time than the rest of the class. I decided to give her that time, and permit her to work on them for a whole week. The next week Bessie had every one correct. I gave her an E and told her in front of the class how proud I was. Next day, she got all problems of the day and again got an E with a comment on the paper, "I am very proud of you." The following day she made an E again and I drew a smiling picture on her paper. By the end of the week she had made an E every day. The class was elated. I sent her to the office to show her paper to the principal. She came back saying that Mrs. S was proud of her too. One could see the feeling of success in her flushed face.

C O M M E N T . How did the teacher accomplish this change in attitude and performance? First, she spotted one source of discouragement after the other. She realized that the child had been afraid to recite because the others were waiting to jump in whenever she failed. The teacher stopped that, and consequently the child lost her fear of reciting. Then the teacher removed every pressure and gave her time to solve the problems at her own speed. As soon as Bessie discovered that she could solve problems, her speed picked up and she could do them at the same rate as the class.

But the teacher also saw to it that the accomplishment was recognized from the beginning. In other words, she made her comments dependent on the child's discouragement and not on her *absolute* accomplishment. Other children got E's too, without anyone making so much fuss over it. They did not need it, but Bessie did. And since the teacher, through her group discussion, had already established an atmosphere of mutual help, the class did not resent Bessie's success but was elated by it. They considered it their own achievement. Another factor is barely evident in this example. Defeated children who have given up altogether may still be overambitious. Bessie's pride in her accomplishments indicates how ambitious she actually was. And the teacher utilized this dormant ambition, even though the child had not displayed it when she first entered the class.

Example 47

Ronny, a slender, pale, timid lad of 8 was placed in my special-help class because he failed in the first-year reading program. His second reading year was a grim struggle to iron out confusions and acquire a phonetic background. He read first and easy second readers that year.

His actions and expression during the first week were those of extreme tension and frustration. He was fearful and insecure, tried pathetically hard to do his assignments, but showed great dependence in new situations, had tremors and profuse perspiration of the hands. He did not smile at all.

The second week his mother came for an interview. She admitted that she had overprotected Ronny. "I babied him too much." He was her third child, but the first to survive. The foreign-born parents came from a cultural background which kept children dependent longer than necessary. The devotion of the mother who waited on him constantly was accentuated by her fear of losing this child also, particularly since he was of poor health. She was determined that he must survive. Therefore, she did everything for him, decided for him, cared for him, and thought for him.

COMMENT. This short explanation of Ronny's background brought forth important details. Ronny's precarious start in life, the reason for his insecurity, dependency, and helplessness, is well described. Any child who is born after the death of an older sibling is in a precarious position. In Ronny's case two older children had died; and the mother's overindulgence was aggravated by cultural trends. He had no chance to experience his own strength.

Ronny's brother Pat was only one year younger, but aggressive, energetic, and active. He was even larger and taller than Ronny who is soft, quiet, inactive, and rather passive. Almost every time Ronny tried to compete with Pat he lost out.

COMMENT. Because of Ronny's childhood history, his younger brother found it easy to get ahead of him. The more active and aggressive Pat became, the more subdued became Ronny. They stimulated each other to develop in opposite directions. It is more than coincidence perhaps that Ronny became sickly and Pat grew taller and stronger. This, in turn, constituted another source for Ronny's inferiority feelings.

I tried to quiet the mother's anxiety, told her that Ronny was doing well academically and that she need not be concerned about the length of time it took him to do his tasks. Neither should she worry that Pat might catch up with him. I was more concerned with Ronny's inability to relax, his unhappy-looking face, and the tension when he tried to work. I was also troubled by his dependence on others.

COMMENT. It is not certain whether the teacher made clear in her report what she actually tried to convey to the mother. It was important to allay the mother's fears and anxieties, but that should not have been attempted through incorrect statements. There was no indication that Ronny was doing well in school, but we can fully agree with the teacher that his academic development was less important at this stage than his emotional and personal adjustment. She was right to direct her efforts toward that end with the hope of eventually improving the academic deficiencies.

The second week of school Ronny went to the steel cupboard for a sheet of paper. He tugged, but the door wouldn't open in the ordinary manner; the handle had to be moved up first. He looked at me beseechingly and said, "I can't open it." I replied, "Ronny, if the doors wouldn't open for me this way [I demonstrated these motions with my arm] I'd try another way." After a few trials and errors he was back in his seat with a paper—and with a smile of victory.

COMMENT. Pretty good. Giving him a hint in his request for help, the teacher left sufficient unsaid to leave room for the child's experimentation and reliance on his own resources. It was still up to him to solve his problems. We can see how he used "dependency" as a demand for service.

Ronny took much more time than necessary for writing assignments. He was still writing the large primary style. At the same time his writing was beautiful; in fact it had the appearance of having been drawn. One day I told him that the children in third grade write only one space tall, not two spaces as he did. I complimented his reading and felt that in a month he might be ready for the third reader. I commented on the beauty of his letters and suggested that he might switch to regular size. "How about writing your spelling words third-grade and high-school style?" I gave him fifteen minutes of instruction with samples, and he was "on his way" immediately after the first lesson. This reduction of size, and the self-confidence resulting from its accomplishment, has speeded up his writing considerably.

C O M M E N T . The important features of the teacher's approach were the emphasis on the beauty of the writing, although it was still deficient, and the shift from right-wrong to lower and higher grades of performance ("high school style"). Instead of impressing him with what he did wrong, she showed him the possibilities of going ahead. It was also important that she took the time to show him what she wanted, in order to make sure that he did not feel pressed but felt capable of doing what he was supposed to do. In this way she counteracted the boy's discouragement and disbelief in his own ability.

During a spelling test one day, Ronny turned around (I was behind him) and looked at me with terror in his eyes, and with great anxiety he informed me that he had just broken his pencil. His lead had broken off! I said, "Well, Ronny, the world hasn't come to an end." I smiled— and he sheepishly smiled back. Before Ronny could answer my question as to what he should do, quick self-confident Ken butted in: "Go sharpen it, Ronny." I added, "Ronny, if this should happen again, just say, excuse me please, I have to sharpen my pencil. O.K.?" He nodded approval, with a gleam in his eyes—and went.

C O M M E N T . The teacher's attitude was encouraging; however, she displayed in this incident a tendency to talk too much—and to preach. In this way Ronny got undue attention through his "helplessness." This is always detrimental. If she felt inclined to say anything after Ken told him what to do, she could have rebuked Ken, pointing out that Ronny would find out for himself what to do. This would have discouraged the superiority of the other children, and at the same time encouraged Ronny to take care of himself.

Another detail which the teacher overlooked: don't talk or "explain" in the moment of disturbance. This satisfies the child's demand for special attention. To tell Ronny that he can excuse himself and sharpen his pencil is all right, but not at this moment. The less said at such a time, the better. If something has to be explained, the time for the explanation is in a short general discussion. On such an occasion one can bring up the question of what to do if a pencil breaks. Then it is perfectly proper for other children to express their views. But in the moment of disturbance the situation is different: then action counts and words should be limited to indicating action.

At first he had difficulties in reading first and second readers. When he acquired a solid foundation of phonetics, I praised him highly for his mastery of vowel sounds, consonant blends, and other combinations. The second week I gave him a work book with sixty-four pages of reading and phonetics. He was to work in this book after completion of the regular class work—and he finished it in two weeks. The first day when he did twenty pages I remarked, "Ronny, you are going through that book like a jet propelled plane." Did he smile—from ear to ear! And it was an A minus average.

His progress seemed to prove that a good phonetic foundation pays big dividends in word-attack and independence in reading. For the Thanksgiving holidays I gave Ronny the assignment of spelling the 119 words he had had this year—and he did not miss a single word. (And I count i's not dotted or t's not crossed as incorrect!) You can imagine the fuss I made over his work. I graded his booklet with a huge A plus. His face was all smiles. And all his finger tremors or perspiration of the hands were gone. Each time he got some work to do he had an expression of "catch me if you can."

C O M M E N T. Despite the teacher's apparent success with Ronny, her approach raises many questions. We had suspected from his background that Ronny was overambitious and striving for excellence. Even his writing deficiency, namely, sticking to the first year's large letters, indicated his perfectionism; when the teacher remarked how beautifully each letter was written, in an effort to "encourage" the boy, she was appealing to his perfectionism. (Could it be that she was a perfectionist also, being critical of the undotted i's and uncrossed t's? Maybe they were two of a kind, and that was the basis of their mutual understanding and response.) At any rate, one wonders what will happen to Ronny again if he cannot get a huge A. Will he get discouraged again? That is the danger of such an approach.

Furthermore, Ronny got so much special attention from this teacher that he again became dependent on her, perhaps not so much on her *help* in doing things but on her *praise*, which is equally detrimental and dangerous. The teacher's mistaken approach is rooted in her misunderstanding of Ronny's family situation. When she spoke to his mother, she did not suspect or recognize the special role he had gained. And since she failed to understand his desire and ability to get a special place, she let him establish the same pattern in the classroom. One may well ask, did *she* influence him more than *he* her? She taught him spelling and reading; from this point of view she was successful. And if the mastery of subjects is regarded as the prime purpose of school, she could be highly satisfied. However, she herself recognized the importance of being concerned more with his emotional adjustment than with his academic progress. She may point out that even in this regard, namely, in regard to his tension and unhappy look, she had apparently succeeded. The tremors and perspiration disappeared and he smiled more and looked happier. But was this progress achieved through a greater integration into the group, or through his dependency on a teacher who "understood" him so well that she made a fuss over him?

These are the pitfalls the teacher must guard against. These are subtleties which can only be grasped when the psychodynamic patterns of a child are clearly understood. Discouragement may have many different reasons and causes; consequently, encouragement, although always beneficial, must be gauged by the motivations of the individual child if it is used as a specific approach to the solution of his problems. In this case the teacher was successful in encouraging Ronny, but not, perhaps, in helping his personal adjustment.

Example 48

Ted and Ned were twins, 8 years old. Ted missed quite a bit of school through sickness, and consequently was far behind his brother. He developed an inferiority complex about this. When he was asked a question he promptly suggested that his brother be asked because Ned was smarter. Actually, Ned's IQ was lower than Ted's. I was aware of this situation when the two entered my third-grade class.

Recently Ted was having trouble with the word "smart." I had him sound it out, and he got it. I told him that he was smart to have figured it out so fast and well. He beamed and went back to his seat. A few minutes later he came up again and thanked me.

COMMENT. The profound impression which the teacher's simple encouragement made on Ted probably tells the whole story. He was handicapped at first by his absence from school, and therefore fell back. Then he had what became a misfortune, a higher IQ than his more successful twin. One can well imagine the destructive effect the combination of these two factors had on Ted's teachers—and probably also on his parents. They could not help but try to impress him with his potentialities, criticizing his deficiencies and putting pressure on him. The net result of these only too frequent procedures was increased discouragement. Telling a child, "I know you could do better," is a left-handed compliment. It implies: "but why don't you?" It is criticism and not encouragement. This teacher apparently broke the chain of detrimental experiences to which the boy had been exposed. Otherwise, one could not understand his profuse thankfulness for her simple praise without any strings attached. (The good effect of encouragement is often entirely lost by some supplementary remarks like, "If you always worked like this . . . ," and so forth.)

Through encouragement of this sort, I felt that Ted had gained self-confidence. He not only completes his work now; he never has mentioned once that he felt Ned was smarter. Sometimes he makes even better scores than his brother who now may develop some difficulty with which I will have to cope.

COMMENT. The teacher is right in anticipating some troubles for Ned in such a teeter-totter situation. The two boys have obviously been in competition or Ted would not have felt that he lagged so badly behind his brother. Now that he is coming into his own, his brother may feel discouraged; and the teacher is well advised to watch for such a turn of events and be prepared to cope with them, in the same way that she coped with Ted's discouragement.

This example points to an important factor that often leads a child to give up in discouragement. It is not important to the child how good he is and how well he is doing; what is important is whether he is better or worse than others. The sense of inferiority, the conviction of not being good enough, bears no relationship to ability. Some children may respond in this way because they are actually unable to keep up with others. In many cases it is the proven fact of an *ability* which is responsible for the child's giving up in despair, as in the case of Ted. It was his ability which induced parents and teachers to demand from him more than he felt he could accomplish. Similarly, it is overambition, the desire to be superior and excellent, which may bring about the moment of despair where the child sees no value in continuing any effort because he has no chance to be as good as he wants to be. Parents and teachers do not convey to a child that he is good enough as he is; and children are always being impressed with the fact that they are *not* good enough as they are, because they could be better. This drives innumerable children to the point of giving up any effort, because they are convinced that they have no chance to do well enough, which means as well as others (competition), as well as they ought to do (pressure), or as well as they want to do (overambition).

Frustrated overambition is perhaps the most frequent cause for giving up. Children who are trained to believe that it is important to be ahead of others will shy away from any activity that does not provide them with the opportunity to prove their superiority. Naturally, their ambition is not apparent after they have given up. For this reason, many parents and teachers find it difficult to accept a psychological interpretation of overambition in a child who does not try at all. But as soon as discouragement is overcome, the overambition becomes evident.

CHAPTER 9

Group Discussion

E ACH TEACHER MAY have a different technique for conducting group discussions. She may or may not play an active part. In any case she must know when it would be a mistake to let the children continue unaided, as there are other moments when interference with the trend of the discussion would be ill advised. The crucial factor is the shared responsibility, a process of thinking through the problems which come up for discussion, and an exploration about alternatives. Shared responsibility is best accomplished with the question, "What can *we* do about it?" The teacher can stimulate the children in the proper direction by asking the right question. The technique used by Socrates, i.e., influencing contemplation of pointed questions, is worth imitating.

Some teachers have developed their own specific introduction to group discussion. The following are some examples.

Group discussions could start as soon as the teacher becomes acquainted with her class. She might invite the students to suggest how the class should be decorated, what they would like to do in the first two days, how to plan the work, organize committees, assign responsibilities. If the teacher considers homework advisable, she has to discuss the pros and cons before she assigns homework. She has the obligation to listen to the criticism of her students if they think the work is just "busy work," without any practical benefit. In lower grades some simple problems need discussion, such as going to the washroom, the order in the hall, and so on.

The teacher must invite all children to give suggestions or voice opinions. If a child is shy or completely passive she may ask his opinion. The teacher should never ask for advice or suggestions unless she is prepared to take them seriously. It is important not only to ask each pupil for his opinion, but to invite the others to comment on what he suggested. Later on the teacher may introduce for discussion and for mutual help the problem of getting to school on time, taking care of the belongings, or doing some part of the school work.

Many young children would like to partake in a discussion but do not know how, for at home they are either ruling or obeying orders without question. They seldom have experienced a friendly discussion. If the children are not yet ready to discuss real problems, the teacher may train the group to analyze and understand behavior through the reading of stories in which the characters have problems in social adjustment. Many such stories are found in reading textbooks. An excellent story for such discussion is "Tippy Elephant's Hat."[1] It is the story of a young elephant who likes to snatch the hats from people and smash them. The following is a discussion which took place after reading the story.

Example 49

Teacher: How do you feel about Tippy's smashing everybody's hat? Do you like it?
[*Most children will express that they do not approve of such behavior.*]
Teacher: Why not?
A child: It is not nice.
Teacher: Why do you think so?
Child: It is not fair to the people.
Teacher: Why does Tippy behave that way?
A child: He has fun that way.
Teacher: Some children feel that it is not nice and not fair. Why would somebody have fun doing things to others which are neither nice nor fair?
Child: Maybe he likes to make others unhappy.

---

[1] June Morris, "Tippy Elephant's Hat" in *New Streets and Roads*, Chicago, Scott Foresman, 1958. (For this example as well as others in this section we are grateful to Mrs. Bernice Grunwald of the Gary School System.)

Another child: He doesn't care if it's nice or not.

Teacher: Why would anyone like to make others unhappy?

A child: Maybe when we are angry with them.

Teacher: Is Tippy angry with the people who come to see him at the zoo? Do you think he would prefer that they should not come?

A child: I think that he wants them to come because how could he smash their hats otherwise? I don't think that he is angry with them. He is just having fun that way.

Teacher: Is Tippy getting anything out of this besides having fun smashing the hats?

A child: No, because his mother and the zookeeper scold him for it.

Teacher: How many of you believe that Tippy does not like to be scolded by his mother and the zookeeper?

[*The amazing thing is that only a few children hold up their hands.*]

Teacher: Well then, does he or doesn't he enjoy being scolded?

A child: I think that he enjoys it.

Another child: I do too.

Teacher: Why?

A child: Well, it's like getting attention, and he likes that.

Teacher: I wonder about that too. From whom else does he get attention?

A child: From all of the other animals.

Another child: I think he wants to make the other animals jealous.

Teacher: How does it make him feel when he gets so much attention?

A child: He thinks that he is the most important of them and he deserves more than they do.

Teacher: Maybe you're right. He thinks that this makes him a big shot. Do you know any children who behave like Tippy?

Children: Yes.

[*The observant teacher will notice many eyes lowered, avoiding the teacher's gaze, or snickering, which is equally admission of having been "caught."*]

Now and then a child offers voluntarily to admit that this is precisely what he has been doing. Once one child makes such an admission, many others have the courage to speak about their faulty behavior. These discussions never fail to have an effect and to bring some results.

Almost every story lends itself for a discussion which involves social relationships and analysis of the character's motivation to behave as they do. The teacher skilled in conducting discussions will succeed in bringing out the points which touch upon the problems existing in the class, without putting the student on the spot at this particular time.

Through the discussion of characters in stories, students can be trained to question and understand their own and other children's behavior. As they learn to accept the fact that everyone makes mistakes, that mistakes can be rectified, that one should not feel embarrassed to discuss one's problems, the teacher may start bringing up for discussion specific problems of specific children in the class.

After the group has had some training in discussions, they should have their own "government" in the form of a student council which meets once or twice a week and where they may discuss anything they want to. This suggestion is always received with great enthusiasm. The student council always works out very successfully, but usually only after some trying weeks. There is considerable confusion at first, which may discourage teachers who do not have sufficient confidence in children.

Two or three members are selected by the group for a certain time limit. Usually, it is for two weeks. All grievances and suggestions are brought to them first. They then bring it up for discussion with the entire class. The opinion of the council carries more weight than the opinion of the teacher. If the council discusses the disturbances John creates by tapping on the desk, the problem is invariably solved more satisfactorily than if the teacher had reprimanded him. Every two weeks the group elects a new council until all children in the class have had a chance.

It takes time before the children are trained to conduct their discussions in an orderly and democratic manner. As the child learns to accept the values of the group, his concept of himself and that of his relationship to others change. Thus begins a solution to some of his problems.

During the first part of the year the teacher must participate actively as a member of the group. When the discussion strays, the teacher may have to lead it back to its original purpose. The teacher may point out to the student council that some children have not been called upon to express their views, or that they have allowed some child to talk for too long. Sometimes the teacher may have to have a special meeting with the members of the council in order to point out specific problems existing in the group, which they can bring up for discussion. The student council meetings must be held at regular times and must be considered an important part of the general school activities.

Some people may ask what sort of grievances children bring up. Children should be able to bring up anything that concerns them. This may be situations which are threatening to them, for example, exams or teacher-parent discussion of student misbehavior.

The better the relationship the teacher has with her class, the freer the child will be in discussing anything that bothers him. Some children bring up for group discussion problems they have at home. The following are but a few of the problems which were discussed in class.

Patsy asked the class whether she should invite a girl to her birthday party even though this girl did not invite her to hers. She was advised to disregard what the other child did, and invite her if she really would like to have her. Patsy took the advice, and later reported that she and the girl became close friends and had good times together.

Harry wanted to know how much work the other children have to do at home. He thought that his mother demanded too much help from him. This developed into a discussion about family belonging and responsibility. The conclusion was that we cannot compare the amount of work children do in their respective homes, since each home is different; in every case we must do our share, according to what is necessary.

Sue wanted to know if it was fair that she should have to go to bed at the same time when her younger brother did. During the discussion it became evident that she misbehaved at home every time she had to do more work than her brother. She demanded that the chores be divided equally. The group felt that under those circumstances she had no right to demand special privileges for herself in the evening. If she wanted to be treated as the older, with more rights, then she must also assume more responsibilities than the younger. Sue promptly discussed this with her parents and accepted the group's suggestion.

Example 50

This is a partial transcript of an actual discussion.

[*We will now hear a student council meeting of a third-grade class. Our class number is 33 and our teacher's name is Mrs. G. My name is Maria and I am one of the chairmen in the student council. Every child gets a chance to get into the student council. Each time anyone wants to come up with a problem, he just signs up in our book, and we call only on those who sign up. We don't always talk about problems, we talk about people who have been improving and those who haven't been tardy any more. Then we talk about puppet shows and parties. Then we vote on it.*]

Maria: Will the class please come to order. We will start our student council now. The following people who are signed up for today are [*several names are given*].

First girl: I have something to say about the bathroom. Well I think that somebody is always writing in them and I don't think that's very nice. And I know who the person is but I don't like to mention their names.

Maria: Well, does anybody have anything to say about it?

Boy: Well, I think whoever does that, we should ask him not to do it, whoever did it.

Another boy: We should give him another chance and if they keep on we should start a council.

Another girl: Well, I have something to say. I think Paul has been improving in listening and he has been doing his work faster.

Maria: How many people have something to say about that?

Another girl: Well, I think Paul has improved in his work too and listening.

Another girl: Well, I know Paul from another building and he hasn't liked school very much. And he couldn't read so good. He was a bad boy and now he's a lot better.

Maria: Anyone else has to say anything?

A boy: Well, I think he likes school better than he used to like it.

Maria: Paul, what do you think about it?

Paul: I think I have improved and I like school better.

Maria: The next person is. . . .

Girl: Well, everytime when I go to school and pass the Dairy Queen and I went through the alley, why these boys they want to hit on me and I can't go in the front because there is that big old dog. Well, he keeps on barking at me and I'm scared.

Girl: I think she lives pretty close to our church and she could cut through our yard. I think no one will mind if she can cut through our yard.

Boy: Well, why don't you call the person that owns the dog and tell him to keep it locked up until you go past their house.

Girl with problem: John, I think I'll do that.

Maria: [*calls next name*].

Boy: I like to say that you helped me with my problem at home.

Maria: I'm glad to hear that. Does anyone have anything to say to that?

Other boy: What was the problem?

Boy with problem: My problem was that my sister used to keep on bossing me around, but now I just do the things I think is right.

Teacher: What do you mean, you think you do what's right? I don't quite understand what you mean by that.

C O M M E N T . This is a typical example of the teacher's sensitivity. She did not let the child get by with generalizations or moral pronouncements. She wants to get to the meaning of his "improvement."

Boy with problem: Well, like when she tells me to do something, if it's right I will do it. Or when she tells me something that I don't like, I won't do it.

Teacher: You don't do what you don't like, or what you think is not right?

Boy: If she tells me something which is not right, then I don't do it.

Teacher: But was this not the same before? What's different now?

Boy: Well, before I argued with her and did what she said; now I just don't do what she says if it is not right.

Teacher: What is different now?

Boy: We don't argue anymore. And she stopped bossing me.

Maria: [*calls on the next boy*].

Joe: Well, everytime I go over to my friend's house my brother, he goes after me and he starts hitting me.

Another boy: Why does he hit you?

Joe: Because when I come over there to play he doesn't want me to go over, he starts hitting me, he doesn't want me to go over, that's why.

Girl: I don't think you should say that because if he knew why his brother would hit him he wouldn't bring it to the student council.

Another girl: Well, I think that your brother thinks that you don't never play with him and all that.

Joe: Yes I do, in the house. I play with him in the house. And we run the train together.

Girl: Well, we know how you act in school, Joe, and maybe you're making your brother mad so that he will hit you.

Joe: Well, I don't make him mad. Well, everytime I don't make him mad, well, he just constantly bothers me.

Girl: You should play with him some more and he will quit bothering you.

Teacher: So far no one has come up with something definite for Joe. After all this is what he is talking about; he needs some help. What do you think he could do?

Girl: Well, you should tell your brother that you'll play with him for an hour or half an hour and then stop it.

Another girl: Well, I think that Joe's brother is jealous because the teacher probably tells a lot about Joe.

Boy: Why don't you tell your mother your brother is hitting you?

Joe: I ask him why he is hitting me and he says forget you and all that stuff.

Maria: What you said is wrong; you shouldn't let Joe's mother get mixed in.

Another girl: She is right, Joe's mother should not mix in because maybe Joe's brother will think that mother likes Joe better and he will probably do more bad things.

Boy: When you buy something, give your brother part of it.

Girl: He shouldn't try to get so much attention, then his brother wouldn't get kind of jealous.

Teacher: You all told him what he should not do. But nobody told him what he should do. And giving his brother presents is bribing him. That's not the way to make friends. Maybe Joe has a solution? What do you think you might do to become friends with your brother? Have you any ideas?

Joe: No, I don't think so.

Teacher: Anyone have an idea?

Girl: Well, I think Joe should play with his brother so he won't do nothing bad to him.

Teacher: How should he play with him?

Girl: Be kind and let him do part what he wants and then Joe do what he wants to do.

Teacher: Isn't there more that Joe can do? Does Joe know how often he made his brother mad? He thinks he does not, but what do you think?

Girl: Maybe he acts big because he is older and his brother doesn't like it.

Teacher: What do you think Joe does when his brother hits him?

Boy: He hollers and gets mad.

Teacher: What else could Joe do?

Girl: Joe could show him that he is not a big shot, that he wants to be his friend.

Teacher: You mean that they should share?

Joe: Well, I think that's a good idea.

Girl: You try it and if it works you can tell us.

Joe: Thank you.

Maria: [*calls on the next girl*].

Girl: Well, I think we should have some new goals because the other ones we had them for a long time.

Another girl: I think she is right, we have had those goals on the wall for a long time. I think they should be changed.

Another girl: I think we need to work on like be quiet when the teacher is out. We improved a little but I think we should work on it more.

Another girl: Well, I think that we should improve not to write in the bathroom any more.

Boy: Well, I think we should be much quieter going down the stairs instead of running up and down the stairs.

Girl: I think we have improved on not talking. We could at least make a little less noise with our footsteps.

Another girl: I agree with her, let's vote on it and see.

[*The vote is taken.*]

Maria: Most people agree with what she suggests, so we'll have that for a goal. This is the end of our student council meeting and that will be all for today.

C O M M E N T . This is an example of a class which had learned to discuss and solve their problems with a minimum of interference on the part of the teacher. The seriousness and the concern the children have for each other is not as clear in reading as it is in listening to their voices. It is an experience of being a part of a group, each one responsible for the other, and all acting as friends even if they don't agree.

Example 51

While we were collecting arithmetic books, Bob came up and wanted to tell me something. I told him to wait until our materials were collected and we were settled.

Bob wanted to know how to stop fights that he gets into when his cousin who is 8 years old, as he is, comes to his house. (Bob fights a great deal at school—the boys don't want to play with him. He complains that the boys pick on him.)

I asked, "What do you fight about when your cousin comes over?" He remarked, "About toys." I asked Bob to repeat his question to the class and tell us more about those fights. He told us that at one time he threw a metal wastebasket at his cousin and cut him quite badly. I asked the class if anyone had ideas on how Bob could stop these fights.

COMMENT. This is an example by a teacher who had begun regular group discussions with the children about pertinent and interesting problems as they occurred. This injection of the problem whenever the child feels like presenting one is not recommended. It is better to have certain times set aside just for such discussions, as the rest of this report will illustrate.

The teacher started the discussion correctly. She asked the boy to repeat his problem and then to elaborate on it, which he did. But then she jumped into finding a solution before she and the children could investigate why Bob was fighting. A good way of keeping the discussion alive and bringing out new ideas would have been the question, posed to the class after Bob's report, "What do you think about this?" Then the children themselves would have ventured some ideas, both about the causes of the fights and possible solutions; and then it would have been up to the teacher to pick out first the remarks which dealt with the possible motivations and reasons for these fights.

Tom said, "Bob doesn't have a very long memory. We had a movie in the auditorium about settling fights." He continued, "In the movie two boys were fighting about riding a bike. They were fighting so much that neither one was able to ride. Finally, another boy came down the street and told them to settle their fight by taking turns riding the bike. The boy said if they shared the bike there would be no fight. The boys decided to share the bike. One boy rode around the block and then the other. By switching turns, the fight was settled."

Bob said, "My situation wasn't like the one in the picture. Those were *my* toys!" Tom replied, "Bob doesn't understand that it was the same as in the picture. If he had called his father, I'll bet his father would have told him to share the toys instead of fighting. They didn't have to play with the same toys at the same time. They could have shared the toys like the boys shared the bike."

Bob still insisted that his situation was different; and in the next breath he wanted to know why the boys always ganged up on him. Mary asked, "Do the boys have a good reason for ganging up on you?" The bell rang. We stopped at this point.

C O M M E N T . This is bound to happen if the teacher does not take the proper time for discussion. As soon as it becomes interesting and important, the bell rings. It is unfortunate that the discussion could not be continued at this point, because it left Bob with the increased feeling that the others did not understand him and ganged up on him. Probably the same ready assumption of unfairness was responsible for his fights with his cousin.

Actually, there was little group discussion. The teacher merely permitted Tom to preach and to humiliate Bob. Tom should have been interrupted, or at least his remarks should have been opened for discussion when he referred to Bob's poor memory. As it was, the discussion did not contribute anything to a clarification of the problem, nor did it improve the relationship between Bob and the other members of the class. Mary started to raise this point, but it got lost. It will be more difficult to start the discussion again where it was left.

Example 52

Ramona, age 13, thinks that many members of the class dislike her. She often complains that other pupils pick on her and make fun of her. One day a girl from whom she had borrowed a pencil asked for its return a moment before a spelling test. Ramona tossed it back to her, two rows away. The class quickly reminded me that they had been cautioned about the dangers of throwing things. They thought Ramona should be punished for disobeying the rule. But how? I took the opportunity to have a discussion on this subject. The students thought Ramona should be paddled. I asked for other suggestions, or what the children thought about paddling. A boy asked for a vote as to whether Ramona should be paddled or not. Theresa, the owner of the pencil, remarked that this would not be fair because many of the kids in the class didn't like Ramona. The murmur in the class indicated disapproval, and I was somewhat disturbed by the turn the discussion had taken. So I said, "No, Theresa, if you will pardon me, I disagree with you. I don't think the group dislikes Ramona." Then as an afterthought, since Ramona was now standing at my elbow, I said, "Well, let's see. . . . Ramona, would you mind turning your back to the class a moment?" Ramona did, and I stood beside her. "Now I would like the members of the class who really, honestly dislike Ramona to raise their hands." We waited a moment, but none did.

"Just hold it that way," I said; then turning to Ramona I said, "Ramona would you care to turn around and see how many of your classmates dislike you?"

She turned around slowly, saw no hands, and then said, "But Theresa doesn't like me."

"How is that possible? She is the one who said a vote would not be fair to you. She defended you."

Ramona turned and walked quietly back to her seat.

C O M M E N T . There are a number of important points in this incident. First of all, the teacher, sensing the total class situation, did not consider Ramona's transgression as an isolated incident, but rather as a welcome opportunity for a class discussion, dealing with the relationship of the other students to Ramona. The teacher proceeded adequately, letting the children express themselves freely and still directing the trend of the discussion. He showed imagination and courage, which are always essential qualities in dealing with children. He did not fall for the temptation to exhort those who suggested paddling. He did not preach or advise. He merely produced action, and this action was encouraging for Ramona. It is obvious that any one such experience will not suffice to change the child's mind about the unfairness of others, or keep her from provoking the others so that they will offer her new proof for being disliked. But experiences like the above will go far to make both Ramona and the others stop and think—and perhaps reconsider their opinions and their actions.

Example 53

The following example is taken from the notes of a teacher who experimented with a series of group discussions.

The five boys of this experiment were selected by their home-room teacher on the basis of poorest adjustment. They were all overage for seventh grade, and were in a so-called special, or low learners, group. Four of the boys were troublesome behavior problems in all their classes. One, Roy, was not a behavior problem, but refused to put forth any effort to do his work in most classes.

The boys were told by the principal that they would have an opportunity to talk over their problems and learn more about themselves. If they chose they could give up two study periods a week for this purpose.

The teacher meeting with the group was also their teacher in one subject. The group met for three weeks near the close of the school year twice a week for approximately forty minutes, and had one concluding period during the fourth week. There were seven meetings in all, held in an empty room next door to the teacher's classroom to give the idea that these meetings were different from a class. Chair desks were arranged in a circle.

The discussions were written up by the teacher as soon after the meeting as possible to retain the "feel" of the sessions as well as some accuracy in recording; the recordings were used by the teacher as review material and to determine the starting place for the next session.

C O M M E N T . These discussions were set up as a special project and, therefore, have aspects of group counseling. Adjustment teachers, guidance counselors, and the classroom teacher should eventually be trained to conduct similar discussions with the same effect, as part of the regular curriculum. It is obvious that such regular discussion periods cannot be classified as "therapeutic." Although the methods used may resemble closely those used in group therapy, the procedure is unquestionably an educational process.

First session. Harry explained the purpose of the meetings to Roy who had been absent yesterday when the principal told the boys about the plan. I told them we would be like a small group of close friends who could say to each other what they wished. They might express their wishes as to this room and the sessions. It would be different from a class because there were fewer boys and there was no need to finish an assignment. Nothing they said would be repeated to other teachers without their permission.

C O M M E N T . That was a good way to establish the atmosphere. What is not clear from this report is whether the teacher just made these statements or had a discussion about them. If she went on from here without letting the boys express themselves about what they expected from the sessions, what they thought about the procedure, and so forth, then she neglected one important point, essential for all group approaches: the warming-up process. In order to get full cooperation, the boys have to be induced to participate from the beginning. In this sense it was excellent that one boy explained to another the purpose of the group at the beginning of the session. But a discussion about it should have followed immediately—and perhaps did, without the teacher's recording it.

The boys were asked to tell about their families so that they might become better acquainted and I could know them better.

C O M M E N T . That is an excellent start, provided the teacher is trained in understanding the family constellation and the significance of interpersonal relationships within the family.

Harry is the oldest of three, has a sister of 12 and a baby brother. In contrast, Ernie is the youngest of six with two older brothers and three older sisters. Two sisters live at home and work; all others are married. Roy is the sixth of eight. He has a younger brother who is also in seventh grade. One brother, a year older, is considered a nonreader, and Roy is nearly so. Hugo is the youngest of three. One brother is in college, and one brother plays on our school basketball team and was recently elected vice-president of the ninth-grade class. Randy was absent at this first meeting.

C O M M E N T . Let us see what detail of this limited information is significant. Actually, each piece of information has considerable meaning, if properly evaluated. Harry is perhaps less influenced by his position as the oldest of the family than is Ernie as the youngest of so many much older ones. Roy's younger brother has already caught up with him, being in the same grade. This probably is significant. Most revealing, however, is the situation of Hugo who is not only the youngest of three boys but has two older brothers who are apparently highly successful, particularly the one just ahead of him. This is a difficult position to be in.[2]

[2] These facts about each boy should be kept in mind in order to understand his behavior throughout the discussion.

They told a little about their families. Hugo sometimes feels like running away. Harry agreed. Hugo's father uses a strap on him, but not so much any more. Sometimes he has to stay in. Staying in was a usual punishment also for the others. Harry said about his father, "When he gets mad, he really gets mad."

The boys were asked what they liked best about junior high and what least. They liked having different teachers during the day and disliked most having a teacher nagging at them.

C O M M E N T . It would be possible to regard these questions about their families and their reaction to school as part of a warming-up process. However, they were raised in a rather abrupt way, the teacher suggesting one subject after the other. Maybe this was necessary with this group of boys. It generally is advisable to ask the children what they want to talk about first. Only if they are not sufficiently productive should one suggest a subject. That may have happened here, too, without the teacher reporting it.

I asked them what gave them a good feeling. Hugo said when he played ball; Harry, when he had his cast taken off after wearing it from his neck to his waist. I suggested that this made him feel free. He said, "Ya, free!" Roy and Ernie felt best while swimming or fishing.

We talked a little more about families, and then Hugo switched to the subject of dead bodies in coffins. We discussed dead bodies for about five minutes until the bell rang.

C O M M E N T . The boys finally took over and talked about what they wanted. Hugo, on this occasion, established himself as a leader. And the teacher was right in following this lead.

As a whole, this was a good warming-up session. All participated, and some initiative was evoked. A similar discussion could have been held in a first session of a series of group discussions within a regular classroom. The only difference might have been a greater limitation of subjects so that more children could have a chance to express themselves.

Second Session—Next Day. Randy, absent yesterday, was present. Harry gave an accurate summary of yesterday's discussion. Ernie said, "Then we ended with dead bodies."

COMMENT. It would be interesting to know why Harry gave the initial explanation at each session. Did he volunteer or was he asked to do so? He certainly exerted leadership of a constructive kind. We can see that the spontaneous part of yesterday's discussion provided considerable delight to some. Apparently Harry, concerned with the constructive aspects, omitted what interested Ernie and Hugo, who has brought up the problem. Is this an incipient line-up of two factions? A sensitive group discussion leader could have well raised this question at that point. Why did Harry omit and Ernie emphasize it?

I reviewed the idea of freedom in this discussion. Randy introduced himself as the youngest in the family of four, one sister married, the other two in college but living at home.

COMMENT. This is also an important piece of information, the only boy among so many women, and—to make it worse—the baby. He probably had many "mothers," some of whom might have spoiled and overprotected him.

The boys were asked to tell their earliest memories. Harry told of having a tricycle when he was only three or four. His sister was just born then and the bike was his "best friend."

COMMENT. The teacher evidently did not give an interpretation at this point, although, being trained, she probably knew the significance of this recollection. Here was Harry, the oldest, being dethroned by his sister and feeling pushed out. The only friend that remained was his tricycle. He was now on his own, being left out by the family.

Hugo remembered running away from his aunt, with whom he stayed when his mother went away. Randy remembered riding a bike and a little auto which belonged to a neighbor. Ernie remembered being brought back from several blocks away, where he had wandered in his sleep.

COMMENT. Ernie's report is a true recollection of an incident, in contrast to the two others, which are too unspecific to permit a reliable interpretation. But we can see Ernie as a little baby who cannot take care of himself, who has to be brought back. And we can also see him expressing his hostility, wandering away in his sleep, a subtle form of rebellion.

Roy remembered when his family lived in a small town; the boys would hit turtles on the head, and the Indians would get mad at them.

COMMENT. For Roy the world seems to be a free-for-all. This is the information which the teacher has solicited so far. Now she is beginning to discuss it with the boys.

I suggested that we start talking about Harry, if he didn't mind. He enjoyed being free of his cast, riding his bike as a little boy. What did that tell about him? They said he wants to be free, independent, on his own, his own boss. Randy commented, "He likes to be the boss."

Harry: "Aw, not all the time." We talked about wanting independence; was it bad? No, all grown-ups want to be independent. Harry, "I don't quite agree with you, because when I boss my sister she doesn't do it anyway." I asked, "Why not?" He immediately answered that she wants to be her own boss too.

Randy: "You know the thing that I hate, it's being alone. I like camp—a group of fellows." I asked, "No girls?" He, "Yah-a-a. But if the director makes me do something alone, I hate it. You know, when you make me sit all by myself in class, that's worse than being paddled."

COMMENT. The teacher missed an opportunity to make an important point clear to the boys. Why did Harry want to be independent and Randy hate to be alone? Because Harry was the first dethroned boy who did not feel that he could rely any longer on any one, and Randy was the baby who got his place only through others, relying entirely on his mother and/or one of his sisters. But in general the discussion was well conducted. It evoked participation and interest.

We talked a little about how all of us like to be noticed. Harry said, "Mr. ———— [the principal] said I do, but I don't. If he would put me in a room by myself, I'd tell him I'd like it, and I would." I asked, "For what purpose would you tell him that?" He didn't know, but Ernie commented, "He is trying to be bigger than Mr. ————." I asked Harry what he thought about it. He coughed out, "I want to be the boss, I guess." I: "That came out hard, didn't it?" And I praised him a lot for being such a good sport as to let the group talk about him today.

COMMENT. This is a nice example of an impressive discussion. The crucial step was the question about the purpose of telling off the principal. And Ernie helped to clarify the issue which Harry could finally see himself.

In the meantime, Hugo was poking Roy. I commented, "We have someone right now showing us how hard it is to be forgotten. Who do you think it is, Hugo?" He said, "Ernie." The other boys grinned. Then he looked behind him. We all agreed it was a kid in a yellow sweat shirt [Hugo wore one]. I said, "Yes, he tried a little trick, and I fell for it. How did I fall for it?" They said, "You talked to him just now."

COMMENT. One can see how clever the boys are in sizing up purposive behavior, particularly when the teacher gives them a hint. This example shows how one can direct the children toward important conclusions.

I had to leave early, so they roughhoused for the remaining ten minutes. Afterwards Hugo said, "Gee, I like to talk like this." [The English teacher reported that Harry and Hugo were especially disturbing later this morning.]

COMMENT. It is not clear whether there was any causal connection between this session and the later disturbance. However, there could have been, though the discussion was probably less responsible than the ten minutes of rough play.

Third Session—One Week Later. The boys seemed restless at first, and Hugo entertained us with his yoyo for a few minutes. It stuck and we laughed at him—and they settled down.

COMMENT. This was a good beginning. It is apparent that the teacher used Hugo's fooling around as a focal point for organized activity: they all looked at him while he played with his yoyo. It was this establishment of an integrated activity leading to general laughter which facilitated the "settling down" of the group.

I asked what they remembered from last time. Harry couldn't remember anything at first, but Randy and Hugo remembered talking about Harry wanting to be the boss and feeling free. Then Harry remembered about being free from his cast.

C O M M E N T . Isn't it interesting that Harry, who had always recapitulated the previous discussions, suddenly did not remember what had happened when he and his problems were being discussed? This a frequent occurrence in therapy. Does this first lacking and then obviously limited recollection indicate that Harry did not benefit from the previous discussion and explanation? Not at all, only it takes a certain time before insights like those provided by the discussion can be fully integrated and applied.

I continued by pointing out that we had talked about someone who was the oldest in the family, and now we could talk about those who were the youngest. Hugo pointed at Ernie. Ernie, Randy, and Hugo are all youngest in their families. They were asked how it felt to be the youngest. Harry and Roy had younger brothers and sisters and they, too, would know something about it.

C O M M E N T . That was a nice shift from one principal aspect to another. It is interesting to note how Hugo again mentioned Ernie when he meant himself, as he had done in the previous session. Such identification and inclusion in a larger group of boys with similar problems is extremely important for the group process. It not only saves face but permits increased receptivity.

Randy was anxious to talk. He said "Older sisters always make you do things, and people say, 'He is the baby of the family.' How I hate that!" Ernie agreed. Hugo said, "You get more privileges. Your mother takes you along and the others have to stay home because it seems like your ma likes you, 'cause you're littler." Harry thought the littlest one got more things at Christmas and didn't have to give things. "When you're big, you have to buy things out of your money and you don't know if you are going to get anything or not."

C O M M E N T . The teacher did not take full advantage of an important fact which revealed itself at this point: Randy saw only the disadvantages in being the youngest and Harry only the advantages; neither was willing to see the benefits of his own position in the family. Only Hugo was aware of his favorable position—and probably took full advantage of it. The boys may have seen how each was inclined to regard the position of the others in the family as more beneficial. Such impressions can only be gained in a group discussion where various members of the group are in different positions and can compare notes.

I asked the boys whether they preferred being treated as big or little. All wanted to be big, of course. "How do you show you want to be big? What do boys do to show they want to be grown up?" Hugo said by wearing engineer boots, Randy, by wearing your pants real low, pulling them down. He got up and demonstrated. Hugo suggested also by wising off sometimes. Harry commented, "You try to make people mad."

I asked, "Why does that make you feel good?" Hugo likes to make Miss ———— mad; she looks so funny. We discussed how it makes us feel bigger and stronger if other people get mad at us. Randy added, "You can fight a kid and win and feel bigger." Harry: "Clothes can do it, too, like ———— [*the name of another boy*]. He takes junior sizes. I went to buy a belt with him. He acts big, but his belt is so little. I can tease him now about being junior."

I asked if you had to win a fight to feel big. Hugo said, "No, if the kid is bigger than you and you lose, but you fight good for your size, you still feel good." Then Randy reported that Hugo tried to be big Sunday, Monday, and Tuesday. "Oh, how?" He grinned and said, "Oh, I can't say now."

I said, "You can say anything here, you know. Do you mind, Hugo, if he tells?" He shook his head, and Randy said, "He ran away." Hugo quickly added, "I did it for fun. They had detectives and everything." I asked him to tell us a little about it. He told how his mother came to get him at the quarry where he was forbidden to swim. She threatened him with Pa, "Wait till he gets home—you'll get it." He waited around a while, but his father didn't come home, so he went out on his bike with another kid. They got a traffic ticket for riding double. That made him madder. "I got to thinking about what they'd do at home, so I thought if I don't go home for a while, they'll sort of not do so much. So I stayed at Ralph ————'s; nobody but a couple of kids knew where I was—Roy here and Pat."

I asked how it worked out, if he got the fun and attention he wanted; he said, "Ya, when I came back kids asked whether I had fun and I said, sure. But it wasn't so much fun 'cause I was alone so much." The group talked a little about liking to be with the gang again. I asked if Hugo was acting grown up or like a baby running away. Randy said, "grown up," but Roy said, "baby." He added when I asked him why he thought so, "because he was afraid." "Aren't grown-ups ever afraid?" Roy, "Ya, but he ran away instead of staying and taking it."

While we talked Hugo was breaking off a piece of candy and eating it. At Roy's answer he almost rolled himself into a ball halfway under the desk. I praised Hugo for being a good sport to let us talk about him.

COMMENT. One may ask what the benefit of such a discussion could be. It is all centered around the question of how one can feel big. And taking this desire as a yardstick for evaluating behavior, particularly antisocial behavior, is important. It removes the moralistic evaluation of behavior to which boys of this type are more than accustomed and immunized. In this way they gain an understanding of their motivation. And it is then inevitable that the question comes up which Roy raised on this occasion, namely, whether one is really as big as one thinks. As soon as the discussion is focused on motivation, the door opens for reconsideration. The child may discover that he actually did not accomplish what he thought he did, and further, he may consider better and more adequate ways of accomplishing what he wants, being big, important, or whatever the case may be. Moralistic preaching and condemnation cannot have such results. The child knows that he is doing something wrong, but he does not care, or he does not know what else to do to gain his ends.

The only objection which one could have in regard to the preceding discussion is the fact that not all the boys participated. Ernie, if he was present, did not say anything, and Harry and Roy said little. To ensure that all members of the group are drawn into participation, it is wise to stop at any important point and ask each one to say what he thinks about it. (There are some counselors who oppose such pressure and direction; they would like to see the discussion unstructured and free. But teachers who do not follow such more or less nondirective methods could use the suggested approach.)

I asked Hugo how long he had been called "Tootsie." The boys explained that they all called him that because it was his nickname. Hugo reported that, when he started school, the teacher asked him about his name. He said "Tootsie." She said, "No, it's Hugo." "But," Hugo went on, "I'd never heard that before." His folks still call him Tootsie because his father's name is Hugo too.

C O M M E N T . This discussion was not followed up by the teacher. She missed, thereby, an important cue. Here is Hugo, deprived of his right name, of his right to bear his father's name, and instead getting a baby name. This makes the contrast between him and the two older successful brothers even worse. It explains also his desire to be big and his acting like a frightened baby in the process. All this could have been brought out through a well-directed discussion and, thereby, become clear to him and the other boys. But perhaps the teacher was right in going slowly at this time.

The group talked a little more about running away. Harry said his father had done it too, so there would be one less mouth to feed. It wasn't really a bad thing to do—sometimes boys or girls did it to get even with their parents for something. I suggested that for tomorrow, our next session, we could think of some way to show parents and teachers that we wanted to be grown up. Randy injected, "Like acting your age—not too grown up, not too babyish."

C O M M E N T . It is not a bad idea to suggest a subject for next time. Such suggestions are not commands, and do not stifle spontaneity.

Fourth Session—the Following Day. I asked the boys to review what we talked about yesterday. Hugo: "We talked about me and why I ran away and being a baby. Say, why does everybody, like the detectives, ask you so many questions when you run away?" Randy explained that they did it to try to help him. I asked whether I had scolded Hugo yesterday. Randy: "Well, a little." The others shook their heads and Harry said, "No, only explained so he'd know why he did things." I followed up: "You mean explaining that running away and hiding out are ways of getting attention or, perhaps, of showing other people that we want to be the boss, or maybe we want to get even with someone? What else do you do to keep from doing what other people want you to do, to have your own way?"

Harry: "I get sick—a headache, things like that, when I don't want to come to school. I never get a headache when I am going to have some fun." Hugo: "You can bribe people. My brother tries to bribe me into doing dishes, but I don't fall for it." I asked, "Randy, when your sisters tell you to do something, do you show them that they can't make you do it, and how?" Randy came back immediately: "I don't listen." Ernie, Roy, and Hugo all agreed that not listening was a good way.

Ernie said, "You can play dumb, too." "For what purpose do people play dumb?" Harry and Ernie both felt that then people don't expect you to do anything—"like Dorothy." [Dorothy is by far the slowest pupil in the home-room group.]

C O M M E N T . Now the discussion is really under way, dealing with important psychodynamic mechanisms. The boys express themselves well and frankly. Note Ernie's comment that playing dumb is a way of getting out of things. (Ernie is the youngest of a large family, and apparently played dumb also during the previous discussions by not participating. This could be pointed out to him.) Note also how the boys begin to recognize the mechanisms discussed in other children, an excellent way to gain insight into oneself.

We discussed Dorothy for a few minutes. The boys thought she must be pretty unhappy. They decided some people don't talk because what they say is always wrong, and somebody makes fun of them, so they don't try at all any more.

Harry injected, "I know a boy who won't drink milk. I think that's dumb." I said, "For what purpose won't he drink milk? Do you think his mother tells him to?"

Randy showed the muscle of his arm and said, "He wants to show how strong he is. He won't do it because his mother tells him to."

C O M M E N T . It is interesting to see how the boys themselves, if they do not understand the behavior of another child, assume the typical adult way of derogatory criticism. Harry could not understand why a boy would not want to drink milk, so he called it "dumb." Note how skillfully the teacher injected the question of the purpose and how Randy immediately caught on. Perhaps he understood because he did similar things at home.

At this point I said, "I've been wanting to tell you boys how well I think you have done in these discussions. You have shown really good thinking. I think we are about ready to see if we can make some of these things pay off. You boys are intelligent fellows. You have been wanting attention, and you have been wanting to show others how strong and grown up you are. You had some little tricks worked out for yourselves that you have been using for a long time; but these tricks got you into trouble because they were bothersome to other people. Now that you know more about what you've been doing, I am going to make an assignment for our next discussion, a week from yesterday."

Ernie: "Do we have to write out something?" "No, I'd like you to put those good minds of yours to work, to see if you can do exactly what you have been doing, but figure out a way that will be acceptable, that people will like instead of dislike. Would you be willing to try?" They all would like to, but, "What do we do?" I continued, "Pick one place either at home or at school to practice, maybe one class to start with; go on showing your power or your ability to get attention, whichever you want, but in an acceptable way. Where do you want to begin?"

Harry: "I'd like to show Miss D how grown up I am." Randy would like to try it in Miss M's room, "I could be grown up there." Ernie also chose Miss M's room, "I'll work there." Hugo said he would try to get attention in Miss D's room, "but I'll get it in a good way." Roy didn't know.

The bell rang and we stopped without enough definite help to the boys. I kept Roy a minute because he felt discouraged and I tried to give him a little buildup.

COMMENT. This suggestion to the boys to put their purpose to some useful end was rather daring, at least at this point. The teacher was right; the boys began to understand. And she certainly put it on pretty thick in appealing to their intelligence to find ways and means toward useful expressions of their purposes. Nevertheless, the question arises whether this procedure did not present premature pressure. It takes considerable courage and self-confidence to abandon the easy destructive methods and venture into useful activities.

Fifth Session—a Week Later. Roy was absent from school. Harry and Ernie had been suspended from school for cutting music class yesterday; at that time it was discovered that this was not the first time this had happened. Harry had not yet returned.

I asked the boys to report on how they got along with their assignments of improving in one class since last week. Randy reported that he had been out of math class last week but had seen Miss M on Friday and been allowed to come back—and for two days she hadn't hollered at him once.

Hugo started talking about a squirrel he'd hit with a stone. Ernie reported that on Friday Miss M had said something to him once, and that was all, and after class she told him and Harry that she had enjoyed them in class that day. He added, "I showed her I was grown up." Hugo began to tell us about hiding out with other boys in a woodpile where they "even had a mattress." Other boys knew about it now, so they are going to dig a four-foot hole for an entrance. "Then the other guys will never find us."

I asked if Hugo was lazy. They all said, "No, he works real hard at that stuff." "Is he fun to know and to talk to?" "Oh yes, he's fun."

"Well, Hugo, how did you make out with your assignment?" "I forgot." "Why did you forget? Was it convenient to forget?" Randy came in, "I know. Miss D biffed him with a book." I asked Hugo to tell us all about it. Hugo said he'd had a pin in the eraser of his pencil, just for fun, but Randy thought he poked him with the pin. But he didn't. It was just the point of the pencil. Randy squawked, and when he wouldn't give up the pin, Miss D biffed him.

"For what purpose did you poke Randy?" "Just to have some fun." I repeated the question for what purpose Hugo poked Randy. At this point, Hugo put down his head and said, "To get attention, I guess." "Did you succeed? Did your trick work?" "Ya; Randy squawked." "Did Miss D consider you grown up or a baby?" Ernie: "A baby, because she hit him." "You mean sometimes you spank babies, but we don't hit grownups?" Hugo: "Oh yes, cops use their clubs on a guy if he is stewed." "Is a guy who is stewed really grown up or more like a baby?" Randy: "He staggers all over like he's learning to walk. You can't talk to him. He is like a baby."

Randy told of a boy at camp who always acted and talked like a baby. Hugo said aside to him, "Did you like him?" When I asked what he had said, Hugo answered, "Never mind. Why are girls grown up at 16 and boys aren't? Girls even look big and grown up then."

C O M M E N T . By now we can distinguish the role of certain boys in the group. Harry had first begun to lead in a constructive way. Somehow he faded out, no longer functioning in this way. Randy now manages to give the right answers; he functions almost as a straight man for the teacher. But there can be no doubt that Hugo is the most disturbing element. He was the one in the first session to switch the discussion to dead bodies in a coffin, and who entertained the group with his yoyo, who ate candy while talking and sidetracked the discussion time and again. He was the only one present who had no useful approach to report. Instead he reported about hitting a squirrel. And when the discussion about his acting like a baby became too hot he switched it to girls. But before he could do so, the teacher was able to clarify his behavior impressively. We can assume that he got something out of the discussion. It is quite significant that he asked Randy whether he liked the boy in camp who acted and talked like a baby. Of course, Hugo knew the answer, and he did not want to go further as he was not ready yet for more insight. This is the reason he switched the topic of the discussion. It is noteworthy how active and persistent Hugo is in his destructive endeavors. He certainly is not less ambitious than his brothers. We saw the admiration of the others for his efforts—he is not lazy. Unfortunately, all his efforts are directed toward useless achievement, like the four-foot hole to hide from the others. His envy because girls are so much more adult than boys of the same age shows his anxiety to be big.

We talked about different growth rates of boys and girls, and how boys catch up and pass girls after 16. They told of older boys who were tall and strong now, but who used to be little. Randy said he sometimes felt real strong, and gave examples.

Hugo broke up this trend again by asking, "What about playing with blocks when you are all alone, and making funny noises with little cars?" We talked about how sometimes all boys, even after they have grown up, felt a little babyish, and that there was no harm in it when it didn't bother others.

We talked a little more about what Hugo could do in English class to get attention in an acceptable way. He suggested he could tell Miss D about how he plays on a major baseball team. "I'm not the best player, but one of the best." "What else?" "I could do my work."

COMMENT. It is pathetic how important Hugo wants to be, and how he has to play with his blocks, or with little cars, when he is alone.

We talked about that and they all felt that they had to have attention all the time. I explained to them that they were good kids to know, even if nobody showed them so by paying attention to them. Hugo immediately replied, "I could go in and just be myself." Asked to explain what he meant he said, "Not a baby, not a big shot."

It is remarkable how the boy caught on. Although at this point his verbal expression may not have reflected deep understanding, without some insight Hugo could not have found such an adequate formulation of his basic problem, namely, that he had not been just himself, but could be. So far he had been a baby wanting to be a big shot.

I asked Ernie to tell us how he felt when he cut music class. "Free and good." Randy said, "Like big shots. I almost went with him, but I didn't this time. You hear kids saying they never go to math class or something, so you want to try it too."

"For what purpose do kids cut classes?" "To show they can't make you stay in school."

We talked a little about why some boys don't like music. "Their voices are funny, and they hate to sing in front of other kids." Randy commented, "They think it's sissy." We talked a little about men singers and men cooks often being better than women. Hugo said he liked to bake especially.

C O M M E N T . This again is a wonderful example of how dynamics can be explained to children when the purpose of behavior is explored. It also shows how well and easily the children can catch on. Then one can discuss the implications in a beneficial way, leading to verbalizations from which the children can profit.

Randy had something on his mind. "I want to tell you that I almost ran away last night, but I didn't." He told of how he wanted a motor bike for a long time, but had to have $100 to pay down, and his mother kept putting him off. Yesterday he found out that he wasn't old enough yet. So he got so mad he walked out, and walked around and around, but went home about nine o'clock. I asked him whether he decided he could take it in a grown up sort of way—and he agreed.

C O M M E N T . This increased tolerance level may well be attributed to these discussions. While walking around, the boy may have recognized his desire to get even with a hostile world—and he did reconsider his plan.

I told them that tomorrow would be our last day. "Oh, no," they all shouted. Randy suggested that we should keep it going for another week, "and then another and another into next year. I like to talk about this stuff."

"Does it bother you when we talk about you here?" "No," Randy replied. "Maybe I like the attention; but when you say 'now let's talk about Randy,' I feel real good."

Sixth Session—the Following Day. Roy was still absent. I asked the boys to tell Harry what we talked about yesterday. Ernie said we checked up on how we got along on our assignments from last week. Harry reported that his was all off.

Randy said we talked more about grownups and babies, and Hugo added, "Ya, we talked more about me."

I asked Hugo if he remembered the suggestions we made to him, and he did pretty well, mentioning first that he could go into English class and be himself. I asked Harry if he could tell us how he got along with his assignment. He started with a story of skipping music class, which he told in great detail. After being suspended he had gone to tell Miss ———— that he wouldn't be in English class, and she said "Good!" —at least that is what he interpreted her as saying. He acted as if he were badly hurt by that. That's why he was angry at her, and why he said his assignment was all off. He concluded with, "Now *she* can make the first move."

I asked for what purpose people say that, and Randy answered, "To put the blame on someone else." Harry suggested, "To show your strength," but he wouldn't discuss it any further.

C O M M E N T . The psychological discussion is now in full swing. The full significance and benefit of injecting the question of the purpose whenever a behavior pattern is set up for discussion should be obvious by now.

The interplay between Randy and Harry became clear in the last responses of each. Randy showed considerable psychological sensitivity, which he had displayed during the previous discussions. Harry, who had taken an early lead in giving the proper responses, still made a feeble effort, but realized that he was somewhat off and then refused to commit himself any further. He conceded victory to Randy. Apparently the teacher was not aware of this, or else she would have done something about bringing Harry in again.

Randy was sitting on a swivel chair which squeaked every time he moved. I said, "My, that chair is noisy." He immediately got up, pushed the chair over where it belonged, and quietly took a student desk. I commented, "What sign of growing up did you just notice in this group, that probably would not have happened two weeks ago?"

Ernie said, "Randy gave up something he wanted." "For whose good?" "For the good of all of us," they all said. Hugo went over to the swivel chair, brought it out again, and sat in it. We went on talking about how pleasant it is when people do things like that without having to be scolded first. Hugo put the chair back and took his own chair quietly.

C O M M E N T . Now the teacher has the group completely on her side. The boys do not merely want to talk; they feel understood and want to understand. The ones who side most with the teacher do not antagonize the others, but help them along. There is no trace of open competition (with the exception of the subtle byplay between Randy and Harry, which the teacher unfortunately did not notice). The group is cooperative, eager to learn and to grow, and the teacher is handling the situation with skill and sensitivity.

Ernie said, "I don't see why you say that cutting classes shows that you want to be strong." We discussed it, as we did in yesterday's discussion, adding that some might do it to get attention, or to get even. Harry said little.

C O M M E N T . It speaks for the sensitivity of the teacher that she noticed and mentioned Harry's withdrawal, although she apparently did not realize its cause.

I asked the boys whether they knew other ways of running away, besides actually running out. Ernie mentioned "running away in your mind." Others mentioned blaming someone else, or changing the subject as Hugo did yesterday when the discussion was unpleasant for him.

We finally compromised on one more meeting, after some discussion. I asked them whether they wanted to keep the same assignments. They did, but Harry remarked, "Well, I'll keep mine, and I'll try a little bit, but not very hard." Harry was hard to reach today, but Hugo seemed especially receptive.

Seventh Session—One Week Later. We checked up first on how well they got along with their attempts to be grown up in classes they had chosen. They all told of not having to be scolded. Hugo said, "I asked Miss ———— for some help, but I didn't bother anybody."

Since this was our last meeting, I asked them if there were any questions they wanted to clear up before we stopped. Harry said, "How about this idea of me? You said I want to show how strong I am. I don't get it." I asked what made us think that Harry possibly wanted to show his power. They answered quickly: "He is the oldest, he likes to be free, he likes to fight and to argue." Harry said, "O.K. O.K., I'd like to think about it." We agreed that that was all right to do.

Hugo wanted to talk about dope. "What does it do to you? Why do the cops always ask you about it?" Harry said, "Ya, they picked me up and said, 'you use dope, don't you?' I never knew anything about it." I told them what I had read about forms of dope, and how it affected people. We talked about the publicity it was getting.

Randy asked, "How come some people don't seem to need to swear and some swear so much?" Harry said he guessed it was like dope, once you get started, you had to do it all the time.

C O M M E N T . Isn't it interesting how Harry immediately stepped in when Randy did not know something? That was his chance to show that he was superior. Such incidents when noticed by the discussion leader and properly interpreted promise impressive experiences not only for the boys concerned but also for the other members of the group. One of the skills that requires the most training is to become sensitive to and aware of the subtle interplay which takes place between the members of the group, be it a small group like this one or a whole classroom.

The question of dope and of swearing led to a discussion of purposes again. Some commented that if you were really able to do something or fix something, you didn't seem to need to swear so much. We talked of why knowing how to fix bikes makes one feel strong and good.

Randy wanted to know whether you could say that a fellow who bought a foreign make of motorcycle was doing that to get attention. We talked some more about why people like to have cars, motorcycles, unusual clothes, and so forth, but pointed out that just knowing one thing about a person is not sufficient to tell us about the kind of person he really is.

C O M M E N T . The last statement is important. While the teacher succeeded in making the boys aware of certain psychological dynamics, she had to curtail the temptation to interpret everything that anyone does without knowing much about it. Another safeguard which has to be impressed upon the boys—and just as much on the teachers and parents who study psychological dynamics—is the danger of using psychological terms freely, particularly in social contacts. Psychological interpretation is mischief if given outside of a period and place where a trained person is in charge of discussion or guidance.

The period ended here. The boys were jolly and friendly, and Harry suggested they should have had a little ice cream or something special "to end our secret club. Will we meet next year?" Then he added, "I wish I could bring Ned to our meetings." [Ned is an active boy in their homeroom group.] When I asked him why, he replied, "I think he needs this too. He acts like a big shot too, sometimes." [Was Harry thinking that if he changed his own behavior, someone else might become leader of his group?]

C O M M E N T . The teacher is right. And Harry also seems to have recognized in Ned some of the problems which he had himself. His coming around at the end suggests that the discussion at the beginning of the session was right for him.

The last day of school Harry, Randy, and Ernie came around to wish me a nice vacation. Randy said, "If I feel like running away next year, I'll come in and talk with you first." Harry said, "I still don't think I want to be the boss *all* the time," and grinned broadly.

C O M M E N T . It is amazing how much the teacher achieved in merely seven discussions. At the end the boys seemed to be bubbling over with questions which they had on their minds. The teacher herself drew the following conclusions:

1. These discussions apparently filled a need for these boys, namely, to discuss questions and problems of their behavior.
2. Even though the boys were called slow learners and uninterested in academic subjects, they seemed quick to comprehend the dynamics of human behavior, and to have definite interest in these discussions.
3. Even though the counselor was also their class teacher, they seemed willing to discuss everything freely and frankly.
4. Had these sessions been held earlier in the year, they would have been more beneficial, and their benefits more easily determined. They

might have been continued for a longer period and the boys would have received more specific help.

5. Roy seemed to be the only one whose personal problems were so deepseated as to be little discussed or affected.

[The teacher made a footnote in October of the following year: I had Roy in my homeroom this year. He was doing good work in all subjects and proved to be a real help in getting the boys who were new to the group oriented.]

6. Some home contact before and after these sessions might have been helpful.

COMMENT. We can agree with these conclusions. Discussions of this type and nature can also be held in the regular classroom, where they have shown the same efficacy as this example demonstrates.

Certain objections are likely to be raised against training teachers to use such psychological procedures. It may appear even more dangerous to encourage teachers who are not sufficiently trained to venture into discussions of this kind. This doubt is based on the assumption that much harm can be done by half-trained teachers and that a little knowledge is often worse than none. But is it really true that a teacher insufficiently trained in psychological methods can do more harm than one not at all acquainted with them? Can we assume that psychological discussions of this nature, even if they are conducted incorrectly, could do more harm than the discussions filled with recriminations, threats, and preaching which go on between teachers and pupils at present in many classrooms? A little psychological knowledge seems preferable to the prevalent lack of it.

There are, however, a few safeguards which may be observed by a teacher who is interested in this discussion method. As long as she uses common sense, as long as she induces the children to express themselves freely, and as long as her psychological interpretations consider possible *goals* and not *causes*, she is on safe ground. Some interpretations may be wrong, but they cannot do much harm. The beneficial effects in building morale, in providing a feeling of togetherness, and in giving the children a sense of being respected and having a voice, outweigh any possible harm.

For this reason, the average teacher can safely be encouraged to experiment with this kind of group discussion. It will take a great deal of training and experience to conduct such discussions in a professionally adequate way. But such a high standard is not necessary. The teacher who conducted the experiment reported here made many mistakes which a trained group therapist would avoid. Nevertheless she did an admirable job and helped the children considerably.

Example 54

Here is an example of a group discussion with adolescents, four girls and six boys, conducted as a demonstration for counselors in training.

Leader: How do you feel about being here?

[*Such a question is usually asked to warm up the group.*]

Boy: I like it but I am nervous. [*Then there is a discussion as to why they are here.*]

Another boy: Because we are average teen-agers.

Leader: And what are these people doing here?

Boy: They are observers.

Leader: They are working with teen-agers. Do you think they know average teen-agers like you?

Boy: They should.

Leader: The girls have not said anything so far. What do you think?

Girl: We are here for a demonstration.

Leader: Demonstrating what?

Girl: You. [*Much laughter.*]

Leader: What do you want to demonstrate about me?

Girl: Your technique of group discussion.

Leader: Exactly, that's what we are here for. Are you willing to help me? [*All say yes.*]

Leader: What kind of problems do you want to bring up for discussion?

Girl: How about extracurricular activities?

Leader: What is the problem?

Girl: We don't have time for it. We try to keep up our grades, it is important to most of us. And we like to have a social aspect in some ways, and some of us get involved and we have a little less time for school work.

Leader: Now, what kind of change would you recommend?

Girl: Less school hours. [*Laughter.*]

Leader: What do the others think about the problem? Do you share this problem?

Boy: Probably everyone has the same problem but probably more with girls because they do more in extracurricular activities than boys do. Boys are in sports. Boys usually don't have the same school spirit, they don't do many things that are connected with schools.

Leader: Would you like to have more time for sports, cars, etc.?

Boy: I am not going to be making my living by having fun all the time. So it probably will be better for me to put in the time for school now and benefit from it when we are older.

Leader: [*calls on another boy*]. I think you had some sympathetic feeling about less time for school and more sport.

Another boy: I feel not exactly that, I feel that it should be more balanced.

Leader: It should be more balanced—in which way?

Boy: School should be arranged so that it leaves time for other things.

Leader: Do you think that there are many young people who feel like that? [*Consent.*]

Girl: The teachers give you homework from your classes and you have all this homework to do at night. One girl I knew stayed up until midnight to do her homework—and that's all she did after school. I think they should have a little more time in class to do the work so you can see where you are making your mistake.

Leader: Do many students feel like that?

Girl: Yes.

Leader: Do you have a student council?

Several boys: Yes.

Leader: Did you ever tell the student council to bring it up?

Boy: I think that everyone has the general impression that it wouldn't do much good. It wouldn't make much sense to bring it up.

Leader: Why not?

Girl: The student council doesn't accomplish something like that.

Leader: Why can't they accomplish it?

Girl: They accomplish things but not like getting the school to work.

Leader: Why not, if that is what the students want?

Girl: Because the students want it, doesn't mean that it's good.

Boy: Right.

Leader: Is it good if you would shorten the school hours?

Girl: Many times they give too much homework.

Leader: Do the kids like to do homework?

[*Most shouted "no."*]

Leader: Do you think homework is good?

Girl: I think you should have a little homework, 'cause you can't do it all in class, you couldn't cover all the material; you could do some work in class and it would leave you free time afterwards for other activities.

Leader: What do you think about homework? Do you agree?

Boy: I disagree. I think it is necessary to have homework because right now our business is school and what we are trying to accomplish is to get through school and get good grades, and learning a lot and I think you can learn a lot if you have more homework.

Leader: Why do you need good grades?

Boy: The reason I want good grades is to get into college.

Leader: Why do you want to go to college?

Boy: So I can get a good job.

Leader: Tell me, how many of you like to study because you enjoy it, regardless of the grades?

Boy: A specific subject?

Leader: Do you have a specific subject you enjoy to study regardless of grades?

Girl: Yes.

Leader: Which one?

Girl: Math. I enjoy working with algebraic formulas.

Leader: How about you?

Another girl: I cannot think of anything, really.

Leader: And you? [*Several answer—English, Spanish, Math, Biology, Graphics.*]

Boy: I don't like to study anything. [*Laughter.*] I can find better things to do.

Leader: What do you think? Is it really the right motivation to study in order to get good grades and go to college and make a better living later on? Is that the reason for going to school?

Girl: I think we're going to school to learn how to think, really.

Leader: How to think—do you think you learn how to think?

Girl: I hope I do.

Leader: Have you ever had such discussion about grades and what you learn for?

Girl: I have such discussions with a bunch of my friends.

Leader: Let us switch to something else. Why are you interested in certain subjects?

Boy: It's just because it's most interesting to me.

Leader: Why is it most interesting to you? I'd like to know.

Boy: You got me, I'd like to know too.

Leader: [*to another boy*]. You were interested in Math and English, why?

Boy: Something I can do *fairly well,* and it seems to be fun. [*Several boys and girls like a subject because it comes easy, because they understand it, or they dislike a subject because it is boring, always the same thing.*]

Leader: I have my own ideas on why students are good in certain subjects and like them. [*To the observers.*] Have you any guess?

Audience: They like the teacher.

Girl: Yes, but not necessarily.

Leader: And why do they like the teacher?

Audience: Because the student is successful.

Leader: Yes, a student who likes one subject, particularly to the exclusion of all else, is usually overambitious. He will do and like only the subject in which he is good. I think one of you said it, You like it because you are good in it. And if you are not so good, you don't care. Are you good in the subjects you like?

Boy: Not especially, but I am poor in all the others. [*Laughter.*]

Leader: Are you one of the best in a subject?

Boy: In Math I was the last time. [*Most students admit that they were on top in their favorite subject, at least at times. A discussion with a girl who did not agree follows. It turned out that she actually liked only the subject in which she was good, but she liked the teacher in another subject which she had not mentioned as her favorite.*]

Leader: You like the Spanish teacher; but since you are not so good in Spanish you don't like the subject.

Girl: I guess so. [*Several boys and girls bring up questions about poor grades.*]

Leader: Why do you make poor grades? Are you capable of making good grades?

Boy: Lack of self-application?

Leader: What do you mean by that?

Boy: Not applying yourself as much as you should. Putting homework off until tomorrow, and it never gets done. You don't get it in and you don't make up. There you go—poor grades.

Another girl: You put it off.

Leader: Now why don't you do the homework?

Boy: Because you have other things to do. [*Laughter.*]

Leader: What is more interesting to you?

Boy: Almost anything besides homework.

Leader: Why do you prefer the other things to homework?

Girl: They are more fun.

Leader: Why do so many kids do what is fun even if it's not good for them?

Girl: It's easier, when it's homework you have to do it.

Leader: And you don't like to do what you have to do because then you give in. That is no fun. And many think the most important thing in life is having fun.

Boy: You got to work sometime to have money.

Leader: And for what purpose do you want money?

Boy: So you *can* have fun. [*Laughter.*]

Leader: Many youngsters do not do the work they are supposed to do because it is unpleasant, and they think they have the right to pick and choose and do only what they like, what is fun. And the people who always must have fun are the same who are bored most of the time. How about each of you? [*They all agree that they are often bored.*]

Boy: I'm hardly ever bored, because I am always looking for fun.

Leader: Are there other reasons why students don't want to work, to apply themselves?

Girl: Pressure, people behind you saying you got to get done, you got to get good grades.

Leader: And what is the consequence?

Girl: Most of the time you don't do it.

Leader: Many children refuse to do their homework or their studying because for them it means giving in. And who wants to give in? [*One girl shows recognition reflex.*] Now who of you is in this category —I won't give in? [*All laugh.*]

Leader: [*to the audience*]. These are the things we have to work out with the students. We have to understand their private logic. What are other reasons why you don't do homework?

Girl: Sometimes you have to take care of younger brothers and sisters or work around the house. By the time you get that done you are worn out, you no longer feel up to studying and concentrating.

Leader: What do you think about what she said?

Audience: Perhaps she is mad and revengeful?

Leader: Right. She is so angry that she has to do these chores, that she gets even with her parents by not studying. How do her parents take it?

Girl: They don't like it when my grades fall down.

Leader: So, if they demand too much from you around the house, it serves them right if your grades do go down.

Girl: I just have to control myself.

Leader: So many of you talk of control; but one can't control oneself, because one always does what one decides anyhow. Since you want to be a good girl, it is difficult to admit that you want to get back at your parents. Then you blame your lack of self-control for your unwillingness to study.

Girl: Yes, I used to feel that way.

Leader: You still do it.

Girl: But not as much, though. [*Laughter.*]

Leader: Since she is not aware of all that, our job is to help her see what she is doing, then she can change it. She would like to control herself, she doesn't like herself that she doesn't do it; she was not aware she was doing it to punish her parents.

Another girl: I knew a girl and she had good grades and she didn't get along with her parents for a while, and then all of a sudden her grades fell down. Could it be the same reason?

Leader: Very often. Only when kids do such things they are not aware of it. Could it be that this little discussion which we have right now will change several of you because you will become aware of what you are doing? Is there another reason perhaps why some of you don't study?

Girl: I got so downhearted about the mistakes on assignments that had been handed back to me that for a while I didn't even bother doing my homework. What was the use, if I was not getting it right?

Leader: Right, that is exactly the other point which was missing. Another reason why children don't apply themselves is because they get discouraged. They don't believe they can get anywhere, so what's the sense of studying? [*Several agree that they feel that way sometimes.*]

Boy: Lots of times I'm just kind of tired and I put off homework.

Leader: You said you often get tired. What would happen if at such a time someone would call you up and suggest a fun thing to do?

Boy: I would not be too tired for that. [*Laughter.*]

Leader: [*to audience*]. You have here a cross section of motivations of the underachievers. Because that is what it is. If the kids don't want to study and to apply themselves, then they don't achieve what they well could with their intelligence.

Leader: [*to students*]. You all could be much better students, I think. Studying is here because one has to, because one wants to go to college to make money, but nobody is studying because one enjoys studying. Learning can only be effective if you like it, if you enjoy it. And often, our children have a false sense of freedom and independence. They have the right to do what they please, and look the other way when something has to be done they don't like. You suffer from that because you make your own work more unpleasant. Do you know that if you would stop fighting against learning, the learning would be more fun for you? You are suffering more from your work by making it more difficult. If you would stop thinking what do I get out of it and were merely willing to do what has to be done you would not fight against it. What do you think of it?

Boy: I think you have to have a little bit of insight of what your homework will bring you.

Leader: What will it bring you?

Boy: You have to think about your future. You got to have something to point at, a goal.

Leader: May I ask you, when you force yourself to do your homework, do you think you learn very much from it?

Boy: What would I gain if I didn't do it?

Leader: Not much less. That is the fallacy of homework. One assumes if one forces them to do homework they will learn more. And they eventually do the homework, but with inner friction, and they don't make better grades. Who benefits from homework really?

Girl: Those who enjoy it, who like to do it.

Boy: [*mumbling*]. There is no such thing.

Leader: Oh ho, if you have a subject which you really like, you enjoy homework.

Boy: There are such subjects, but we are talking about the whole. I don't think there is anybody who likes to sit down and do homework.

Leader: You are all brought up in the way that you don't have to do what you don't like, and then fight with yourself to do it. Even if you do it, you do it reluctantly, with inner friction.

Leader: I would like to ask you how you feel about this discussion.

Girl: I think it's quite interesting. I learned a lot today. I think it helped me. I'm going to do my homework tonight. [*Laughter.*]

Another girl: Everyone should have the opportunity to be in a discussion like it.

Another girl: I think I got a lot out of it. I know I don't feel like doing homework and I know nobody else does either. I didn't know the different reasons why.

Boy: I feel there are certain things I have been doing wrong but haven't realized that I could correct it.

Leader: [*to a boy*]. How do you feel about the discussion?

Boy: I think it was real good. I think that other kids ought to be put into the same situation; then there would be a lot smarter kids around.

Leader: Do you think one should have such discussions in school?

Several: Yes.

Boy: I think it would be good.

Leader: With whom, with the teacher or with the counselor? [*Divided opinion. Some say the counselor, others the teacher because she knows them better. Whoever knows them better.*]

Leader: If you have any questions, please ask them. If not, thank you.

C O M M E N T . This is not a typical group discussion, because in the setting of a demonstration a wider range of problems have been discussed than would come up in a single session in a class or with a counselor. One would usually go deeper into each issue and particularly into the psychological aspects involved. There also would be more discussion between the members of the group than took place here when the leader tried to provide a learning situation for the group as well as for the audience.

As a rule, the participants are usually asked about their reaction to the session and what they have learned; and are also asked at the next session what they remember of the previous one. The discussions are part of a learning process, learning about oneself, about others, and about life. The summary at the end of a session recapitulates the important points and makes them better remembered, as does their repetition at the next session.

Many of these examples show our technique of "loaded questions" which the Greek philosopher Socrates so effectively used to influence people.

CHAPTER 10

Group Situations

S INCE THE TEACHER is not dealing with each child separately but is always confronted with a group situation, he must be equipped not only to understand the interaction taking place between the children but to influence such interaction effectively. Even a teacher not familiar with the intricacies of sociometric exploration can become sensitive to interpersonal tensions and group situations. Knowledge of human relationships and individual motivations can help the teacher to understand the total situation in which each child operates, namely, the group.

One requirement for all good group leaders—including teachers—is the ability to see *everything* that goes on in the group at any given time. This requires a wide range of vision. The significance of this width of vision has been recognized in speed reading. The more a reader is trained to see with one glance the quicker he can read—and the better he understands what he has read. In a particular way, this applies also to the group leader. The better equipped the leader is to notice everything that goes on, the better he can deal with the whole situation and the more effective he will be. The teacher must be trained to be able to encompass the whole class with one glance. The width of vision, varying with each teacher, determines the size of the class with which she can deal effectively. At no time should the concern with one child preoccupy the teacher to the extent that she neglects the total class situation. Trained in the group approach she can deal with each child within the total group instead of singling him out for isolated action.

A simple example is the teacher's effort to calm down a noisy class. If she shouts, she only adds *her* noise to that of the class. But if the teacher lowers her voice, or stops altogether after saying something of interest to the children, they will exert their influence on each other for quiet. Natural consequences always imply action, not verbal commands or reprimands. In fact, the teacher is always more effective the less she says and the more she does. Preaching and scolding are not only ineffectual, they are demoralizing and harmful. Order can be maintained in the classroom without much talking. The teacher may, at the beginning of the year, establish one of many techniques, such as raising the hand, to restore silence without saying a word.

It is advisable not to let any misbehavior go unnoticed. Any disturbance, in the most remote corner of the room, affects the atmosphere of the whole class and becomes a focal point of infection, spreading restlessness and lack of interest. A teacher may be inclined to overlook a disturbance because she does not know what to do about it and would rather prevent further friction. However, if she utilizes group pressure to bring the disturbing child back into the fold, she can overcome inattentiveness, noisiness, and other transgressions which may interfere with class activities.

Fighting among the children is a familiar problem. Several reports deal with such situations and how the teacher tried to resolve the conflict.

Example 55

Ronald, age 7, is the second child in the family. He came to me with the complaint that Mona and Tim were preventing him from being first to get his coat. I asked him if it really made any difference if someone else was half a minute ahead of him. As I expected, it did to him.

I called all three children to my desk; Mona and Tim had complaints too. I told all three children to sit down together and to talk over what they might do about the situation.

When they returned, Ronald reported that they had decided to take turns. He would be first for one week, then Mona, and then Tim.

C O M M E N T . The teacher is correct in indicating the importance of Ronald's position as the second in the family. It helps explain why he resents anybody being ahead of him. She also chose the generally effective approach of letting the children settle their differences and find solutions by themselves. She is to be commended for not jumping in and trying to settle the problem for them.

The solution which the children found on this occasion is not, however, entirely desirable. It does not remove the disturbing need to be first. It would have been impossible to get Ronald's agreement had the other children not given him the right to be first during the first week of the agreement. What will happen during the following weeks is still an open question.

The teacher's initial reaction in questioning the importance of being first was more nearly correct. Devoting several class discussions to this topic would have done more for the elimination of such conflicts than the temporary solution that was found.

Example 56

Hal hung his coat on a hook in the classroom. He picked up a pencil and a piece of paper and went to his seat. Lou came into the cloakroom, took Hal's coat off the hook, put it on another hook and started to his seat with his pencil and paper. Hal came to my desk to tell me what Lou had done. Before I could say anything at all, Lou came to tell me that he *did not* take Hal's coat off the hook. I was suspicious when Lou came so quickly, while Hal was still talking to me—how did he know what it was all about? I asked both boys to come to the cloakroom with me. There I asked them to pick up their wraps, to go downstairs to settle their dispute, and when they were both ready to come in and hang their coats and get to work, they could come back. They both came back, hung up their coats, and quietly went to their seats and started to work.

C O M M E N T . This episode has considerable significance. It was obvious to the teacher which one of the boys was in the wrong. She refrained, nevertheless, from making any comment to this effect. Some may question the wisdom of such procedure, thinking it the teacher's obligation to reprimand the culprit. But what could she have done? Telling the boy that he was wrong is superfluous—he knows that; and it would not have stopped him from repeating such transgressions. Some more impresssive step had to be found—and it seems that the teacher found one.

The skeptic may still object to a procedure which "punishes" the innocent with the guilty. Why should Hal be sent down when he actually did nothing wrong? This is a fundamental point to be clarified. *We are not dealing here with a moral issue, but with one of relationships.* True enough, in this instance Lou wronged Hal; but the teacher has no way of knowing what Hal may have done previously to provoke Lou. And even if the present act of transgression had been unprovoked, a punitive act by the teacher would not have improved the relationship between the two boys. Her staying out of the conflict and letting the boys settle it was bound to have some beneficial effect on their relationship. This was the main problem in the situation, which the teacher recognized and resolved.

Example 57

Ned and Sam were in my special group of 8-year-olds. Sam was typing and Ned wanted his turn and kept pestering Sam. Generally Ned's crying fits got him what he wanted. But the more he talked about getting his turn, the less inclined Sam was to quit. I told them that Sam was to type as long as he wished, and when Ned's turn came he could do so too. But he decided to cry, glancing at me out of the corner of his eye. First I paid no attention; then I remarked, "Ned, I can see how hard you are working to get those tears out. But since it won't make any difference about typing whether you cry or not, why don't you interest yourself in something else?" To my astonishment he stopped crying and started some other project. As soon as Ned showed no more interest in the typewriter, Sam got up and said, "Your turn now, Ned."

COMMENT. It was wise of the teacher not to assume the role of judge in determining the turns. She succeeded in keeping out of interpersonal conflicts; but she paid too much attention to Ned's crying. This example has been included because it demonstrates the extent to which the behavior of one child is interwoven with that of the other.

Example 58

One day recently a fight started outside my office window. The two principals were unaware of being watched. First there were loud words, then shoves, and finally the glasses were removed and the books handed to a third party. I decided the time had come to do something. Just as the fight was about to get underway, I made my way to within a few inches of the fighters. I said, "I am sorry about this, fellows. I think it is a pity that you don't know how to settle your differences without beating each other up." One of the boys looked up and grinned broadly. The other still glowered a little and looked distinctly unhappy. To him I said, "I guess you must really have been pushed around quite a bit." He looked up surprised and asked, "Why?" I told him that he seemed so angry. "I think somebody must really have been mean to you to make you feel so mad." He smiled, "Naw—nobody pushed me around." Both boys asked if they could go to class. I said, "Why not?" and they were on their way.

A comment on this episode was provided by the teacher.

Contrast this with the way in which I might have entered the situation at an earlier time; what I would have done is probably typical of the way many would behave.

Approaching the boys I might have indignantly demanded that they "stop this nonsense." Probably next I should have demanded to know their names and which class it was they were supposed to be going to. Then when I had asked, as I most certainly would have, what it was all about, I probably would have each one trying to shout louder than the other to convince me that the other was wrong. By then it would have been necessary for me to shout louder than the total of their combined efforts to shut them up and instruct them to speak one at a time. And then I would have had to be the judge and decide which one should speak first so that I might adequately decide which one should be blamed. Then after a brief but learned lecture on the evils of fighting I might well have sent both boys to the office where they might have had to go through the same thing all over with the principal who would finally demand that the two gladiators shake hands and remember to act like gentlemen hereafter. After that they would have entered their classroom twenty minutes late and had to explain to the teacher why they were late.

COMMENT. The present handling of the fight took far less energy, commotion, and friction. But more was accomplished than merely the end of this particular fight. When the teacher expressed sympathy instead of moralizing condemnation, most of the deeper motivations for this encounter were removed. It was not merely a covering up of smoldering emotions; the fire was extinguished, at least for this time. This approach may well have impressed the boys more with the nonsense of settling their differences with fighting than preaching and lecturing would have. But most important, a teacher who approaches the children in this way appears as a friend, and can be effective as such.

Example 59

Here are the answers which a teacher received from her third- and fourth-graders when she asked them to write—at regular intervals—what each pupil liked or did not like about her. In many instances complaints were such that nothing could be done about them—the child merely disliked part of the routine. But even the possibility of expressing his dislike openly may go a long way in reducing a child's resentment.

When she gives us tests; when we read those "green books"; when she takes our "free period" away; when she calls on the girls all the time, when the boys have their hands up; when she punishes the whole class, when two people "did it"; when we write poetry; when she says we can't write in workbooks that go with our book rental; she doesn't have lipstick on for her afternoon class, but has it on in the morning; when she makes us sit, or read out aloud, or study the vocabulary; when our teacher is sick and we have a substitute; when we have a writing lesson; when I have to work in *Scottie & His Friends*; I don't like to write; I don't like to stay in a room two hours at a time; when you let the other class [*fourth-graders*] do things, and don't let us do those things.

COMMENT. The nature of these complaints indicates the relationship which the teacher has with her pupils. There is not one instance of real hostility. Some of the complaints indicate a slight reference to unfairness—or at least express the feeling of being slighted (calling the girls instead of boys, letting the other class do things, not wearing lipstick in the afternoon), but most of the complaints are about school and work and not about the teacher. From what we know about this particular teacher, she probably used every single complaint as a basis for discussion.

The friendliness which the teacher evoked in her class is clearly manifested in the much larger list of things which the children enumerate as "liking" about their teacher.

She gives us plenty of time to do our work; she helps everybody—not just one person; she discusses things we study with the whole class; she teaches about famous people; she lets us take books home; she does not make us read the whole book; she gives us good grades if she thinks we are doing the best we can; she reads the "giggle page" in the Play Mate and tells us jokes and riddles; she displays our work uptown and in school, and shows our work to other classes; she lets us make things, booklets to take home to our parents; lets us see things—passes them around; lets us do interesting things; lets us work on our stamp collection during our free period so we can trade; lets us write our own poetry; puts names and addresses of pen pals on the blackboard so we can write to them; puts poems on the board and lets us draw pictures around them; lets us do almost all the things we like to do—gives us nice things to do; she reads at the end of the hour; she reads about Dr. Doolittle and lets us read the weekly reader; shows us movies about things we are studying; lets us play games that we bring to school during free period; lets us make reports on things we are interested in; lets us work on big jigsaw puzzles and helps us; lets us help her clean paste jars, cupboards, etc.; lets us check papers for her, especially arithmetic papers for class D; lets us pick our own seat; lets a monitor choose a person to take his place, instead of choosing all the monitors herself; lets us use the big board mops; lets us have big paper mops at our desk; lets us pick the books we want to read; lets us use her books; lets us sit in the back of the room for a week; lets us make a monthly newspaper to take home to our parents; lets us use the dictionary; lets us go down the fire escape; when I bring things to show the class, she passes them around—not just looks at them and gives them back to me; gives us short pencils to take home.

COMMENT. These are some of the things which the children write down spontaneously. Stimulating such expressions of pleasant experiences arouses awareness and appreciation for them. Letting a child openly express his grievances diminishes the anger; letting him express his pleasure increases it. Sharing has beneficial effects; it evokes a feeling of mutual consideration and belonging. For this reason bringing such feelings up for class discussion unites children and teacher and brings about a harmonious group atmosphere.

Example 60

I had trouble with one class. It was always noisy, and sometimes it was even difficult to give the assignment. After about four weeks of this I became desperate. So I told them something had to be done, and that I had been thinking about the situation and had reached one solution, but that we would spend a few minutes that day in class working out other possible solutions. We all talked it over, but I decided to use the one I thought would work—and it did.

COMMENT. Even if the procedure did work, the total approach to the situation was not good. First of all, why wait four weeks? A class discussion is in order at the beginning of a disturbing situation, as soon as it arises and continues. Then there would be no need for the teacher to become desperate. The way the teacher arranged for a group discussion was not constructive either. She already had reached a solution, still wanted to talk it over, and finally decided for herself to stick to her original plan. The plan may be good, and it may work, but this is not the way to win the cooperation of a class and establish a democratic procedure in which everybody shares the responsibility and takes care of his share.

This was it: I promised the children that I would let them have twenty-five minutes of the art class to talk while they work, if they would give me the first fifteen minutes to explain the lessons and to pass out supplies. They all agreed. Also in the compromise it was decided that if I wanted the class to start or stop, all I would need to do would be to raise my hand.

Now when I walk into the classroom, I raise my hand and the room becomes still enough to hear a pin drop. They let me talk for fifteen minutes without interruption or even talking, and all during the work period I leave them alone without interrupting them. It really works.

C O M M E N T . We can understand why it works. First, the agreement showed mutual respect and consideration. Second, the mechanism of raising the hand to establish silence is effective. It is even better to have an agreement by which each child who sees the teacher or leader raise his hand also raises his own and keeps quiet. In this way those who are slow in responding are coaxed by the others to do the same. This procedure stimulates greater mutual responsibility, instead of mere submission to the sign of the leader.

Despite the autocratic approach, the teacher had obviously won the children's cooperation. There was general agreement about the routine which the teacher correctly termed a compromise.

Example 61

This is a classroom situation which was made the basis of a study project by a teacher-student. She first stated the problem as she saw it, then tried to analyze the reasons, and finally outlined the possible solutions. This outline was then discussed in teaching class and followed up by the teacher.

The Problem. My first-grade reading readiness class has periods of fighting. The fighting shows both the conventional variety of "two to a bout" and the petty picking on each other. Generally, one or two focal personalities are apparent; these change with different periods. The fighting is mostly concentrated during recess, in line, at the lockers, and in the bathroom. My class is very transient, for when a child can be put into another room he leaves and I get a new slow reader in return.

Analysis and Diagnosis. I found different kinds of fighting. Each seems to fit different goals in different children.

1. There is the friendly sort of fighting which does no harm unless it progresses into a more violent conflict. This kind is mostly for attention; the child tries to impress either me or his friend. This is a testing, a matching of wits. Examples of this are mild pestering of the neighbor in line, teasing like taking a child's hat on the playground, or standing near the teacher and playing rough in a pretended "cowboy" fight. Tommy knows of no other way to play since his father has always roughed him up in playing with him. And there is Danny whose mother ran out to save him from every fight. These two are always in some

sort of roughhouse, never actually hurting anyone. They get attention in this way.

2. Then there are those fights where someone gets hurt. They usually express a desire to hurt a child in the room. These children are in a state of revenge; they no longer care if they get hurt in the act. Their main purpose is to hurt others. They get pleasure in being beaten up, for then they can wear badges for living in this cruel world. They are the "left-outs" who try to punish those who are in. I have noticed that in some of the more obvious cases of this sort, the child will choose an opponent who is much too big for him. These battles recur, with the same principals involved. Right now I have a new boy in just such a state. Donald is out of the group and cooperates little with it; as a matter of fact, he works always against the group. He never follows any of the organizational rules, always grabbing all the turns, always calling out the answers. He starts the worst fights, just by picking on someone, and gets all the more angry if the other one will not fight back. When he gets hurt he runs off the playground and goes home to mother.

3. Then there are the fights that come from children who would rather be the boss than have friends. They would like to direct the movements of all their friends. They are power-drunk. Letitia is just such a child. She has few friends for she smothers children by hanging on to them or by teasing them to death. When they try to get away from her she will start a fight. When questioned she is always right and it is the other one who is hurting or bothering her. Lately, Letitia has found no support from me in her fights. Now she is slowly showing a little more imagination in "winning" friends; but she still tries to be the boss.

4. Then there are those fights which are in self-defense. A child may feel justifiably annoyed by some child who behaves in either way described above. Margie has many times hit back when Letitia started a fight. This must be considered as adequate behavior and a natural reaction to provocation.

COMMENT. This analysis was discussed in the teaching class and it was agreed that the description of these four types of fighting was probably correct. It might not always be so simple to decide accurately in which group the child belonged—such "diagnosis" requires skill and experience—but it was felt that the teacher was moving in the right direction by trying to understand the dynamics of the fights. She then presented her *Plan for Action*.

Group Approaches. I have tried several different approaches to fit the different situations, appealing to the whole group. I asked at the time of lining up that only those who could be good neighbors should line up. I let them go down the stairs by themselves to see if they could do it, and I have let the troublesome children be the leaders. When I used this approach, it was generally effective.

C O M M E N T. This indicates that the teacher used some imagination. It really was "an appeal to the whole group." Instead of scolding, she made being a "good neighbor" a desirable goal; she gave the group the responsibility for taking care of itself, which actually implied each one's taking care of the other. Finally, the troublesome child who was seeking status, or at least acceptance, could find both by being a leader; thus the teacher redirected the goal into the useful side. She continues:

We have had group discussions on fighting and how one can change a potential fight into friendly play. These discussions usually cover such items as "why children fight," "how children feel who do fight." We had a dramatic play where one child showed how he turned a fight into a friendship. This approach seems to be best for a lasting effect.

On the playground we have tried games to build a class feeling, to take attention away from personal grudges, to develop in the child a feeling of sportsmanship, and to give vent to his desires to match physical prowess with others.

C O M M E N T. Playground activities of this nature are not unusual; however, using them deliberately to offset strife among the children and to get at the roots of isolation and antagonism is noteworthy. This kind of group discussion which explores and explains purposes is not yet widely used.

Individual Approaches. In regard to the attention getters, I have resisted their efforts to attract my attention. When they wanted another child's attention I said things like, "your friend would like you to look at him." This usually brings a smile.

I have also tried to build alliances for the children who are left out. This is done by reseating and by an appeal to another child to help the one in question.

I have also encouraged the children sometimes to let some of those who are always pestering "have it." It seems to me this is a form of natural consequences. I have made sure that the child in question knew beforehand that he was on his own by letting him overhear my response in this way when a child came complaining about him. In such instances I sometimes just told the child that I would not stop any more of his fights.

COMMENT. The last approach aroused considerable discussion in teaching class. The teacher had maintained previously that sometimes fighting was an adequate reaction to provocation. We all agreed that a child should be able to fight back when attacked, but we questioned the advisability of considering fighting as such as an adequate solution of any conflict. And we questioned particularly the teacher's encouragement of such fights. We felt that her report on the group discussions where other responses to provocation were discussed was a more adequate approach and contradicted somehow her attitude of letting the children fight it out. On the other hand, it was emphasized that fighting does not have to be regarded with such alarm as is often the case. One can be much more casual about a form of interaction as frequent as fights and often not too harmful. It seems to be a cultural pattern to frown upon open expression of hostility, while oblique and subtle hostility is generally tolerated.

The teacher was encouraged and asked to report on future developments. Toward the end of the semester she reported the following results.

I have hardly any fights anymore. I consider this the result of several factors. The games on the playground and the building up of a gentlemen's agreement about how we play together was one. We also had discussed the three goals of showing off, wanting power, and trying to hurt others as revenge, and we did some role-playing in acting them out.

When we discussed the attention getters it was not easy to get the whole group into the discussion. However, they seemed to absorb enough to see that attention could be obtained either through "good" or "bad" behavior, and that one could use this desire for doing useful things. They became sensitive to the constructive and destructive forms of attracting attention.

I was pleased with our discussion of the revengeful child. We had quite a lot of true confessions without any censoring. One boy even admitted that he considered burning the school down to hurt all of us. We had a lot of fun acting this out. At first, I had to play the child in order to get the point across.

It was much easier for the children to recognize the child who always wanted to be boss. They pointed out examples and realized how unpopular this child was. Now when a child has a conflict with someone and comes complaining, we give him several alternatives for settling the conflict, and almost without exception the child chose the most socially accepted one.

C O M M E N T . Unfortunately we have no detailed example of this point although the teacher has submitted some reports included in previous chapters (e.g., Example 16).

CHAPTER 11

Effective Procedures

THE PROJECTS in this chapter demonstrate what a teacher can accomplish with children in a relatively short period of time, even with comparatively little training. Each advanced teacher-student who has had at least one semester in this method submits an outline for discussion, containing a description of a problem that she is currently encountering in school. The outline also contains a tentative evaluation of the dynamic factors involved and a tentative plan of action. Progress reports are presented from time to time to the whole teaching class and discussed there. The reports presented here are final drafts of such projects, with comments and interpretations added for the purpose of this book.

Example 62

Ken is an 8-year-old child in a third-grade class. He poses a problem by not being a part of his classroom group. He is reluctant to join his group, even on the playgrounds. He is extremely quiet. There is no life or sparkle such as one may expect of an 8-year-old. His facial expression never changes. He could easily be forgotten in a large classroom. He sits in his seat like a statue with a blank and oblivious expression. His academic work is poor.

He is under treatment with a speech therapist because, as his record states, he has a severe articulation and voice disorder—"no control of tongue." In order to avoid speaking he simply shakes his head in the negative or the affirmative. The blank look remains on his face as he shakes his head.

His learning grade is classified as low average. He is poor in reading, language, and physical education. He has poor work habits. He works slowly and clumsily.

Background. Ken has two older brothers, Pete, 20, and Dick, 18. The kindergarten records indicate that he wets himself at night. The first-grade teacher recorded: "Ken is mature physically. His social and mental attitude are below average for his age. His citizenship is poor."

The physical education teacher had been quite concerned about him. He suggested taking Ken as a case study. The gym teacher made many attempts to get Ken into the group at play, but invariably Ken ended up at the sidelines, standing with his hands in his pockets or chewing his nails.

Evaluation. In order to find the reason for Ken's maladjustment, I plan to have short talks with him to get a clearer picture of his role within his family group. He is the baby in the family—and apparently is acting the part of a baby to get special services.

Ken is a problem not only in the school situation but also to himself. His infantile actions in school are probably the results of overindulgence and pampering in the home. His behavior would indicate that he attempts to get attention and the services of his teacher in a passive-destructive way, the way he gets it at home.

COMMENT. The teacher may be right—but from the little we know so far Ken may already be beyond the stage of demanding attention, and is demonstrating his utter inability in order to be left alone. A child "who could easily be forgotten" is not demanding attention but getting the reaction he wants: nobody expects anything of him. But the teacher is right in assuming that the position of baby, with two so much older brothers before him, has something to do with his behavior.

Plan of Action. During short private talks I shall try to learn about his feelings toward school, playmates, and his relationship within his family. Consistent encouragement is of utmost importance in developing a feeling of self-confidence. This boy needs friendship, someone to give him worth and treat him as a special friend, not as a problem child.

Incorporating the help of the group may prove rewarding in helping

Ken "to get out of his shell" and feel that he belongs. Calling on him when he is most likely to be prepared will give him status and permit him to feel part of the group by contributing. He needs a few words of praise when he contributes, to have the confidence that he "can do it," with an occasional pat on the shoulder or head when he is contributing or achieving something.

To develop his friendship and his self-respect, he must not be threatened. All conflicts must be avoided. Nagging and scolding for his lack of effort or for his reluctance to recite will only strengthen his passive resistance.

COMMENT. This outline is somewhat general but correct. It emphasizes the obvious discouragement of the boy, the need for avoiding further discouragement, and the stimulation of self-respect.

Follow-up. The first week of school in September a new speech therapist came into the class to screen out speech problems. Ken would not leave his seat to be screened.

COMMENT. This episode was discussed at length in teaching class. Was this a sign of a power contest? The teacher reported that the speech therapist had asked the children to step in front of the class; some teacher-students suggested that Ken might not have been so reluctant to leave his seat if he had been asked to go to the back of the room. He probably would have been more willing to "disappear" than to be conspicuous.

During the first two weeks Ken has done no reciting. He completes his written work in his work book; but when I call on him he simply looks at me with a blank expression.

September 22—Third Week of School. Today Ken came to school with a new colorful flannel shirt. As he picked up his pencil and paper from a table where I was sitting, I said, "I like your shirt, Ken. What pretty colors." He looked at me as though I were a stranger—started toward his desk, then turned around and said, "Thank you." He seemed surprised that I spoke to him.

COMMENT. That was an ingenious approach. What startled the boy was not that the teacher spoke to him but that she pointed out his being conspicuous—and in a positive and pleasant way. He could be noticed without suffering. And this surprise made him thank her explicitly, although belatedly.

September 23. I tried to find out how many children were able to complete a page of addition and subtraction in a specified time. I praised one of these, Ralph, for he had been a "slowpoke" since school started. Ken stood near by. I asked him if he too was able to finish. He did not use his voice; he nodded yes.

September 28. As I sat at the table watching the boys and girls pick up their papers and pencils, Ken leaned over to show me a bandaged arm. I asked him twice before he told me what happened. [I know I should ask only once.]

C O M M E N T. How right the teacher is! Immediately after she did it she realized that she had fallen for his provocation to do something more for him before he would respond. This incident is typical for a child who wants attention and is unwilling to do anything for himself.

When a child recites I remind him to stand at the board until he has good listeners. Ken went to the board, but went to extremes waiting for the class's attention. But he was not passive any more; he pointed the ruler at the child that wasn't giving him his complete attention. Well—there was "life" in that gesture!

And he did recite. Afterwards I asked the class, "Did anyone notice if Ken made any mistakes?" All agreed that he made no errors. Then I asked, "How many think that Ken did a nice job of working his problems and reciting?" Ken showed quite some interest in their reaction by looking at the hands as they went up.

C O M M E N T. The report does not suggest why Ken was suddenly willing to recite. But it was important that the teacher not only praised Ken for his accomplishment but asked the class to express their approval. In this way Ken could feel accepted by the group.

Today a new boy came to our school from another state. I placed him across from Ken, and asked Ken if he would like the job of helping Shelly around the building during the day, and helping him in the classroom. Ken nodded yes, but did not attempt to help Shelly head his paper or show him the page we were working on. Later, however, I saw Ken sitting with Shelly and showing him in his clumsy way how to fold his paper into eight columns.

Ken did not do a good job with Shelly on the playground. The gym teacher found Shelly on the sidelines. But Ken did show Shelly where the washroom was and where to line up for his next class.

C O M M E N T . Our discussion of this episode with the teacher-student pointed out how this opportunity to feel that he knew a little more than the new boy might have been the crucial step that made Ken ready to recite in front of the class. The teacher reported that she almost made the mistake of helping Shelly when she saw that Ken had fallen down on his job, but she stopped herself at the last moment and let Ken do as much as he could.

September 29. I have attempted to give Ken board work where he has the opportunity to recite before the class and, therefore, to contribute. I do not detect a severe speech defect. His presentation is in a kind of lazy and monotonous tone. I am inclined to think it is due to lack of practice in speaking.

Today I started to select my October classroom monitor. I asked for hands indicating which ones wanted jobs. When I saw Ken's hand I asked him which job he wanted. He wants to be Captain Slip Monitor. That is a good job for him. He is responsible for seeing that the captain slip is taken to his various teachers, and finally getting it in to the office at the end of the day. In the morning he is to bring it back to his register teacher.

Ken is not consistent in shaping his "m's." Sometimes he has two hills and other times three. Apparently he doesn't believe in rules; he believes in doing things one way one time and another way another time.

C O M M E N T . This is characteristic of children who are poor spellers and poor writers. Here we have, besides, a child who is a poor "doer" in anything.

He wants me to notice him in the hall. He manages to come close to where I am standing. I usually nod my head. I winked at him a few times. He just looked.

September 30. Today I got the surprise of my life. I was in the hall as usual during passing time. Ken came down the hall, saw me watching him, stopped dead in his tracks for a moment—and winked at me. The antics this child went through made me feel that this was the first time he had ever attempted to wink.

C O M M E N T . It speaks for the psychological perceptivity of the teacher that she realized the significance of Ken's *doing* anything to get attention. This is a shift from a passive to an active approach regardless of how minimal and insignificant the extent of the movement.

The speech therapist was in our building today and had Ken in her office. She thinks Ken does not have much of a speech problem, but is just a "baby" and does not want to talk. He does have a slight difficulty in making some letter sounds, but nothing serious. The therapist will help him if he cooperates, but feels that the boy is dull, and she would rather spend her time with a cooperative, average child.

C O M M E N T . This finding, as opposed to the diagnosis of the first speech therapist, confirms the teacher's impression. Could it be that the speech impediment has changed since the first therapist made his diagnosis?

October 1. Today as were were lining up I noticed Ken's zipper only halfway up as he came out of the washroom. Another half-done job to induce service! I whispered to him to go back to the washroom to complete the job.

C O M M E N T . In this laudable approach, the teacher did not say "zip your zipper," which would have been the reaction Ken was begging; nor did she say anything in front of the other children which would have humiliated him. She gave him the responsibility for taking care of himself.

During recitation I am now calling often on Ken. On several occasions he volunteered by raising his hand. He started his Captain Slip Monitor job today. He did very well. He waved the slip in front of me to let me see that he wasn't forgetting to take it from one teacher to the other.

C O M M E N T . He still shows how much attention he wants—but he is moving from a passive to an active approach, from the useless to a useful one.

October 5—Fifth Week of School. Ken can manage to be the first one to finish his arithmetic assignment. I let him place his problems on the board while the others finished.

COMMENT. It is now becoming apparent how ambitious the boy is. Who would have suspected such a drive to be first in a boy who had been so completely passive and inconspicuous? Again we note the teacher's sensitivity. She immediately seized the opportunity to accentuate his being first with his assignment.

The girl Captain Slip Monitor forgot the captain's slip this morning. Ken brought it up to her. He let me know that she forgot it and that he had brought it up. So far he has been a fine Captain Slip Monitor.

COMMENT. Another example of Ken's ambition. He is trying to be ahead of the others and to make sure that it is noticed.

Last week I wrote "good" on Ken's spelling paper and I drew a smiling face because he made 100. He told me he was going to tell his mother about it. Today he reported that he had shown it to his mother and his mother showed it to his father, and his two brothers had a peek at it too.

COMMENT. The desire for attention is obvious—and Ken's ability to get it. However, this is probably the first time that he has been commended.

October 6. While we were passing our materials in arithmetic class, I saw Ken for the first time in mischief. He was hanging over his desk, pestering the boy in front of him, who in turn was hitting Ken on the head with a pencil. This is the first real sign of "life" I have seen in Ken.

COMMENT. There are probably few teachers who would be as delighted in seeing a boy in mischief. But the teacher is right: for Ken this is progress. He can assert himself, he can be active, even if this activity is not always constructive.

October 11. Ken did nothing for several days. He did not speak and simply shook his head yes or no. I examined what I had done. I did not give him any board work where he would have an opportunity to recite. I deliberately did not call on him unless he volunteered—and he did not volunteer.

It seems that Ken did not attempt to contribute on his own unless he got the extra attention he desired. This indicates that he still could not count on himself without being dependent on someone else.

C O M M E N T . It is crucial that the teacher examined what she had done when the boy did not function well. It may not have been her fault, since the boy was exposed to other influences, many of which might be detrimental and discouraging. But it pays to analyze what one may have done without realizing it. And in this case the teacher found the answer.

She had decided to stop giving Ken special attention and wait for his own contributions, because she was correctly afraid that he depended too much on her praise, that she might be stimulating his overambition unduly by letting him be the first. This danger existed, without doubt. But she found out that she had moved ahead too fast. The boy still needed considerable special attention before he could be weaned. Of course, it needed to be obtained in a constructive way. Her premature withdrawal may account also for the mischief previously mentioned. However, Ken was not even courageous enough to continue his mischief to get special attention, and instead withdrew again into passivity.

October 13. The children recited a Hallowe'en poem. Ken was called upon when he raised his hand. He recited in a monotone voice, but did a nice job. When he was through, he walked to the back of the room where I was sitting, instead of going to his seat. Apparently he was looking for further approval. Or was he, perhaps, rebelling against order?

C O M M E N T . We can assume that it was this reaching out for the teacher which prompted Ken to go to her instead of returning to his seat. But it is wise of her to keep her mind open and consider other possibilities also. At this point, she does not say that it was rebellion against order; she merely makes a mental note, watching the development to see whether there is such a trend.

October 14. Again Ken brought not only the boy's captain slip but also the girl's. And again he let me know that the girl had forgotten to bring hers. Another example of how he is looking for approval.

October 15. Today I did not wait for Ken to volunteer the answers, but I called on him. When he realized that I had called on him, he looked at me dumbfounded; he sat looking at me with his mouth open and jaw hanging. He looked stupid. As I waited for his answer, the class was getting impatient; they started to point to their books. He finally realized he was to recite. His answers were correct. He knew what was expected of him, but was seeking an additional reminder, without getting one.

COMMENT. Again the teacher resisted falling for his "stupid look" and refrained from comment or pressure. The class pressure was sufficient. And when Ken realized that no additional move was forthcoming from the teacher, he complied.

October 20. I checked Ken's arithmetic book. Problems he did not feel like doing, he omitted completely. He didn't read his directions carefully. For instance, when he was to count by 2's, he counted by 5's or 1's. When the problems involved writing, his writing was poor in some cases. This seems to indicate rebellion against order, doing things as he pleases.

COMMENT. The teacher is watching for confirmation of her assumption. She is probably on the right track. As Ken becomes more courageous, his rebellion against his unfavorable position in his own family may become open. One has to watch for that.

Today the office girl and I watched Ken on the playground, standing on the sidelines biting his nails, occasionally jumping into the games, but jumping right out. The office girl commented, "He just doesn't seem to know how to play."
It seems to me that Ken wants to be a real boy, but feels he isn't. I have the impression that he feels defeated by his two older brothers, one who runs a service station, and the other who does a man's job of repairing cars in a garage next door. His father works in the garage too.

COMMENT. This is an excellent demonstration of the difference between a psychologically untrained observer and a trained one. All the office girl could see was that Ken doesn't seem to know how to play. This is true enough. But the teacher immediately searched for a possible reason for such behavior. Maybe he does not feel he is a man—and immediately her mind wanders to the other three men in the family, a father and two much older brothers. He is male also, but he cannot compare with them.

November 3. Ken was absent yesterday. When I asked him why he was absent he said, "I was waking my mother at night. I was sick."

C O M M E N T . This is a significant remark. Apparently, it was less important for Ken that he was sick than that he could awaken his mother. This is his way of finding a place in his family, through being small, helpless, or sick.

November 4. I had a short chat with Ken while the class was working. I asked him what he did after school. "I go to the store for my mother." I asked him if he played football or other games with the boys in the neighborhood; "No." He said he watched his brothers at work. I asked him how he got along with his brothers. He fights with them. I asked why; he didn't know. What did he fight about? He couldn't tell. It was time to recite, and I had learned nothing more at this time.

Next hour, while expecting my class, I was in the hall early. Ken came early too from his gym class to wash his hands. I asked him to sit on the bench with me. "You told me the first hour that you had fights with your brothers, and I have been wondering what you were fighting about." He looked at me, but said nothing. Then I asked him what his brothers did (knowing it well) and he told me all about the service station and the garage. And then he volunteered, "My brothers call me *Stupid*."

C O M M E N T . One can visualize Ken pestering his brothers and they pushing him down. He preferred to watch his brothers at work to playing with the neighborhood boys. Despite his unpleasant relationship with his brothers, he accepted this relationship as his sphere of life.

Education Week. I finally had an opportunity to talk with Ken's mother when she came to our PTA meeting. She talked very little. Asked about Ken's activities after school, she said there were no children in the block with whom Ken could play. She showed much interest in Cub Scouts which were listed in our school newspaper; she asked me to find some boy who could get Ken interested in it. Maybe I could ask a boy to pick Ken up at home to go to the meeting. (Obviously the mother is overprotective and wants me to do something for Ken as she does.)

I asked her about the relationship between Ken and his brothers. She complained about the great difference in their ages. When I said that the brothers called him stupid she showed an expression of resentment. "They only kid"—but then she went on to say that she had talked to them about it. That was all.

Her main complaint about the school work was his poor handwriting. I explained to her the difficulty in changing from manuscript printing to cursive writing.

COMMENT. That is all the teacher reports about her conversation with the mother. It is interesting that this conversation was as unproductive as was her talk with Ken. She did not get much information from either. But she spotted the mother's overprotective attitude. She sensed some conflict between the mother and the brothers, but she did not pursue the issue. She might have been more persistent in her questioning, but maybe the attitude of the mother was too forbidding to make further probing feasible.

November 16. Today Ken showed me a new watch. He simply held out his arm—not saying anything. I liked the watch, and thinking of getting one for my son, I asked him where it was bought. His answer was "a store." Only after I questioned him for a while did he tell me what store it was. I asked him to keep me informed as to how well it kept time because I wanted a similar one for my son.

COMMENT. It was good to give him such an assignment, but it was not so good to press him for an answer. When he first answered "a store," some explanatory comment on the reason for his short and noncommital answer would have been preferable to the pressure for more detail. So far, there is no evidence that the teacher interpreted to him his avoidance of saying one word more than he chose.

It is also questionable whether she should have said anything when the boy merely held out his arm. It might have been better to answer also with gestures. That could have been in fun and not a reprimanding, and would have shown him what he was doing.

This afternoon Ken brushed up against me with a jacket on his arm. He didn't say anything, but indicated by his action that he wanted me to see his jacket. It was new. I didn't talk with him about it. I was talking to a teacher at the moment, and simply nodded that I saw it.

COMMENT. This was a better response.

Several weeks ago he got a new bike. I asked him today why he was getting all these things, wondering whether they were birthday presents. He said no, and continued, "I don't know why she [mother] is buying me all these things. I guess she just wants to." I was wondering whether Ken was being showered with gifts because he was improving.

COMMENT. Another possibility is the mother's resentment against the way Ken is treated by his brothers, which she may see more clearly now. And she may be trying to make up for that. It could well be that she is in alliance with Ken against the three strong men, and holding on to him as a baby who still needs her.

November 17. I asked an older Cub Scout to take Ken to a meeting. I brought a copy of the Cub Scouting book to Ken, and he examined it with interest.

COMMENT. Although the teacher is doing things for Ken, we have no indication of her doing so in an overprotective manner.

November 19. We have been making maps on pieces of glass, out of flour, salt, and water. Ken showed much interest. He kept walking to the back of the room to watch others mixing their dough and coloring it with vegetable dyes. He asked if he could stir some of the batter to make it smooth. Even while working at his seat, he would "sneak" to the back to see how things were progressing, while others were working at a back table.

Despite his obvious interest, I wondered if he would ask for a piece of glass, flour, and salt to make a map of his own. He did not for several days. Only when I suggested that the Cub Scouts could take their maps to earn arrow points did Ken finally announce that he was going to buy a piece of glass. He, too, wanted to earn arrow points.

COMMENT. We can see the teacher's interest in stimulating Ken and at the same time her patient waiting for him to come around. He is still waiting for stimulation and offers of reward before he moves into action, even if he is interested. It is obvious that he believes others can do things and all he can do is get a vicarious satisfaction from their achievement.

The gym teacher asked Ken why he didn't have gym shoes when he was getting a new watch, a new jacket, and a new bike. He answered that he had gym shoes at home but didn't bring them to school. It seems that Ken is still trying to avoid gym activity which would show him as not being a real boy.

End of November. Ken had joined the Cub Scouts. He brought two cigar boxes to make a shadow box for his mother. He painted them, and is going to take them to his next Scout meeting to earn points, before giving it to his mother for Christmas. The paint job he did wasn't neat, but I was happy to see that he went to the trouble to scout around for cigar boxes and bring them to school. However, he has not brought his piece of glass for a map thus far.

C O M M E N T . How careful the teacher is in avoiding any possible discouragement by criticizing the paint job or questioning his working on the cigar box instead of bringing his piece of glass.

Ken's grades for the first ten weeks indicate satisfactory work in arithmetic, spelling, reading, and the arts and crafts. He needs to improve in self-expression, social living, music, science, auditorium, speech, and gym.

December 1. Ken used to lag into the classroom when school started in September. Now he is usually the first one in. He is more friendly, hangs over the desk, and chats with me about himself and his family.

He is most anxious to help me to prepare the back table for project work. He is not avoiding his academic work by helping with the project, but enjoys project work genuinely.

Yesterday four children were cutting crepe paper to make crepe clay with salt, flour, and water. After the four had worked hard I asked them to choose someone else to take their places. Ken had his hand up high to be chosen, and was by one of the boys.

Ken does fine work in arithmetic. He and other fast workers have been given the opportunity to work easy fourth-grade problems in a fourth-grade book. (This is a third-grade class.)

C O M M E N T . Quite a change within three months from a boy who was completely withdrawn to one who is ahead in his arithmetic. One cannot assume any more that he is dull.

The principal, who stops in occasionally, noticed Ken working with a group in the back. She expressed her wish that he could stay with this class all day, but he needs the other subjects. (He spends three hours with me doing his academic work in my classes.)

December 9. Other teachers in the building are noticing that Ken is participating more in his group. In fact today he had a fight, a good old-fashioned boy-to-boy tussle, in gym class. He made his glass map last week, and plans to give it to his older brother for Christmas. He's told me three times that he was going to give it to his older brother. Apparently Ken and his older brother are in an alliance against the middle brother.

C O M M E N T . The teacher's plausible interpretation of Ken's alliance with his older brother might be important if one could reach the older brother to help with Ken's development.

December 17. Today is very cold. Ken came to class excited and full of pep. Four other boys came at the same time. In a *real loud* voice Ken said, "There are only five boys in class." That's the loudest voice I have heard from Ken since September.

C O M M E N T . The type of voice a child uses is often extremely significant, expressing his self-concept and his approach to life.

While he was working some arithmetic problems which involved reading, he came to me for help on a word. I asked him to work it out for himself. As he walked back to his seat he stopped at another boy's desk and asked him what the word was. He still wants the service of others. I did not give him the word because I knew he had come to me simply to put me into his service. During reading class he works out words easily.

C O M M E N T . The teacher did not say what she did, or whether she did anything, when Ken asked the other boy. We can assume that she made no comment, because making a fuss would not have improved the situation. Then Ken really would have gotten the attention he wanted. However, it would be advisable not to let such incidents go by entirely, particularly in this stage of development, but to have a private talk with Ken about what he was doing and why.

December 18. Again Ken came to me for help with a written problem. I asked him to read the problem to me; he did. By the time he had finished he gave me the answer immediately. Again he didn't need help—he wanted the services of others.

C O M M E N T . This seems to be a general pattern in this case: Whenever the teacher refrains from giving help, Ken no longer needs it.

Today Ken had completed his assignment and was looking for a book to read. I gave him a poetry book from which I often read to the class.

When he returned it he asked me to read a poem he liked. After reciting and collection of the materials I told the class that Ken had found a poem that he liked and asked me to read it to the class. I asked them if they would like to hear it. They assented—and enjoyed it very much; in fact they asked for more.

COMMENT. This was a nice way of integrating Ken into the group. He stimulated it himself.

Ken asked to take the poetry book home over the Christmas holidays. The Christmas present he gave me was wrapped by himself. It had scotch tape all over it. He had addressed the card to me, but his writing was covered by another card signed by an adult. His mother probably thought he had not written it neatly enough, so she covered it and wrote herself.

COMMENT. This shows the training he had received at home. Nothing he did was good enough. And the mother has not changed. This would be an assignment for the teacher.

Ken's behavior in the hall, passing from class to class, is quite different now in December than it was in September. He comes down the hall swinging his coat around his head, taking long, although awkward, steps, and not following all walking rules to the letter. We have lines marked on the floors to keep hall traffic moving smoothly. Ken has attempted to walk right on top of the line—or slightly on the wrong side of it. He talks in the hall which he never did. This is permitted between classes if it isn't noisy.

January 5. Ken asked for the poetry book again, and again, when returning it, wanted one to be read to the class. He asked for a poetry book to take home, and I gave him one he hadn't seen before.

Ken's den mother at scouting told me that he enjoys coming to the meetings and is a good helper. She visited me in class one day and he came up and stood next to us. She bragged about Ken in front of us, that he was one of her best helpers. He likes her. She gives him a pat on the head—but she tells me she "shoves" him into activities too.

COMMENT. The teacher is sensitive—and correctly so—about another adult's unwarranted pressure on Ken. This is the more detrimental since it not only prevents the boy from standing on his own feet but may also push him into more rebellion and resistance.

Since the end of the semester was approaching, the teacher summarized the development of this case.

Ken has found his place within his group. He has learned to smile and to take a part in group activities. He no longer sits "like a dummy." He "chimes in" often, always ready and willing to help.

He no longer waits for others to do things for him—only occasionally falling back into his previous pattern, but even then more active in his bid for service. But he is willing to help when the occasion arises. One day he helped the children to select books, and offered his services. He asks if he can pass out material.

He shows much interest in his work, is always anxious to look on the board to see what the assignment is for the period. He completes his lesson quickly—and correctly, too. He is interested in reading stories and poems, and enjoys sharing them with his classmates.

He is no longer afraid to talk to me or his friends in class. And he has some real friends, friends that select him to take their places as monitors, for instance. In December he was selected Book Monitor—and he is on his toes to be right there to collect the books when the discussion period is over.

Cub Scouting has done a great deal for Ken.

His handwriting is still poor, but has improved by leaps and bounds. His reading and arithmetic work is very good, and it has become obvious how ambitious a boy he is.

The gym teacher reports a great change in Ken's gym activities— even having real tussles with his classmates.

The speech therapist tells me that Ken is a changed boy. He does not hesitate to come into the clinic for therapy, and is cooperative there. "Ken is a changed boy, not the boy I met in September," said the speech therapist. Apparently she changed her mind about his being dull.

I have learned a valuable lesson from Ken—a case study I was going to drop like a hot potato when I did not get a peep out of him for weeks. The first two weeks I was completely discouraged—and did not see where I could ever be of any help to this boy.

Now we are real friends, and I think our friendship has brought a closer relationship between the school and his parents.

COMMENT. This case shows how much a classroom teacher can do if she understands the child's motivations and knows the methods of counteracting his mistaken goals.

While the results of this case are gratifying, there is still more that can be done. One has the impression that Ken is still managing too often to put his teacher into his service.

Example 63

The Problem. Betty is a bright and ambitious girl, 16½ years old, and a senior in high school. She has had difficulty getting along with her classmates for at least 4 years. Although she worries about the fact that they don't like her, she does things to antagonize them and gives the impression of feeling superior. A number of teachers have tried to reach her, but claim that it is impossible to get her to see where she is wrong. Since she is a member of the Honor Society which I sponsor, I have been asked many times to talk to her about her tardiness, loitering in the halls, and outbursts of temper. I would like to help her learn to solve her problems, for she is interested in teaching and may have difficulties in college that may discourage her from continuing her education.

Background. Betty is the younger of two. Tom, two years older, graduated last year and is in college on an athletic scholarship. Betty has had much better grades all the way and has been a conformer—the teacher's pet. In her sophomore year we had a discussion and Betty complained that she had to obey rules, such as piano practice, and getting home by a certain time, while her brother "could get by with murder." Last year Betty complained whenever she did not get an A, but her mother did not sympathize and she came back the next day as if nothing had happened. It seems that her mother had succeeded in the past in forcing Betty to obey, but now she has little luck and gets so upset when Betty gets into trouble that she "doesn't know what to do."

In the lower grades Betty always volunteered to do things for teachers. Her classmates resented her helping out in the office and in grading papers. Valentine's Day this year has been the first that she did not receive a "rub" for being teacher's pet. Last year I talked to her a number of times and she seemed to be more pleasant with her classmates. In fact, she was elected cheer leader at the end of last year. However, she was not satisfied and wanted several other offices in clubs. When the Honor Society elected officers, she was absent and afterwards she was very much disappointed. She told some of the students they should have postponed the meeting. Later a business club was being organized, and she was so anxious that she nominated herself. The girls laughed and proceeded to nominate someone else.

Evaluation. It seems that Betty's goal is attention getting, and that in some areas she is in a power contest with adults. Some teachers think that Betty considers them as too idealistic and cannot understand that high school could be fun. She has the notion that to be somebody one must always be on top. She is a poor loser in contests. Often she tries to get attention by acting loud and silly. She has often wanted to transfer to another school, and feels that it would make her friends happy. Her father has insisted on her staying.

COMMENT. The evaluation describes more problems than it evaluates. There is much more that we would like to know about Betty, although we know a great deal. She surpassed her brother scholastically. Her social adjustment suffered from her overambition and desire to gain intellectual, and perhaps even moral, superiority. One wonders whether her brother, not driven as she was by such high standards and ambitions, was socially better adjusted, more popular, and better liked, which may have in turn discouraged Betty's confidence in her social relationships. It would be important to know her relationships to mother and father, with which of the two she sided, and who stimulated her ambition. So far, we have no clear indication of a power contest with adults, although both her achievements and her failures may be more than a bid for attention.

Plan of Action
1. Win her.
2. Encourage her.
3. Try to get her to see that it is unnecessary and impossible to be on top at all times.
4. Natural consequences.

COMMENT. This is a good general outline, but not sufficiently specific, with the exception of point 3. The girl seems unsure of her place in the group; otherwise she would not direct herself so much toward the teacher and toward her superiority. What are the reasons? Why is she so discouraged, particularly socially?

February 5. I saw Betty in the hall during her sewing period, talking with one of the basketball boys. Later I met her upstairs and asked why she was there. She said she was up to see the guidance teacher. I found it was not true and decided to have a talk with her, as many teachers had been complaining about her doing as she pleases. She always pretended she was not doing anything wrong. I found out that she had been upset over several incidents in the past week. Several boys had skipped school and were caught. The rumor got around that Betty had reported them, and when the class began to accuse her, she "threw a fit," banging the piano keys a dozen times.

Betty told me about this and cried. She said no one would now speak to her. Everything seemed to happen to her, and the harder she tried the more the kids disliked her. She said even teachers misunderstood her. I told her that perhaps she was trying too hard and that it might be helpful to stop and analyze what she does to create this "wrong impression." I told her I would be glad to talk it over with her if she wished.

That night she was upset and told her parents that all the teachers were against her too. She did not come to class the first period the next day.

C O M M E N T . This was a good beginning—not too much and not too little. The teacher did not preach or scold but offered a program of help. That was all she could do at the time; but it had to be said and done even if the girl resented this personal "intrusion."

February 8. Betty came in early. She had been taking a scholarship exam the last two days, so I asked her if it was difficult. She nodded. Later she came up for paper and stopped to look at some pictures on the desk, making some comments. This seemed to break the ice. I gave the class some transcriptions knowing that Betty did well on them. Then I told the girls with the best scores, including Betty, that they were doing well and, therefore, might work more on dictation while the rest practiced transcription. Betty was pleased, and proceeded to improve her work the next few days.

C O M M E N T . This was good, as far as establishing a good relationship was concerned, but so far there was no follow-up to the first talk. Perhaps the teacher sensed Betty's reluctance.

February 13. Betty was late. She came running in with her note, saying, "This is the *last* time."

C O M M E N T . Although there is some indication of the girl's friendly attitude, the development is still slow. Half a month has already passed since the original talk. Apparently the teacher wanted to wait until the girl came of her own volition.

February 25. The class ranks were distributed. Betty was fifth. The salutatorian was a junior who had enough credits to graduate by taking additional summer work. There was some talk that this was not fair, although the girl ranking third did not seem to complain. Betty took it upon herself to campaign in the third-ranking girl's cause, and there was talk that the community was petitioning a reconsideration. This was stopped by a class meeting at which regulations pertaining to ranking were explained. Betty had gained new friends through this.

C O M M E N T . That was one instance where fighting against "unfairness" brought not enemies but friends, where sitting in judgment was not provocative. But for Betty this was not a good lesson. Too bad that the teacher did not point out to her that the good result should not mislead her.

March 1. Betty stopped me in the hall and asked if I wouldn't talk to Jane, who—she thought—had started a rumor about her and the boys. I asked her if she was worried that others would believe it. No, she didn't care. But she and Jane had been rivals for some time. She said nothing more to me about this.

C O M M E N T . The girl almost asked for a talk, but apparently the teacher was still operating merely on point 1 of her plan for action, namely, trying to win Betty.

March 5. I called Betty out of her sewing class to arrange for another scholarship exam. She came out with a suspicious smile and said, "Is this going to be good or bad news?" I laughed, and she seemed to be relieved.

C O M M E N T . We can see the policy and concern of the teacher: to overcome Betty's suspicion of all teachers. She is certainly succeeding in establishing a friendly relationship, but so far not in utilizing it.

March 13. Betty came early to make up the rest of her time. When she checked with me I remarked that we were now squared up, and she added jokingly, "if I don't come late tomorrow." She then asked if there was any chance of getting an A for this period. She said she wanted to make straight A's to prove to her mother she could still do it.

COMMENT. The teacher has succeeded by now in winning the girl's cooperation, but she has not attempted to change her outlook. However, one should not overlook the implied encouragement and consequently increased self-confidence which the girl experienced during this period.

On April 2 the case was brought up for discussion at teaching class. The teacher-student was commended for having broken the pattern of Betty's other teachers, reproaching her for her wrong-doings. The dynamics of the case were discussed. Betty is paying the price for having tried successfuly to be better than her older brother—and hence to be better than anyone else. She seems to have envied his ability to do as he pleased. If she cannot be specially good and get recognition for it, then her desire to do as she pleases becomes apparent.

She looks down on classmates and teachers. Her fantasy of being a perfect schoolteacher expresses her criticism of her teachers. Her action in nominating herself shows her apparent belief that she is the best one, and if no one else knows it, she will show them. Her interest in being on top is exceeded by her desire to sit in judgment. Both can be accomplished by becoming a teacher.

The teacher has succeeded in winning her over. She should continue her discussions with Betty. The teacher confirmed the impression that she was reluctant to do so without waiting for Betty's request, because the girl appeared so defeated the night after the first talk. It was pointed out that Betty actually made some advances which were not recognized as such; and that the teacher could safely go ahead now and help Betty to see that it is not necessary always to be right. Since Betty overreached herself because she felt utterly defeated if she was not completely right, she must learn the *courage to be imperfect*. It would be wise for the teacher to tell her that she did not understand her yet fully and that the punishment of making up time was perhaps not necessary. And, most important, she must provide Betty with the experience of being liked and having a place even if she was wrong. She must learn that even criticism did not mean that people did not like her.

April 16. When I arrived in the morning Betty came in saying that she has been here since 10 minutes before the hour. She was indicating that she was making up time.

During the second period that day, I went into her bookkeeping class. While I was with her teacher she came and interrupted us to ask me a question in bookkeeping. I pretended that I thought she was talking to her teacher and waited; but she looked at me for an answer. After she left, he told me that he had explained the problem to her before, but she didn't seem to accept it. He is teaching bookkeeping for the first time, and I had had the class before. Now Betty is critical of his inexperience. Later when I talked to her about this she seemed to realize his predicament but not that she had hurt his feelings in the above incident.

That afternoon I decided to talk with Betty. I asked her if she had given any more thought to the things we had discussed before—why she was having difficulties with her friends and teachers. She was slow to respond. Then she said everything seemed to be going along better. She gave as the reason that she and Jane were no longer friends. Even her mother noticed the difference since they were never together.

C O M M E N T. It is possible that Jane exerted a bad influence on her, although we have no indication for it. However it is more probable that the improved relationship with the teacher was responsible for Betty's improvement; but she did not know it and would have probably hesitated to admit it. Such an admission would have implied that she had been at war before and her difficulties were her own fault.

I mentioned that I was worried about her repeated tardiness, even though she made up her time. I said I felt that this method of making up wasn't working. She replied, "Oh, I think it has. I now get up early from force of habit. The last time, I was up a long time, but after Mom left for work I dozed off." I told her that it seemed to me as if we were just playing a game to see who would win. She smiled. I explained to her that things such as tardiness are not just accidental. There are always reasons behind them, and I wondered if she might be able to see them. She didn't respond. I said that these might be the same reasons that she has had for doing things that annoy her friends and, therefore, would be worth discovering.

"You have wanted to be a teacher for a long time. I believe you have some ideas about teaching—I know I had when I was in high school. You probably know pretty much in your own mind what teachers do that is right and wrong." She smiled and said, "But I don't express them." I proceeded, "I used to think the same, and when I look back now it is true that I avoid some of the errors of my teachers; but I also make mistakes they didn't. It's impossible to be perfect." I told her that although she didn't express her opinions, they were as obvious as if she did. If she expected her teachers to be perfect and her classmates to be perfect she could never be satisfied with them, and therefore would make them feel that she felt superior. One's attitude affects one's behavior. She said, "Oh, but I don't think I am superior." I said, "I know you don't, but that's the impression you give."

As an example I brought up the incident about the bookkeeping problem. We talked some about it, but I didn't feel I got anywhere. We concluded the conversation on the idea that perfection is impossible and unnecessary, and that we must accept ourselves and other people as imperfect. I also stated that I was glad to see that she had progressed so much in gaining new friendships and that she was so much happier. I assured her that she had great possibilities and that college would be a lot of fun.

C O M M E N T . This discussion was handled well. There was perhaps some preaching and not enough opportunity for the girl to express herself and her opinions, an opportunity which she might not have used at that time anyhow. She was still defensive. This is the reason why the teacher felt that she did not convince the girl.

There was one important moment when the teacher missed the point. When Betty could not see that she felt superior, it was correct to retort that she gave the impression, but the teacher should have explained why she could not see how superior she acted. At this moment it could have been indicated that she herself could not live up to her demands of perfection. And since she never was sure that she was good enough, she did not really feel superior, she merely pushed others down in order to elevate herself. In other words, it was essential for the girl to recognize the extent of her inferiority feelings and her doubt about her own adequacy. Mistaken compensatory measures cannot be eliminated as long as the source, the nagging doubt in herself, is not removed.

For this reason, the manner of terminating this interview was excellent. It implied encouragement and faith in the girl. Remedial measures should be directed first toward trying to raise the self-confidence of the child, rather than toward the elimination of transgressions. It is this effort of the teacher which characterizes all her dealings with this girl and which constitutes an effective corrective approach.

April 22. Making arrangements to rehearse for the honor society induction we ran into conflicting plans for that period. Betty was in favor of telling the other teacher how wrong he was. "We made our plans first. He knew about it; he always does things like that. I'll *tell* him." I said that wasn't wise. This incident showed me that she was still "looking down" at people.

C O M M E N T . The teacher is right. Since she recognized what went on, perhaps she communicated this to the girl. Sometimes little signs or slight insinuations furnish as much information as a talk, provided the two understand each other, as these two undoubtedly do.

May 7—Report Card Day. Betty was late. As she came in she said, "Yes, I know; what a day to come late. But you have to give me credit for not being late for the past four or five weeks." (I later checked the record, which confirmed her statement.) I gave no answer, just smiled.

May 8. We were checking yesterday's transcript and I made a mistake in marking the papers wrong where I had not dictated a word. Betty said, "You are beginning to slip, Miss ———." "Beginning?" I remarked. We went on with something else. I was trying to get her used to the idea that everyone makes mistakes.

May 12. Betty scored in the third quartile on the national scholarship test. After talking about it she said, "Oh well, there were still a lot below me." She didn't seem disappointed.

May 13. Betty's attitude seems to have changed. She seems to show more respect. I cannot give any particular example or incident; she merely seems to display a feeling of warmth. She smiled a lot more today.

May 19. Betty came a bit early to discuss a job which I mentioned to her earlier. She asked me if she could use my name for reference.

May 28—Conclusions. I feel very much satisfied with Betty's improvement. She still has many things to learn, but seems to be moving in the right direction. There are a number of girls and boys who now like her, and she makes few bids for attention. She also now comes on time. She has made plans for college for the summer without advertising them, as she did when she first got the idea early this year. I feel my talks with her "rang the bell" somewhat.

COMMENTS. Comparing the last incident with the description of Betty made in the beginning indicates the progress she has made. And one cannot doubt that it was the consistent effort of the teacher which brought about the change. According to her original plan for action she succeeded in both winning Betty and encouraging her. One can assume that the teacher has succeeded in her third goal also, helping Betty to see that it is not necessay to be on top all the time. The girl's reaction to her score on the scholarship test would indicate that. There was little evidence of the teacher's use of natural consequences. But on the other hand, the teacher had succeeded in overcoming the girl's feeling of social inferiority, as witnessed by her increasing number of friends and better relationships with them. Greater skill in conducting interviews, which is so essential for teachers of adolescent students, could have further increased the teacher's effectiveness.

Example 64

This is an English class consisting of twenty-five sophomores; it meets the last hour of the day when both teacher and pupils are tired. Except for a minority who prepare their lessons beforehand and work during the class period, the group is noisy and works only under pressure.

The range of ability is greater than in a normal class, extending from students who are superior to those who are barely literate. Particularly the retarded members show a passive-destructive behavior pattern. Bernie, a big boy, seeks and gets attention through loud and irrelevant comments. His father has set up impossible intellectual goals, and he is out to prove his inadequacy (which is not entirely assumed). Another focus of disorder is bright but emotionally disturbed Alice. Unhappy at home, she frequently lapses into a dream world, coming out of it with a loud surprised "huh?" or a guffaw. She does not seem to resent derogatory remarks from other pupils, since any attention is better than none.

I give Alice constructive outlets for her desire for attention. For instance, she gets to write assignments on the board since she has a fine hand. (This idea occurred to me after she had filled the board during the intermission with "Mary loves John," etc.) She seems almost pathetically eager to please me, but she continues to be a center of disturbance.

We have here a tired, discouraged class and a tired, discouraged teacher. Both need to feel the joy of accomplishment. No doubt, the discouraged members of the class should be given assignments they can do and be complimented for accomplishment. A unit system with low minima and graded optional assignments might work here.

C O M M E N T . This is the report as it was read to the teaching class. Various aspects were discussed. The teacher-student's use of the word "irrelevant" in describing Bernie's remarks was criticized first. They were perhaps logically irrelevant, but certainly not from a psychological point of view. Bernie's wisecracks seemed to indicate a desire to defeat the teacher, to show superiority. He probably is continuing in the classroom the power contest he has with his father. He defeats both by his display of inadequacy, and thus excludes himself from functioning in the area in which he cannot get glory. He might be overambitious, but only on the useless side. The teacher was, therefore, advised to assign him a project which might give him glory. English lends itself easily to such a project.

Then we discussed the question of a unit system. It was decided that such an approach would eliminate any chance to create a group feeling in this class. The wide range of ability was another obstacle. But without group integration there could be no satisfactory class procedure. Under these adverse conditions one could not continue with ordinary methods; the situation called for imagination. And the first task of the teacher was to find a way of integrating the class and winning interest and cooperation.

The teacher was inclined to give up. The odds were too great against winning cooperation, much less stimulating enthusiasm. And there was nothing the pupils had in common.

Was there really nothing they had in common? When this question was posed to the teacher-students, they pondered it—and finally had an idea. Of course, the class had something important in common, and the teacher had already mentioned it without realizing the significance of her statement. They had a class at the last hour of the day, and their interests and abilities were so divergent that it seemed almost impossible to work together. They all were in the same boat, that is what they had in common. Their common problem was, therefore, how to make this experience as pleasant as possible for all concerned. Such a proposition should catch their fancy, wake them up, and stir up some enthusiasm. Because if they did not do something about it, it would be a miserable experience for *all* of them.

Consequently, the teacher was advised to have a frank discussion with the class. She should ask them whether they would like to make this experience more pleasant for each other. And if they wanted to, they would have to find ways of doing it. The teacher should be frank in expressing her own discouragement, and show understanding of the discouragement of others.

She could give an assignment asking the children to write what they thought about the class, the teacher, the other students. This would evoke some interest. Those who were too discouraged probably would bring no assignment; they should be invited to make an oral comment.

It was suggested that the problem of Alice should wait for further discussion, and the teacher should first try to set the stage for a fruitful class experience, to establish an atmosphere conducive to learning. The teacher-student submitted the following report one week later.

I asked the group to form a circle. I laid my cards on the table, stressing always the "we," "our," and "us." I told them I was discouraged about our class and knew they were too. Several members are in the Spanish class with me the hour before. They agreed that morale was high there, that any sound there was "in the line of duty." When asked to write their ideas as to what was wrong with us, several asked if they must sign their names. I told them that these papers were not to be graded, therefore the names did not matter; but it was important to write clearly and to spell well enough to get the message across. (I saw a dictionary being used by a boy not in the habit of using one.) Good essays were handed in. Three pupils who had been absent added oral comments, after I had read the papers to the class, again in a circle. There was consensus as to the poor discipline. "There is too much noise." "We yell out." "I am as bad as any," they wrote. Another wrote, "We have been on word study long enough." "You are too lenient," was a frequent comment, sometimes with "I like it that way." Alice (I recognized her paper from her handwriting) voiced most forcibly the need for punitive measures. There was a decided minority of boys, one of whom tried to put the whole blame on the girls. Another one commented that since there were more of them (the girls) they would naturally make more noise. One boy made the suggestion (in writing) that the more gifted should help the weaker, such as him.

I tried to get the group to see that punishments were no good, that the only thing which would help was the group's intent to cooperate. If they would agree, all I would have to do would be to mention the name if someone got out of line; however, if he did not take the hint, I would take further action.

I said their comments made me feel hopeful, and asked them if they didn't agree. Only Bernie saw no hope for improvement. "If everyone would help it would work; but everyone won't, so it's no use." We discussed that and he could see a ray of hope; it was suggested that self-discipline is possible.

C O M M E N T . Although this is not a detailed description of the group discussion, and although one has the impression that the teacher did most of the talking, the overall result seems excellent. The children had a chance to express themselves freely in writing, and the follow-up was effective.

In search of an assignment which would give Bernie the experience of success, I asked another teacher who had had experience with him, and she told me that Bernie had served well in the previous year's carnival, in some managerial capacity. I asked him to run my "fish pond." I said that I had noticed the other day when he and Al had chosen sides for the word-down that he had chosen very wisely. "Your side did so much better." Someone who passed by overheard this and ribbed, "He's dumb, but he can pick the smart ones." I pointed out that some presidents had succeeded because they could delegate powers to well-chosen subordinates, whereas others had failed because they did not have this quality, so important to an executive. Bernie had already promised to help in the "spook house" so I asked him if he would pick out someone for my job, a boy that really would be dependable. He did—the boy was. I complimented Bernie on his selection.

C O M M E N T . That was an excellent follow-up of the suggestion made in the teaching class. Bernie really could do something which brought him honor. His response supported our assumption that he was overambitious.

Ten Days Later. I phoned Bernie's father to tell him about the great improvement in his son's attitude. The father said he had had a talk with Bernie, telling him to be a man and snap out of it; he had expected a change. "Life begins when you don't care who gets the credit, as long as good is done," I have read. I did not discuss my part.

C O M M E N T. It was gracious of the teacher to let the father think it was he who produced the improvement in Bernie. However, modesty can also be a fault. This father needs some awakening; the pressure which he puts on Bernie will have the opposite effect. And what he had told his son did not give him any justification to expect improvement—on the contrary. Someone will have to tell him; otherwise the teacher's best effort will be jeopardized by his continued pressure and humiliation.

The Next Day. Alice was the only one who disturbed the class as we sat in a circle discussing our reading. I moved her twice. She passed a note to another girl; I asked her to give it to me. I put it in the back of the book I was using. Later I read the note and found it so full of what appeared to be homosexual content to warrant my discussing it with the counselor of the school, who has had contact with her and her family. He suggested discussing the problem with Dr. D. The same day Alice asked me (while in the little informal study group that I meet each day) if I had read "that note I asked you not to read." "What note?" I asked, feigning a poor memory as I did not want to do or say anything before getting Dr. D's opinion.

C O M M E N T. The following day the teacher reported in teaching class that both Dr. D and the counselor were of the opinion that Alice had wanted her to see the note. It was suggested in the class that she have a conference with Alice; that she avoid behaving as an authority but rather stand by as an understanding friend; that she refrain from preaching, from probing which would appear as curiosity, and avoid any approach that would harm their relationship. She should admit that she had found the note and read it; she should also admit that she learned a great deal from the note about things she knew nothing about. She should recognize Alice's apparent importance in the group and ask her whether she wanted to be important; and if so, she could appeal to her ability. Such a capable girl does not need *this* kind of importance. And finally, she should ask her what she thought of the class.

Two Days Later. I had a conference with Alice. I told her I had found the note and was impressed with her knowledge; I had to inquire as to the meaning of some of the terms she had used. I said that I had noticed how many friends she had and what an important role she played among them. I wondered if she had wanted to impress me with the note, and if it was very important for her to be outstanding. Alice thought it was not so.

Our conversation brought up many of her pet hates. The principal, the home visitor, the counselor (who also teaches a class), her mother, her brother. Her father and she get along, she said; but a later comment seems to disprove that. She exclaimed, "My father thinks he is going to make me go to college; but he won't! I am not going." She said of the counselor-teacher, "I hate her because she thinks she can move me to the back of the room when I talk and make me study. She can't. She can't make me."

I suggested that she seemed not to like people in authority. Should our wills clash I was afraid she would resent me too. "Maybe you like to be the boss." I pointed out that when the English class had sat in a circle, she was the only one who did not conform. She did not see this psychological slant, but seemed interested when I said I realized that I too had always wanted to be the boss. I spoke of conscious and unconscious attitudes and of how revealing certain psychological concepts have been to me. She seemed interested.

C O M M E N T . Identifying herself with Alice's intentions was a wonderful twist. It can be questioned whether the girl really did not see the points the teacher made or merely did not want to admit the correctness of the interpretation. In offering herself as an example, the teacher removed the obstacle of pride and superiority in recognizing such motivation.

I suggested that she turn her ability to write into useful channels. "All of us are to write an essay for the American Legion Contest on 'America, Land of Opportunity'; you could win." With vehemence she replied, "Nobody is going to make me write an essay."

C O M M E N T . The girl is clever enough to sense the trap. This is probably the reason why she does not want to "understand." She fears being influenced. Therefore, the previous discussion of wanting to be boss was to the point.

I learned that she was young for her grade, having had a double promotion. She hated children, never wants any. Her young brother made her realize "how awful kids are." She never wants to marry. She had no plans for the future, except escape from home after high school. I suggested she think about the power angle and told her that I would ask her about it again some day.

C O M M E N T . Whatever other benefit this discussion may have had, the most important aspect was that the teacher permitted Alice to open up, to express her resentments. This was the first step toward a relationship of friendship. It is obvious that the girl is at war, first at home, then in school, and finally in society. The main enemy seems to be the mother, who apparently sides with her younger brother. Despite a certain alignment with the father, she rebels against him too. He is a man, like her brother, and she is only a girl. Her unwillingness to play the feminine role indicates a strong masculine protest.

In Spanish class the same day she was well behaved beyond the class standard. Lest the customary informality should lead her to talk out of turn, she sat stiffly giving 100 per cent attention to me during the whole hour. The English class followed. When the assistant was absent she asked me urgently to let her check the attendance. While she was doing so, I told the class about the essay. "At least one of our members knows about the project and is against it. I am anxious to know how you feel about it." I told them that though the subject given by the Legion was "America, Land of Opportunity," they could write quite negatively if they so chose, as far as the class project was concerned. They would receive credit for an essay that condemned everything, although I would not submit it to the contest. I asked each member of the class for his opinion (Alice was busy and I did not question her) and all agreed to cooperate in such terms as "I'll sweat it out," or, "I'll write something," and so forth.

When I asked Alice later in the period to write a notice on the board, she complied eagerly, erasing and rewriting at least three times before she was satisfied with her results.

COMMENT. The whole procedure showed the teacher's sensitivity and imagination. Whether she actually had identified herself with Alice, as she verbally at least pretended to do, she felt the girl's needs and met them. She let her check the attendance, gave her special significance as the only one who knew about the project, acknowledged without criticism that she was against it, did not press her for an answer, permitted negative essays, in line with Alice's general condemnation of everything—in other words, she opened all the doors for her. And the girl responded.

In due time, Alice handed in her essay on "America, Land of Opportunity." It was a conventional one. I had not asked her anything about it.

COMMENT. This was apparently a turning point. The teacher refrained from putting any pressure on Alice and she conformed, not only in submitting the essay but also in its content.

From time to time I have remarked to the class, "Isn't this change wonderful?" And they looked pleased. I spoke to Bernie privately, expressed my happiness and amazement at the change, both in the group and in him. Incidentally, despite a week's absence he made a C minus on his make-up test upon his return.

COMMENT. The teacher's enthusiasm—if sincere—is contagious. We cannot doubt her sincerity nor the change which took place, although she did not report too many details supporting her observation.

About a week later I found another of Alice's notes which indicated both homo- and heterosexual interest, if not activity.

COMMENT. That is all the teacher wrote. We would like to know whether she made any comment or let it go by unnoticed. Some people might think such incidents warranted more serious action and concern, but Alice's problem does not seem to be primarily of sexual nature; therefore, it is wise not to emphasize this aspect, but rather to help the girl in her general adjustment, as the teacher is attempting.

The report card grades show general improvement. Two pupils—not the two special problems—continued to be dilatory or delinquent in their assignments; but their work, too, is generally better than before. Two students who realized that they had improved were unhappy at the C they received although they had been making D's and F's previously. I tried to show them that their earning a C showed tremendous progress.

C O M M E N T . The improvement in grades as well as the obvious concern of the students with their grades is an indication of progress. It is interesting to note that the students who apparently did not mind their D's and F's (otherwise they would have done something about them) were now dissatisfied with their C's. This shows again the overambition so often found in failing students and which probably was a factor contributing to their failure.

The report up to this point was presented in teaching class. The teacher-student was praised for her excellent grasp and her utilization of the principles and techniques which we had discussed. She was advised to give more detailed reports about certain situations and her way of handling them. Some of the examples follow:

After each test I let the pupils form teams of two, consisting of one who had more or less mastered the subject and one who had not. I held "teacher's meetings" with the stronger pupils, suggesting helpful approaches. I stressed the importance of respecting their "pupils" and encouraging them by comment on what was done correctly. There was considerable improvement.

C O M M E N T . This is one of the crucial features of the teacher's approach to the class which was not clearly expressed in her previous reports. She had indicated that she had given up her idea of a unit system consisting of students of the same attainment level. The above detail clarifies how she integrated the more and the less advanced students into one group. The significance of such an approach cannot be sufficiently stressed. A variety of beneficial results is achieved in this way. First of all, differences of skill and accomplishment within a class, which so often cause disintegration by pitting the good against the bad, the dull against the bright, are no longer a handicap but an asset. Instead of competing with each other, the students help each other. *Being ahead no longer means glory; it entails responsibility.* Asking the advanced student to assist the slower impresses both with some basic elements of proper human relationships: respect for the fellow student, even if he is academically behind; the need for encouragement and the method of providing it, operating on the horizontal plane of one toward the other, instead of the vertical plane of one trying to get ahead of the other. All was an obvious by-product of the teacher's approach. Her method of mutual help was carried from the general but unfavorable classroom situation, in which all helped to make it pleasant, to the details of academic instruction.

I reduced the number of sentences which must be mastered in punctuation drills from groups of twenty-one to groups of fourteen. This gives the class a chance to achieve and to gain encouragement, which was impossible for many under the heavier budget.

COMMENT. She provided opportunities for all to experience achievement, an important consideration.

I asked for written compositions on home problems, suggesting titles like, "My Family: A Problem," or "My Brother Is a Pest," or "My Biggest Headache." Only one student said he had no problem and wrote on another subject. All the others poured out their conflicts and their hates. Alice's essay was full of gall and acid about her younger brother; Bernie's problem revolved about the family car and his conflict with his sister for the use thereof. A mild-mannered child (or such I had thought her) lamented that the law had unfairly put her sweetheart in jail, and now she would have to wait until he got out, to be married and go away.

The essays appeared to have a cathartic effect on the pupils. They gave me some insights as to why they have not always functioned well.

COMMENT. A psychologically trained teacher can make the written assignment a source of understanding each child. Not only the child's problems can be spotted and assessed in this way, but his personal make-up, his life style. Themes about "early recollections," about the "family constellation," and the like, can provide the teacher with valuable information. This can be followed up both in group discussions and in short personal talks. The need for discretion does not require emphasis since every teacher has the obligation to keep her information about her pupils confidential.

Bernie was having difficulty in identifying compound word forms. I was teaching him alone. After a little explanation I wrote five examples and said, "These are pretty tricky; if you can do two sentences, you will be doing well."

He did four—and smiled, "I ain't so dumb, am I?"

"No indeed," I replied, "but you had both yourself and me fooled for a while." He beamed.

COMMENT. This is an interesting example of the intricacies of encouragement. It shows how the teacher can turn the correct answer to four out of five problems into a success story. But only a teacher who is fully aware of the significance of self-confidence and courage will see the possibility of considering a not perfect answer as "success." It is less important that Bernie, at this stage, know all the answers than that he learn to believe in himself.

Alice is anxious to help check papers. She wanted to check spelling. I told her that I found it unsatisfactory to have even good spellers correct spelling because they often miss errors. But I asked her whether she thought she could do it accurately. She said she knew she could. And I gave her a chance.

She is so accurate in this kind of work that I have asked her to be my assistant next year. She seems to be very happy about the prospect.

COMMENT. Remember this is the girl who has been a focus of disorder, who lapsed into a dream world, and who had gotten attention by showing off in a destructive manner. The teacher has succeeded in providing status for her *within* the group and not against it, within society instead of outside of it. The teacher writes the following conclusions:

Bernie is now functioning, because he knows he can. Alice is a cooperative member of the class. We now have a happy class, and—believe me— a happy teacher.

While a better spirit is the most significant achievement, I think the grade chart shows that academic achievement has, in the main, been greater also.

The teacher then presents the grades for each student, comparing the first semester with the second, of which three weeks still remained.

Interestingly enough, the three best students showed a slight decrease, from A to A−, A− to B+, and B+ to B. Only one B student improved to A−, two B students to B+, and three B students remained B.

Quite different is the situation on the opposite end of the scale. All of the six students who had D in the first semester got passing grades; one improved from D to a B−. And three of the six C students got a B or B+. This is the significant part in regard to academic achievement.

This experiment shows what a teacher can do with a most unfavorable class situation and with student material far below average. She demonstrates both the utilization of group dynamics and individual motivations for the benefit of each individual and the group as a whole.

Epilogue

DURING THE PERIOD in which this material has been collected, our deficiency in coping with the problems of youth has become increasingly obvious. We are witnessing a crisis in our approach to education, which cannot be resolved without major changes that amount to a revolution in teaching. The basic premises on which we operate in our schools have not been adjusted to the contemporary needs of young people. Consequently, our influence upon youth has diminished, and the resulting emergency becomes more obvious from year to year.

The increase of juvenile delinquency, both in numbers and the intensity of transgressions, is only part of the picture, although it arouses the public more than any other aspect of our present predicament. More important is the great number of children who can be classified as "vulnerable." Emotional disturbances in children have become so commonplace that they are often not recognized as such. Relatively few children are free of shortcomings which need correction. Psychotic or borderline cases have increased within the last few years, according to clinical observation. All these disorders are part of a general maladjustment reflecting the rebellion of children against society, against authority, against order and social demands.

How can teachers cope with such problems? Let us be frank: They often cannot and do not, because they are not sufficiently prepared. Teachers are expected to know how to influence children. For many, it is a rude awakening when they come to the realization that they do not know what to do when individual children misbehave or fail.

The ensuing discouragement makes teachers and school administrators sensitive to the abundance of criticism that comes their way. Much of this criticism is unwarranted but not all of it. One can well understand the reaction of the harassed educator and his inclination to deny all charges and to ignore them, but that does not help to recognize and to correct deficiencies.

It is often disputed, but there are definite indications that an increasing number of children are failing to learn to read and to write properly. Disciplinary problems in the classroom, which the teacher cannot master, often hamper learning altogether. Teachers who try their best to do a good job, with enthusiasm and persistence, who are confronted with often insurmountable difficulties in the classroom situation, are bound to consider such criticism leveled against the school as unfair and insulting.

Although compulsory education forces children to attend school, many are expelled because they are troublesome and unmanageable. These are often children with normal or superior intelligence who are by no means sick or pathological. They are restless and unruly, defiant and provocative. The schools must accept their responsibility for these children and develop means to deal with them adequately.

What do school administrators think of this predicament? Some object to what they consider the impossible burden of the schools, because parents, church, and community agencies have added their duties to the job of the school. They say that the schools are being asked to do too much, and teachers are loaded down with duties that parents should have discharged. To quote one, "We are expecting teachers to handle emotionally disturbed children in the classroom between the appointments with psychologists. Schools are not supposed to be a residual agency, a dumping ground for all the chores no one else wants to do. The schools should be concentrating on what is peculiarly their job—teaching the subject matter that parents cannot be expected to teach. They should not be expected to be clinics, nursery schools, and character building enterprises." This opinion of one administrator is supported by another who states that "because the schools are trying to be all things to all men, they are merely skimming the surface and doing everything poorly." Another voices a similar complaint that parents are passing off their responsibility onto the school. "They want their children in school to keep them out from under foot, and they assume that if they are in school they are learning all they need to be taught." Another claims that "the schools should not take responsibility for the whole child. If they do, they will fail."

These statements express the opposite point of view from that of this book. True enough, parents have often failed in the first place and teachers are confronted with the consequences of those failures. Eventually, parents, in their effort to raise children in a cultural atmosphere which makes traditional methods obsolete, will learn techniques to raise socially and emotionally well-adjusted children. But teachers and schools cannot wait until that has been accomplished. They must take on the responsibility, because they cannot discharge their duty to impart academic knowledge unless they understand the whole child and help him in his adjustment. For this, teachers *can* be trained. They need not be therapists; but they can become skilled in the use of psychology in the classroom.

Neither "back to the woodshed" nor efforts to restore old-fashioned discipline can bring results. Our children no longer respond to autocratic methods. We must go ahead and devise means by which we can stimulate cooperation, responsibility, and growth. This cannot be done without the application of psychodynamics and group dynamics in the classroom. The principles outlined in this book may help to produce a change in the atmosphere and to open new avenues for reaching all children, making school an enjoyable and rewarding experience for teachers and pupils alike.

INDEX